Who Gave You Permission?

Manny Waks was raised in Melbourne, the second oldest of 17 children in an ultra-Orthodox Jewish family. In 2011, Manny publicly disclosed his personal experiences of child sexual abuse within the Jewish community and undertook extensive work as a victim advocate, culminating in a royal commission public hearing into Australian Jewish institutions. He is currently CEO of Kol v'Oz, an organisation he established to address child sexual abuse in the global Jewish community. Prior to this, Manny held several senior leadership positions within the Australian Jewish community.

www.mannywaks.com
www.facebook.com/MannyWaksPublic

Michael Visontay has worked for over 30 years as a journalist, author, and lecturer. A former assistant editor of the *Sydney Morning Herald,* he has ghost-written four books of memoir, including *The Happiest Refugee* and *Undies to Equities: the remarkable life of Henri Aram.*

Who gave you permission?

the memoir of a
child sexual-abuse survivor
who fought back

Manny Waks

with Michael Visontay

SCRIBE

Melbourne • London

Scribe Publications
18–20 Edward St, Brunswick, Victoria 3065, Australia
2 John St, Clerkenwell, London, WC1N 2ES, United Kingdom

Published by Scribe 2016

Printed and bound in Australia by Griffin Press

 The paper this book is printed on is certified against the Forest Stewardship Council® Standards. Griffin Press holds FSC chain of custody certification SGS-COC-005088. FSC promotes environmentally responsible, socially beneficial and economically viable management of the world's forests.

Scribe Publications is committed to the sustainable use of natural resources and the use of paper products made responsibly from those resources.

9781925321623 (Australian edition)
9781925307665 (e-book)

A CiP entry for this title is available from the National Library of Australia.

scribepublications.com.au
scribepublications.co.uk

To my wife and children—
and to the victims and survivors
of child sexual abuse

Contents

Preface

In writing this memoir, I have endeavoured to be authentic in every way. This has led to some internal conflicts about what I could and could not share with readers. Ultimately, I decided to be forthright about everything that I felt I had a right to share — warts and all. Particularly confronting were my very personal challenges, especially those I've had to deal with in recent years.

They are not the ones most readers will assume — the intimidation and ostracism that I and my family have endured due to my public advocacy regarding child sexual abuse within the Jewish community. Rather, it's the challenges I've never spoken about publicly, and have only recently started sharing with those closest to me.

The biggest deterrent to sharing these very personal challenges has been the need to protect my wife and three young children. I don't want to impact them detrimentally any more than I may have already done, whether it was my fault or not. This is why I have taken the decision to protect them by not including them in the book. This is my story, not that of my wife and children.

There are several other important points I would like to make before the reader delves into the book itself. Despite some of the difficulties I've had with my parents, especially my father—who I'm critical of in the book—I would like to make it clear that I'm now closer to my parents than ever before. And it's not only because of their continuing support for me and my campaign. Most of us make mistakes as parents. No doubt they made a fair share of theirs, which was magnified, considering they have 17 children. But well before my public campaign, we addressed the conflicts of our past, and as a result our relationship today is solid.

It is also important to emphasise that, despite my terrible experiences with the ultra-Orthodox community, I greatly respect and appreciate some aspects of Orthodox Judaism—such as having a break from work on the Sabbath and spending time with the family, something you're compelled to do if you're prohibited from working and using electrical appliances.

I just wish that Orthodox Jewish leaders would be less hypocritical and more tolerant of others. They also may want to wake up to the disturbing fact that many within their community have left due to having been sexually abused as children—so many people I've spoken to have shared this terrible experience with me. But the Orthodox community also contributes to something that is important to me: Jewish identity and continuity. As a proud Jew (and Zionist, a believer in the right of the Jewish people to exercise self-determination in our historical homeland), this identity is a core part of who I am, and I will do my utmost to ensure our Jewish continuity is passed on through my children.

Chapter One

The reluctant troublemaker

People often ask me why I am so driven, why I have spent so many years calling for retractions, resignations, and apologies. Why have I chosen to become such a 'trouble-maker'? When people hear my name, they nod their head. *Oh, that guy. Yeah, I know him, the abuse victim fighting Chabad or Yeshivah in Melbourne.* To the general public, and even to some of my own family, I am Manny Waks, the sexual-abuse advocate, the nuisance who won't go away, the irritant who won't shut up.

It's not how I want to live, or be known, and it's certainly not how I imagined my life would unfold. So back to my question. Why me? Other people have been sexually abused, in other schools and religious contexts—many of them far worse than I was, and over a much longer period of time. Most of them don't turn into a one-man band for justice. It was never my intention either. When I went public with my allegations in 2011, one of the reasons I did so was to put a face to the experience and, by doing so, to encourage other victims to do the same, or at the very least to take whatever form of action that best suited their needs. Although I was taking a major personal risk, I backed myself. I was experienced in public life, not short of chutzpah, and I could be forceful and candid. I knew how to stand up for myself, and for others.

Yet here we are, over five years later, and there is still only one surname linked with child sexual abuse within the ultra-Orthodox Jewish community in Australia. For most of that time, it's been just me. A year ago my brother revealed publicly that he, too, was abused. Two victims, same name. No wonder people think it's the Manny Waks show.

If others had come forward, the spotlight would have been shared more broadly, as it has been in other communities. Why haven't others taken the plunge—at least not in Australia? The reality is that most victims don't disclose their abuse, but here there's the additional stigma of speaking out against the closed world of ultra-Orthodox Judaism. And they have seen what happened to me and my family. Many victims have told me how they thought of disclosing their names. *But we've seen what you're going through. Why do that to ourselves and our families?*

They fear being cast out from everything they hold dear. Like them, I grew up immersed in the ways and words, values and rituals of the Chabad movement. Chabad was not just my way of life. It was my world. I was saturated, enveloped, and almost suffocated by it. My family lived across the road from the Yeshivah Centre, which includes the Yeshivah College where I went to school. My daily life was defined by a walk of 20 metres, from the house of my Chabad family to the extended family of Chabad a stone's throw away.

It was a straight and narrow path from my family to the Yeshivah Centre. The rabbis and teachers who nurtured, taught, and shaped me were not like teachers at a public school, or even a private religious school. We regularly interacted—including outside of the classroom—and these men loomed as giants to my youthful, fragile mind. Fierce and friendly, they were figures of awe-inspiring authority, my moral and ethical prophets in a complex world.

In the Chabad universe, if a man is not sure how to resolve a problem, if he needs help about how to conduct himself, or how to deal with conflict, he asks his rabbi for advice. This is what my father did; it's what I saw him do while I was growing up. I saw my friends' parents doing the same. If the rabbis said something, it had to be right, and it would be true—at the very least, their advice always had to be followed. Whatever their verdict, their authority was formed through the wisdom accumulated from years of learning the Torah—the Bible of the Jewish people—and other religious scriptures. I was learning from the same scriptures, trying to gain the wisdom that shone forth through their beards and spectacles. My leisure time, my weekends and holidays, were defined by Chabad, as were our family celebrations. It filled every part of my waking life.

Having been brought up in such a self-contained world, the sexual abuse I suffered inside the physical and emotional boundaries of Chabad shattered everything I knew as an 11- or 12-year-old boy. When the men in charge of my world, men whose power was absolute, refused to apply their wisdom and authority to my experience, they betrayed me (and my family) completely.

It was a betrayal of everything I knew and had been told. It was a betrayal of everything they stood for; it was a betrayal of the future that lay ahead. Their denial of my experience, and of the sickness within their midst, was a betrayal of my life and well-being, and that of all the other children in their care, and a betrayal of the trust that thousands of parents had given them over several decades.

When I challenged the leaders—religious, secular, and communal—to acknowledge the scale of the problem, to address it and ensure that others didn't have to experience what I did, when I asked them to do this in the name of human decency, how did they respond?

First they ignored me, then they downplayed it, and then they said it was being addressed. When I demonstrated that they were wrong on all counts, they shunned me. They ostracised me—not just me, but my family, casting me and my parents out of the only community and life that we had known. When I think about this treatment today, their authoritarianism, lack of internal accountability, and intolerance of dissent sounds more like a cult than a religious movement.

I am bruised but I am still standing, my life a rollercoaster with ever-increasing greater highs and lows. I can start the day in despair and end with hope, savour fleeting joy that gives way to inexplicable sadness, and grind my teeth with frustration until I gain a smidgin of satisfaction. That is the nature of the journey I am on, an unpredictable search for something better than before. My story is about family, leadership, and responsibility. Like all parents, I want my children's life to build on mine, to reach further. Most of all, I want them to realise that integrity, compassion, and justice must always come before blind loyalty.

Chapter Two

Day of reckoning

From my early teens, I wore a white shirt, black pants (later a dark suit), and black hat nearly every day of my life. Most of the boys I knew—certainly all my friends—wore the same clothes. It was the uniform of our religious group, Chabad, and its main purpose was to make us feel part of one big family. It's a long time since I've worn the Chabad uniform. Today, I am wearing a grey suit. In the secular world, this is also a uniform. But for me, these are the clothes of an outsider. Today, I am appearing before the Royal Commission into Institutional Responses to Child Sexual Abuse at its first public hearing into the Jewish community. It's difficult to believe that this day has finally arrived, and I am filled with a great sense of vindication, of achievement. I've been hoping today would happen since the inquiry was announced just over two years ago, and I am looking forward to receiving some belated justice.

Stories like mine are now well known across Australia and the wider world through the bravery of victims and survivors from other religious communities—primarily the Catholic Church, but also the Anglican Church and related institutions such as the Salvation Army, the YMCA, orphanages, and other children's homes run by these Christian institutions. The royal commission, instigated by the Gillard government in 2012, has shone a powerful spotlight on the leaders of these organisations, and to some degree has brought them to account for the actions and inactions of individuals acting in their name and the duty of care they failed to administer.

But this spotlight had not been focussed on the Australian Jewish community—indeed on any Jewish community worldwide—whose handful of ultra-religious Jewish schools in Sydney and Melbourne had always tried to deal with these problems from the inside, without help or direction from the outside secular world. Just as the Catholic Church had done, Jewish religious leaders operated under a law unto themselves. Literally. The code of behaviour governing ultra-Orthodox Judaism, which dates back to Biblical times, includes an ancient tradition forbidding Jews from going outside the community to seek solutions to criminal and ethical transgressions.

To some degree, to break this law was considered a crime worse than the original offence, worse than molesting a young boy. In July 2011, I broke that law. I told my story to *The Age* newspaper in Melbourne, which published a report about it on its front page. All hell broke loose, and so began my campaign to bring the weight of the law on to the men who abused me, and other victims within the Australian Jewish community, and to call to account the leaders of the religious schools, councils, and institutions.

Today is the culmination of my mission. It's my day, our day; it's the Jewish community's day, too. It's justice writ large, and the broader community has a strong appetite for this moment of reckoning. As I walk with my lawyers and my father out of our legal office on Lonsdale Street and across to the County Court of Victoria, I know there will be a throng of media waiting for us there. I know because I ensured there would be. I sent out a flurry of media releases to alert them to the hearing about to begin. Today, justice feels most real, yet it also feels surreal. I have come home to a Melbourne that is no longer my home. I'm living a paradox, and I feel confused. I am caught between two worlds, belonging to neither. I have no home to come home to. I have been driven out of the city that I grew up in, forced into exile.

This time last week I was in the Loire Valley in the French countryside, about two hours south of Paris. It will be our home for several months, in a tiny village of several hundred people. It's a universe away from Carlisle Street, St Kilda, where I grew up, across the road from the Yeshivah Centre. The locals speak no English, and we don't speak French. The nearest synagogue and kosher food are at least an hour's drive away. Not that I mind about either. So far we keep to ourselves, and have not yet had time to meet anyone. We moved there just a couple of weeks ago to start the next phase of our life, away from the unending scrutiny and harassment that have followed us around Melbourne over the past four years.

In regional France, nobody whispers when we walk down the street. No one points at me; I don't have to steel myself every time I read the paper, or worry about what the children may be exposed to each day, or wait for the latest instalment from my parents about how they are being frozen out of the Chabad community. This has been the currency of our life since I went public.

We had set ourselves on a new life in France when, out of the blue, on the eve of our departure, the royal commission phoned to confirm that it had granted me a public hearing. I was elated. *It's finally happening.* Although my legal team and I had prepared an in-depth submission to the commission, not everyone who makes a submission gets a public hearing. I knew that if they were going to focus publicly on the Jewish community, I was going to be a central figure because of the information I had gathered over the course of my campaign and the fact that I was the public face of this campaign. Yet it had never seemed real until that phone call, when they gave me a date and it became public.

I am absolutely elated; elated and in turmoil. The hearing is to start in six weeks' time, but we are booked to fly to France in four weeks to start a new life—we have already sent our belongings over and arranged for our house in Melbourne to be rented. Months of careful preparation have to be fast-tracked to get all my documents in order and to contact other victims who may be needed to give further evidence, while managing our plans for relocation overseas. The commission is sympathetic. We fly to France as planned and, a week later, the commission pays for my flight back.

I am not used to treatment like this from powerful institutions. For so long now, it's been exactly the opposite.

I return to Melbourne three days before my hearing begins. The ABC's *7.30* wants to do a story, and I have agreed to let them greet me at the airport, to accompany me to my lawyers, as well as when I stand outside the Yeshivah Centre, and later when I go to my brother Shneur's synagogue—all for the cameras. I am booked into a hotel at walking distance from the courtroom. I meet with my lawyers, and am given a tour of the court in the afternoon, shown where I will sit—potentially cross-examined—and where others will be located during the public hearing. Everything is done professionally, and with great courtesy and sensitivity.

The day is full on. I meet up with Shneur, now a Modern Orthodox rabbi who leads the congregation at The Ark Centre in East Hawthorn, and I go to synagogue that night with him. Another of my younger brothers is also there, and a couple of other siblings join us at his house for dinner.

Most Friday nights when I am in Australia, I go to Tony Fink's house. Tony is my closest friend, and he has an open night every Friday. Often he makes a legendary big pot of chicken soup, and some nights 20 or 30 people drop in. In the summer he mostly makes a large tray of chicken—cacciatore (my preference) or apricot—and rice to feed his many guests. We recite blessings over the wine, and light the Shabbat candles—a ritual Tony insists on preserving, often despite my lack of interest, eat the traditional Challah (ceremonial plaited bread) loaves, chat, drink, and play music. Whenever there's footy (Australian Rules Football) or cricket on television, we watch that. We do so religiously—despite the fact that we support football teams that traditionally despise each other. I follow Carlton, and he's a Collingwood fan—both of us passionately so. I stay at Tony's that Friday night and over the weekend. It helps to feel back in familiar territory, and I move to the hotel during the two weeks of hearings.

As we approach the County Court on the opening morning, the cameras and microphones start bobbing into view. They're waiting for us, anticipating our arrival. *This is really happening.* Until now, justice for me consisted of the arrest and conviction of my abusers. I was able to assist in obtaining justice for other victims. But that was about individuals, the molesters.

Today represents something bigger. To me, and many of the other victims—certainly the ones with whom I've been in contact—this is of equal, if not greater importance, than prosecuting the paedophiles themselves. The royal commission is addressing the enablers, the leaders of the institutions who facilitated the abuse through their inaction, their intimidation, or by covering it up. Ever since my public disclosure, I have been attacked in every way possible in the public domain. Some of the rabbis, leaders, and community members even went so far as to call the media and smear my reputation, and that of my family. 'His family is screwed up … see what his brother says about them,' they would whisper.

Today is the day when we bring these leaders to account. Are they even fit to be called leaders? They are in positions of authority, but have abrogated their responsibility to set a moral example to their flock. Perhaps they didn't take an adversarial role towards me, but those who didn't are complicit by their silence. They have known what was going on for all those years, but chose to keep quiet, claiming privately that it was too difficult to come out, to confront the uncomfortable truth. The oft-invoked mantra by the Jewish leadership, when convenient, that *the only thing necessary for the triumph of evil is that good men do nothing*, was completely ignored.

As I stand up on the first morning to read my opening submission, I scan the courtroom to find an array of lawyers and a sprinkling of supporters, but not a single representative from any Jewish religious or community organisation. Astonishingly, no one is here from any of the Jewish community's peak bodies—those who purport to represent us and our interests. In the lead-up to the opening day, none of these organisations issued a media release acknowledging the importance of the royal commission or endorsing its public benefit. Not one. Even so, I am truly shocked that none of them has turned up at the hearing. From a moral perspective, it would have been the right thing to do, and it would also make sense in terms of public relations—to show, at least symbolically, that they care. But on an emotional level, I must admit I am glad the Yeshivah leaders aren't here. I can be more relaxed without having to face their silent glares.

To put this culture of silence in context, every Jewish community organisation trips over itself to release a strongly worded statement whenever there is an incident on the other side of the world involving Israel, or a case of anti-Semitism here at home. They compete to be the most outraged, to offer the strongest message of support, to be quoted in the media. On this matter of child sexual abuse, though, you can practically count the number of public statements over the years on one hand.

Instead of being 'out there', the thrust of the Jewish community leadership's response has simply been to attack me, to discredit my evidence and that of other victims—to shoot the messenger. They have ignored the substance of my campaign, burying their heads in the sand over a scandal that is beyond religion, and is an issue that strikes at the heart of all human decency.

On this opening day, the public gallery is full. I am prepared—in fact, I am itching to speak—and most of the time I feel strong, despite the constant reminders that I have entered uncharted waters. The commission insisted on clearing my opening statement before I read it, and struck out the name of my first abuser, Velvel (Zev) Serebryanski, instead giving him the acronym AVP, because he is living in New York and has not yet been charged. I was not happy about this. I like to discuss things publicly, even very private things—probably as a result of having been silenced for decades. My style is painfully obvious: *Don't tell me to be quiet. I will scream as loud as I want.*

Sometimes I lose my composure in the courtroom, although it's not when they ask me about the abuse I suffered. No, I have mostly learned how to deal with that when I speak about it. Horrible though it was, and still is, I have generally learned how to pack those experiences away emotionally. No, what causes me to break down is my recollection of the bullying and the incessant vilification, the smears and attacks against me and my family. Although I do my best to hide the scars, they linger just beneath the surface, raw and ready to erupt.

So I am completely unprepared when the commission asks me why we decided to leave for France now. For once, I am lost for words, and tears trickle down my cheeks as I try to come out with an answer. *Take your time,* they tell me. I give them an instinctive response. 'If it was up to my wife, we would have left a long time ago.' It's the truth. Counsel assisting could see the nerve she had exposed, and moved on to another line of questioning.

My father, Zephaniah Waks, is at my side, and will be for the whole two weeks. My father has been my constant and greatest champion since I went public in 2011, and has paid a high price for his support. My parents have been verbally and physically attacked, shunned by the Chabad community that has been the centre of their life for 30 years, and finally ostracised so comprehensively that they have been forced to sell their house. In 2013, they put their house on the market and moved to Israel. Soon after, my father had a heart attack. But he is a strong man, and wild horses could not keep him away from this hearing. More than that, it is critical for him to be here. He has a mountain of compelling evidence, and he has been brought in as a witness at the last minute. So I have had to assist with his submission, find him a lawyer, and so on.

Although my father is my greatest champion, there is a lot of tension between us, and he adds to my stress at a time when I am stressed enough. Even in court he can't be quiet, texting our legal team furiously from the back of the courtroom. One day he sends 50 text messages as he provides a running commentary on proceedings, interspersed with well-meaning tactical advice. I know he means well, but I need a clear head to pursue justice for myself and those who have been abused, ignored, and then vilified. I've been living with the memory of my experiences for more than 25 years. Although this moment of reckoning is a giant step forward, the road ahead is littered with landmines and exposed to enemy fire.

Chapter Three

Welcome to Camp Waks

The heart of my story lies in East St Kilda, where my parents, Zephaniah and Chaya Waks, raised a family of 17 children—11 boys and six girls—in their wisdom and devotion to the Chasidic Chabad tradition of ultra-Orthodox Judaism. My parents say that if they could have had more, they would have. After all, when they got married in 1974, the Chabad Rebbe, Rabbi Menachem Mendel Schneerson, gave them a special blessing to have many children. The Chabad movement encourages large families, as well as outreach to other Jews, as a way of renewing Jewish life in anticipation of the arrival of the Moshiach, or Messiah. In this grand plan I was born second, a year after my sister. I am the eldest son, the first-born boy and role model for the others. Their values, customs, and parenting were tested on my shoulders; I was the standard-bearer for the family's ambitions in the Chabad community. My birthright came with a heavy responsibility.

All my life I have been asked the same question. *What's it like being one of 17 children?* The short answer is that my upbringing often felt like a military camp, with my father as commander and my mother as his second-in-charge. We children were the grunts who had to be raised under strict discipline to make us suitable for the life of sacrifice and mission that lay ahead of us. 'Military commander' is not my phrase. It's my father's, and I agree with him. He was commander first, and father second. My mother's roles were spread a little more evenly. Together they implemented a daily routine governed by two principles: ultra-Orthodox Judaism and the law of numbers.

The daily routine of a Chabad child remains within you forever, the touchstone for everything good and bad in your life. As a boy of 10, growing up in East St Kilda in a house across the road from the Yeshivah Centre, my day started at night because the Jewish day always starts the night before, after sunset. Even the following day's Jewish date commences the previous night from sunset—just as it does for the Sabbath, which commences each Friday at sunset. Every evening, before going to bed, we had to make sure there was water in our *negel wasser* (a bucket dedicated for the ritualistic washing of hands in the morning), and place it next to our bed, as it was forbidden to walk more than three steps after sleeping without first washing our hands. Once the bucket was full, we said the Sh'ma, a traditional Jewish prayer, and went to sleep—not on our stomach or back, but on the left side of our body. This was not as straightforward as it sounds. In the early years there were only two bedrooms in our house: one for girls and one for boys. My bedroom contained six brothers and two triple bunk beds. There was always noise, someone whispering or making a joke. Farts, too. Then you had to make sure you didn't trip over stuff. One day, when one of my brothers was out of bed, he rushed back after hearing one of my parents heading into our room. In the rush, he tripped over and smashed his face on one of the bunk beds. He lost a few teeth and some gum.

In later years, as the family grew, my parents renovated and extended the back of the house to accommodate a double storey, and there were nine additional bedrooms—seven upstairs for the family and two downstairs for guests. We often had guests staying over, mainly on the Sabbath and Jewish holidays, but also on many other occasions, such as when family or friends visited from overseas or when community members needed extra space for them or their overseas guests. On average, there were two children to a bedroom. The house then felt comfortable and spacious, especially since, at any given time, some of us were absent studying interstate or overseas, or living in the local Chabad dormitory. It was rare for all 17 children to be in the house together.

We woke up around 6.30 every morning, and the first thing we did was wash each hand three times: the water-filled vessel was taken in the right hand and placed in the left, with which it was poured on the right hand; it was then transferred to the right hand, and then poured onto the left hand. This should not be confused with the process of washing hands prior to consuming bread. We were not even allowed to wipe our eyes before we washed our hands, because they were considered impure until then. The superstition was that if we wiped your eyes before washing our hands, we might become blind. I genuinely believed that. Later, it was one of the more difficult rituals for me to stop doing—even years after I became secular.

At 7.00 am, I had to go and dip myself in the mikvah, a ritual Jewish bathhouse where people of both sexes—in completely separate locations—immerse themselves in order to cleanse themselves, both symbolically and literally. The mikvah was literally a one-minute walk from our house, on the Yeshivah grounds. Although sometimes I did this with my father or a brother, mostly I did it alone. On the eve of the Sabbath or Jewish holidays, often a few of us siblings went together.

When I returned home, I would hang up my towel and pick up my *teffilin* (phylacteries) and go to synagogue at 7.30 am across the road to pray. As with the mikvah, sometimes it was with my father or brothers, but mostly by myself. This was the first of three times we would pray every day—once in the morning, for 45 minutes to an hour, then in the afternoon for 20 minutes, and then at night for 15 minutes. This excluded the brief prayer before going to bed, and the many smaller prayers interspersed throughout the day—it was expected that we would recite at least 100 blessings each day, which included blessings before and after consuming any food, after going to the bathroom, and when we heard thunder or witnessed lightning or a rainbow. Some blessings, which I took for granted at the time, were more loaded—there was one for not making us non-Jews, and for men, a blessing to thank God for not making us a woman. Yes, there were a lot of numbers in there, but that was how regulated my childhood was.

We would only have breakfast after finishing morning prayers and getting ourselves ready for the day. We always served ourselves. Usually, every older child was responsible for ensuring that they fed themselves and the child 'under their care'—the one who slept in their room. We'd do homework with them, and make them their school lunches. More often than not, we'd eat together; probably not everyone, but most of us. The cereals—typically, Corn Flakes, Rice Bubbles, and

Weetbix, but sometimes home-made granola as well—would be out on the table. Once, when we were young and new to Melbourne, before any of us had tried Weetbix, I decided to prepare them for everyone, so I set them up in plates and poured milk over each dish. By the time everyone was ready to eat, their Weetbix was completely soggy; needless to say, no one ate it, and I copped an earful and more for wasting money and food. I thought I was doing a good deed. It sent me a clear message: stick to *our* routine.

School started from around 8.45 am and finished at 4.30 pm. After my barmitzvah at the age of 13, I was put into a more religious study program, and my daily learning began at 7.30 am and went to 9.30 pm. Sometimes there were other religious activities after that, so from a very young age I became accustomed to long days. We always made our own lunches. My favourite was strawberry-jam sandwiches, and at some point I used to take four of them a day. Those jam sandwiches helped get me through some pretty boring morning classes. Once in a blue moon we got money to buy some hot chips from the canteen. Indeed, getting any spending money was a rarity. Once my mother gave me $2 when a friend came over; we were allowed to go to the bakery to buy a $1 sweet each. I was so excited! I can only remember this happening once during my childhood, apart from modest pocket money for school camps. Each day after school finished, there was more praying, study, and, thankfully, sport. Mostly it was basketball, because the Yeshivah Centre had a few courts, but sometimes we'd play cricket, soccer, and kick-to-kick Aussie Rules. I loved sport, and also played before school; there wasn't much time for recreation in the afternoons, because my parents insisted we eat our family dinner early.

What was 'early'? Five pm. That early. Mostly my parents

did not eat with us. During dinner, my father would be in his home office, working, while my mother would stand behind the kitchen bench and serve us all. When we got a bit older we were assigned duties around dinner. One would serve, one would stack the dishwasher, yet another would wipe the bench, and so on. For the meal, we sat at the kitchen bench, not at the dining table. Although our meal was not 'formal', it was strict, and everyone had to be there—and not just out of respect. If you were late you might not get your preferred food. We were under strict instruction to always finish everything on our plate, even if we were no longer hungry—a habit I have not been able to shake, even now. When we weren't eating, we were talking; the family meal was a noisy affair. You had to shout to get a word in, and no one listened to anything. Often it was mayhem. Everyone spoke at the same time, trying to get the attention of their parents and their older siblings. When it did get rowdy, we were given warnings, then we had to be quiet. After this, one peep would mean you finished your meal prematurely, especially when my father came out. That meant returning to a cold meal or no meal at all, depending on how great your transgression.

Once dinner was over, my parents—mainly my mother, as my father would be working, praying, or studying—started the routine of getting us off to bed, again early. We hated it! I wanted to stay up longer. I guess, understandably, my parents wanted as much time alone as possible.

The dynamics and relationships between the children basically clustered around birth order. As the eldest boy, with five boys in a row under me, I was somewhat of a leader of a gang, and would often direct activities. We were very much into basketball, and played together before and after school, and on weekends. My position of authority was a given, so naturally the younger boys tried to prove themselves against me. Shneur once beat me in a bicycle race and, boy, did that sting. It was a humiliation, and the memory has stuck in my mind to this day.

Birth order seems to count for so much in any family — in mine, even more so. During my younger years, I developed individual relationships with the brothers immediately under me, and my older sister, Shlomit, who took on the role of quasi-teacher to the younger children. I had a natural bond with Shneur, who was born a year after me. We studied, played, and did similar chores. There was also a reasonably close relationship with the next three brothers: Shmaya, two-plus years younger than me; Yosef, three-plus years younger; and Yanki, four-plus years younger. I remember some regular tension between those younger three, who were very similar in terms of size. But I can't say there were meaningful relationships between me and my younger siblings at the time. It was more like: *Who wants to do what?* This also describes life with my sisters. There wasn't a gender separation as such because, apart from Shlomit, the others were born later than me, so that I did not have much practical day-to-day interaction with them — besides, my time was already consumed with around half-a-dozen other siblings closer to my age.

People have often asked me how we could afford our life. My father worked as a computer consultant, and my mother was at home taking care of us, so it took strategy and forward planning to provide for everything we needed. When my mother went to the supermarket, she took a few of us — often around five — and filled a trolley for each child. We easily spent $400–$500 at a time. But you can't bargain at supermarkets, so my parents improvised. They purchased items that were in season or on special. We bought fruits and vegetables from a regular shop on Carlisle St—the main shopping strip for Melbourne's Orthodox community—and after my parents developed a relationship with the owners, they could rely on him to give them the best prices and produce. They'd purchase in-season products by the box. It was a win-win. If cucumbers were expensive, my mother bought tomatoes that week. If apples were expensive, she'd buy oranges.

My father would give the boys haircuts, using a 'zero' blade to keep our hair as short as possible, in accordance with ultra-Orthodox—not strictly Chabad—tradition. We looked like potato heads, and some of us resisted the ritual so, at some point—when we became older and the resistance intensified—he tried to bribe us with rewards. Whoever agreed to a zero cut would get a packet of Nobby's Nuts as a treat. Despite my immense dislike of the zero haircuts, I relented to get the reward.

We were always looking for ways to save. If we went on family outings, my father would get family discount tickets. Once, an amusement park refused to sell us a family ticket because they would not accept that we were one family—they had never heard of a family that large. They were sorry afterwards, as my father proved to them that we were indeed one big family, and they were forced to compensate us with some freebies.

There were five kitchens, each with its own oven, in our house: one for dairy food, one for meat, one was *Parve*—neither dairy nor meat (for example, for making cakes)—and dairy and meat ones in the Passover kitchen. When my parents submitted plans to extend the house as the family grew, the local council thought they were trying to build a boarding house on the quiet, and it took a few months for the planning officers to accept that they really did have 17 children, and that the development application was genuine. Years later, I met one of the councillors involved at the time of the building application, and he recalled the suspicion that an illegal brothel was being built there—they could not understand the need for so many bedrooms and bathrooms (although I'm not quite sure what they assumed the kitchens were for).

Food, family dinners, and celebrations—whether they were births, barmitzvahs, and batmizvahs, weddings, or other Chabad rituals, such as the cutting of the hair of young boys—occupied a central role in our social life. Although we did have some birthday parties, there was no major significance given to the day, other than the birthday child getting to choose dinner on the day. When we got older, the boys used to have a *farbrengen*, a uniquely Chabad get-together that translates as a 'joyous gathering' but was more like an inspirational study session that could be held on birthdays and religious events, when we would drink alcohol, sing, discuss religious matters, and make new resolutions. Celebrations were mainly in a religious context, and our lives were marked by the calendar of Jewish festivals. On some occasions, we sang in Jewish nursing homes, or at public events such as Chanukah in the centre of Melbourne. We went on family holidays, but not that often—mostly to school camps organised within the Chabad environment. But we often did go to the park on weekends, which was a lot of fun. We mixed exclusively with people from the ultra-Orthodox community. When we were sick, we went to an Orthodox doctor; it was the same for dental care, and for legal and accounting advice. I don't think I ever went to the bank as a young boy, or to the post office.

Effectively, I did not have to engage with any non-Jews, in

person or in thought. We weren't allowed to read novels, listen to mainstream music, or go to the movies, because all of these would expose us to the immorality and dangerous ideas of the outside world. We weren't allowed to watch television for the same reason. However, the set we had at home was used to play family, religious, and educational videos. My father actually put a sign on the family TV: 'This unit is used only for kodesh [holy] & (lhavdil) [to make a distinction from] secular educational & family videos.' We weren't allowed to follow sports on TV (and following it in general was frowned upon in my house—it was deemed to be *shtusim*, nonsense), so, although I got my first cricket bat when I was ten, I had to sneak out to watch cricket at my friends' houses. Similarly, I was given a Carlton footy scarf and socks around the same age—somehow I convinced my mum to purchase them for me at the Victoria Market, but I don't think she realised what they were—but could only watch the games somewhere else.

On Shabbat, the holy day of the Jewish week, we stayed at home together and rested, as was customary in Chabad households. That meant no cooking, turning on of electricity, touching a light switch, listening to radio, or using the phone—nothing that could be considered by Orthodox rabbis as constituting labour and against the idea of rest and spiritual nourishment. And if we forgot to turn on the oven, lights, or any other appliance, we were sent to stand at the end of our street to ask a random non-Jew to fulfil this role—but we weren't allowed to be direct with the request, only to hint (for example, 'We forgot to turn on the oven', which often led to confusion about what we actually expected from them). These 'guests' were duly rewarded with a *L'chaim* of whisky or the like.

As part of our Shabbat family ritual, my parents used to

force us to have an afternoon sleep, because, understandably, they wanted to rest. It never occurred to any of us that they might be tired, and I just saw it as plain unreasonable. We used to *hate* that enforced sleep the most. I was so traumatised by the practice that for many years I could never sleep in the middle of the day. I still struggle to do so.

In our family, Shabbat was more than a day of rest. My parents also saw it as an opportunity to influence Jewish friends and others to become more religious. They would regularly invite people—secular and Orthodox Jews—for Shabbat meals. They were beautiful meals, comprising my mother's delicious, Yemenite-influenced food, and plenty of drinking and singing, which occasionally brought out the neighbours to listen and even join. At times we would put on plays for the guests. Shlomit, the appointed 'teacher', would organise the other kids, and we would go off to a bedroom to prepare and dress up, then come out to perform a Jewish-themed show for the guests. My parents took great pride in these events, and the fact that the older kids taught the younger ones.

Another feature of these meals was the way my parents made a point of positioning their children and Chabad friends between the non-religious guests, in the hope that their religiosity would rub off on the others. The preparation was intense and stressful. My parents had very specific ideas about the seating arrangements. You couldn't have a person of one gender sitting in between two people of the opposite gender—irrespective of their age or if they were related. My parents spoke in Hebrew when they were planning the seating so the guests couldn't understand. It was absurd, and as children we hated the fuss, stress, and ridiculous rules. We would look at each other, thinking *There they go again*. At the Friday-night meals, my father had a tradition of peeling garlic and sending some of it across the table to share with my mother. Apparently, we learned later, the garlic was supposed to enhance the potency of your sperm. We would laugh and roll our eyes when they ate it, although we now realise these were aphrodisiacs for the conjugal evening that would traditionally follow in ultra-Orthodox families—Friday nights were referred to as 'Mitzvah night'.

Sometimes my father's idiosyncrasies took us completely by surprise. One day we were driving back from a trip to the country when my father saw a 'Selling Goats' sign. We did not have pets. And having a dog or a cat was anathema in the Orthodox world. They're not kosher animals, deemed impure. (As an aside, perhaps it's the reason that till this day I'm still very uncomfortable around these types of animals—by contrast, I'm very comfortable beside pretty much any kosher animal.) Besides, there were already many children. We didn't need a pet. What did that matter? He followed the sign, got out of the car, and, next thing we knew, we were driving home with a goat in the boot. When we arrived home, we opened the boot, and the goat jumped out and escaped down our street. It ran into the corner house that was being used as a Jewish support service. A Chabad psychiatrist we knew, Dr Mottl Greenbaum, was walking past, and came in to help. Dr Greenbaum caught the goat by its horns, and we eventually managed to chain it and bring it back home. We named it Honey, and soon discovered that she was pregnant with two kids. My parents put the goat in the shed at the back of the house. At the time, I didn't know what they were thinking, and even in hindsight I still don't. The goat would soil the whole yard, and then the shed. We had to put it down after just a few months, which was a very sad day for the kids, especially Shneur, who had developed a close bond with the animal. He cried on that day.

To the outside world, we were ultra-Orthodox. From within the community, my father reckoned we were not *that* religious. In a video about our life made by film-maker Barbara Chobocky, *Welcome to the Waks Family*, which was broadcast on Australia's SBS in 2002, my father described our level of adherence the following way:

> We are to the observant side of the middle, but we're definitely not on the radical side. There are people who dress more radically than us, and will be more inflexible in talking to women. For example, they would not agree to do the video, and engage with the outside world. On the other hand, we're not totally open to the world either. Does that make us extreme? I don't know.

With a family as large as ours, and as religious as ours, group routine and ritual were the mainstays of daily life, and there was no real time for one-on-one relationships with our parents. We didn't engage in small talk in the way that other families would. For example, when other kids walked down the street with their parents, they might talk about football, the weather, what was in the shops, or even school. That was not our family. Instead, my father would often discuss deep and meaningful subjects with me, mainly based around ultra-Orthodox themes: the anniversary of a famous rabbi in Europe; morality tales from the shtetls (Jewish villages in eastern Europe); and other stories all designed to make the children more observant, to feel the spirit of Chabad more fervently. Essentially, they were *divrei Torah*—words of Torah, a broad description of religious discussions.

That was just the way our life was. My mother created individual photo albums for all of us—or at least for the first ten kids. We all took the photos, and my eldest sister would go through them and help write captions for them. As a child, you don't know what you're missing if everyone around you has the same. I generally felt comfortable, and never felt I was missing out on anything. However, as I got older and saw more of the world, and my friends' families, the absence of certain personal familiarities began to dawn on me. For instance, when we were young my mother would assemble us in the living room, one by one, to clean our ears. I enjoyed the ritual, not just because we were all in it together, but probably more so because it presented a rare opportunity to be physically close to my mother. If we were sick, there was no pampering or mollycoddling—we were basically sent to our room to rest until we recovered. It got boring pretty quickly, so we'd be quite desperate to return to school. Often a few of us were sick at once, so the Chabad doctor would come and see multiple patients in one visit.

There was no time for a one-on-one after school. At times, there was a *How was your day?* but it was fleeting. Occasionally, when we were younger, my mother would give us a kiss, but no one ever uttered the words *I love you*. The word 'love' was just not in the family lexicon. My father did not, and still does not, accept the widely accepted view of unconditional love, which he refers to as a 'mantra'. However, he does feel a special relationship with all of his children, irrespective of some of the profound differences between him and them (which I discuss later). I get the feeling that my mother deeply regrets her lack of outward love and affection towards the kids over the years.

Nevertheless, 'love' was profoundly implicit in our way of life. I felt loved, and I never felt unloved. Yet it was love in the context of religion and religious practice. So what did the word actually mean? When my parents spoke about love, it was not in the family context, or between family members. It was always about a love of Israel (the land of Israel, not really the state), and injunctions to love your fellow Jew, love God, love the religious practice, and, seemingly most of all, love the Lubavitcher Rebbe (Menachem Mendel Schneerson).

My birth name is Menachem Leib (Menachem after the Lubavitcher Rebbe, and Leib after my paternal grandfather), and the next brother was named Shneur Zalman (named after the first Lubavitcher Rebbe). We cover most of the previous Lubavitcher Rebbes (Chabad and Lubavitch are interchangeable: Lubavitch is the town in Russia where the movement started, and Chabad is an acronym in Hebrew for wisdom, understanding, and knowledge). That sent a clear signal about who was at the centre of our family universe. On my birthday and other occasions, I would write letters to the Rebbe to ask for his blessing, as was the custom. I felt a special kinship with him because my birthday was the day before his—so when my Hebrew birthday concluded at sunset of the 10th of Nissan, his commenced only minutes after that, on the 11th. To my youthful, impressionable mind, this meant there was a small overlap between our birthdays, creating a bond that not many could claim and which was regularly mentioned to me.

In addition to the love of *Yiddishkeit* (Jewishness), my father also placed a premium on demonstrating respect for your parents. One clear expression of this was the way he designated a chair in the dining room as his, and his alone.

And my mother had one, too. This was customary in Orthodox homes. None of the children could sit on it without first asking for permission, which was only granted in rare circumstances.

In my case, as the eldest son, my behaviour served as a role model for the younger ones, so he expected more of me. From a young age (as an early teen), I was forbidden to enter the house wearing shorts or jeans, and certainly not without wearing my *kippahh* (yarmulke or skullcap) or other religious garb such as *tzitzit*. 'Your younger brothers are looking at you, and will copy you. You have a responsibility,' he told me more than once. I absorbed his messages in surprising ways. One day when I was about 13, he needed a chair to sit on when drinking wine during the Havdalah ceremony, which marks the end of the Sabbath. As there were no chairs in the room, I got down on all fours and made my back into a chair, and motioned him to sit on my back. He actually did it. My father sat down on my back; he didn't put his full weight on me, but I remember how much he appreciated my gesture. 'That is the ultimate sacrifice, a demonstration of respecting your parents,' he said. That moment encapsulated how every activity and decision was intertwined in a religious context, invested with religious meaning.

These practices reflected not only Orthodox values, but my father's tendency towards black-and-white personal judgements, most notably about family relations. For example, my father has two younger siblings, Nathan and Sheree. Both lived in Sydney in their younger years, both of them married non-Jews, and they had two children each. However, because an individual's Jewishness is matrilineal, Sheree's children were officially Jewish, but Nathan's were not. My father would not readily speak to Nathan's wife, my dear Aunty Candice, because she wasn't Jewish — and, from a certain stage, not with their children, my first cousins, either. When I got to my barmitzvah age, my parents decided they didn't want our non-Jewish cousins to talk to us, for fear of them infecting us with *goyische* (non-Jewish) ideas and values. So we were allowed to continue a normal relationship with Sheree's children, but not with Nathan's. That caused massive friction within the family — between my father and his siblings, and also with us, because we really liked our uncle and aunt, and were very close to their children. Even when I was much older, around 17 to 18, my father tried to insist that I not see them.

Chapter Four

From Crown Heights to Caulfield

Amazingly, my father did not have his own barmitzvah, and he never fasted on Yom Kippur during his youth. His parents were middle-class European Jews who raised their three children in a totally secular Jewish environment on the north shore of Sydney, in one of the first houses designed by the prominent Jewish–Austrian architect Harry Seidler. My grandfather named his first son Stephen. As a teenager growing up in the 1960s, Stephen was a keen surfer, went to Byron Bay, and embraced the counterculture. He partied, drank, and dabbled with drugs. He lived the life of sex, drugs, and rock 'n roll.

When Stephen was 18, his father had a heart attack and died. He was 54, and my father's world was shattered. Suddenly, and not surprisingly, his life seemed empty and materialistic; he felt bereft and unsure of his place in the world. As he said on *Welcome to the Waks Family:* 'You start to realise that there are certain things in life which are absolutely beyond your control.' At the time, like many young men in the 1960s, my father was interested in alternative religions like Buddhism as a way of searching for meaning. But then he happened to meet a Chabad family, and something clicked. He realised that the meaning he was looking for lay in his own backyard. This was when he temporarily changed his name to Hasofer, after his adoptive Chabad family in Sydney.

My mother Chaya's upbringing was starkly different. Her family comes from Yemen, and was flown to Israel in 1949, a year after the creation of Israel, as part of Operation Magic Carpet, in which nearly 50,000 Yemenite Jews were airlifted to the newly founded state, to provide sanctuary and a new life. The Chabad community in Israel helped her family (as well as many other Yemenite Jews) settle, and so they also became Chabad. My mother grew up in K'far Saba, my birthplace, in central Israel, near Tel Aviv. Her family was very religious. Before marrying my father, she had not been to the beach, which was nearby, nor touched anyone of the opposite sex outside of her family; she had never heard the Beatles or Rolling Stones, nor been to the cinema or theatre.

In 1970, when my mother turned 17, her father offered her (and all her sisters) a choice: she could either get a driver's licence or fly to New York to see the Lubavitcher Rebbe. She chose New York, got the Rebbe's blessing, and flew back to see him again. On this follow-up visit she met my father, who by that time had fully embraced Chabad and had changed his name to Zephaniah Zelig, the Jewish names he was given at birth by his parents.

She knew practically no English; he knew practically no Hebrew. They went on three dates, communicated through sign language and a mish-mash of the two spoken tongues, and hit it off immediately. Their families approved, the engagement was announced, and they went to ask the Rebbe for his blessing. My mother says, 'He blessed us with lots of kids', and so they were able to have 17 children. A month or two after the engagement, they got married in Israel, where they settled and began their new life together in an ultra-Orthodox area in Jerusalem.

That was code for starting a family, pronto. My sister Shlomit was the first, in 1975, then me in 1976. All up, my mother gave birth to eight children in Israel. I don't know how she coped. On *Welcome to the Waks Family*, she admitted that she panicked after the first three children, and found the early years the hardest. By that time we lived in B'nei B'rak, an ultra-Orthodox city, where we lived on the top floor of an apartment block, with a swimming pool that we loved to splash around in during the hot summers. My parents found life spiritually rewarding in Israel; yet, despite some support from my father's family, it was financially challenging. They decided that life would be easier to manage back in Australia, where my father felt he could succeed as an independent computer consultant after having studied at both Princeton and Hebrew universities. In 1984 he returned to Sydney in advance to arrange accommodation for the family. My mother, who still spoke almost no English, had to bring eight children under the age of ten on the flight by herself. Again, I have no idea how she coped. But I do recall that flight; my mother recalls that, as the eldest boy, apparently I was a great help.

The family settled in Lamrock Avenue at Bondi Beach, and lived there for about a year and a half. We went to the Yeshivah school up the hill in Bondi. Apart from the stress this caused my mother—living in a foreign country where she didn't know anyone, speaking little English, and taking care of eight children while my father was often interstate on work—our life in Bondi passed uneventfully.

As it turned out, my father was having to spend so much time in Melbourne on work that the whole family relocated there, a move they had initially intended anyway. A Chabad friend helped find a house, and we drove down in a van, along with the removalists. My mother, expecting her tenth child any day, drove part of the way. When we arrived in the evening, she went into labour. My father took her to hospital, and a few hours later my brother Avi, or Bobom, as we called him, was born.

While we were young, no one really knew what my father did in his job. Although he was known as a 'computer guy', everyone was content to let this vague catch-all term remain in the background behind his family and religious commitments. His work involved frequent travel, and when he returned home, occasionally he would give us gifts; he once brought a large packet of textas, and we could each choose a single texta, another sign of how we were to make do in such a large family.

A few years ago, he explained that he had two large clients, one a merchant bank and another large company with several hundred employees, for whom he was a one-stop computer shop—analyst, programmer, strategist, and consultant. 'It was lucrative, plenty of work, I was good at what I did,' he told me. He also received some assistance from my late paternal grandmother, who lived much of her adult life with my aunt Sheree at her large waterfront house in Balmain until dementia required her to move to a nursing home. While my grandmother was still in possession of her faculties, she recognised the life my parents had chosen, and decided to help them. 'Why should I wait till I'm dead to help you?' she told my father. While we lived in Sydney, she even gave me a saxophone and clarinet, and arranged for lessons for a few years. Later, she moved to Melbourne, and my father volunteered to build a granny flat for her. However, it didn't last. She couldn't bear to leave the water in Balmain. Instead, Sheree had to take care of her until she completely lost her faculties, before passing away in 2015.

By this time, my uncle Nathan had changed careers from being a world-renowned cellist with the Sydney Symphony Orchestra, the youngest principal cellist in its history, to a successful wine merchant, and spent much of each year overseas. At one stage, he and his wife, Candice, planned to move to France permanently, but in 2015 she was involved in a serious car accident that has tragically limited her mobility, and for which she requires constant care. I have remained close to Nathan and Candice throughout the years. Indeed, when we decided to leave Australia in early 2015, they invited us to stay at one of their properties in the Loire Valley while we considered our options about where to live. That offer helped make a difficult period of transition for us a little easier.

Many people wonder how large Jewish families can afford to pay private-school fees for their children. In practice, the fees at the Yeshivah Centre were not really a problem. Ever since the school was established in 1949 (and the girls' school in 1959), it has been funded by donations from the community (as well as the government), and this funding has been sufficient to cover the real costs of educating students. The Yeshivah Centre would offer parents 'discounts' on fees, later called 'fee deferments', but did not genuinely consider asking for them to be repaid in full. My father told the royal commission:

In our case, you had to send your kid to that school. You had no choice. The school fees didn't relate at all to the cost of what it was costing to educate the kids. As far as I know, no one from core Chabad, which I was, had ever been asked to pay anything back.

The relationship between school and family was much deeper than for religious schools from other faiths. My brothers and I probably spent more time at the Yeshivah Centre than we did in our own home. Between long hours of classes, extra religious study, and playing sport after school, it soon became a home away from home. Education was only part of what it offered Jewish students. Parents sent their children to learn and practise the philosophical and spiritual mission of Chabad Judaism. As part of that philosophy, the Yeshivah Centre accepts all Jewish students, with the aim of inspiring those from outside Chabad to join the movement, or at the very least to become religious. So although it was a Chabad school, a significant proportion of children did not come from religious families.

During infant and primary years, the curriculum was split fairly evenly between Jewish and secular subjects, slightly in favour of general over religious. After their barmitzvahs, boys can be moved into an intensive religious studies program called *Mesivtah*, which was at the time 100 per cent religious. This was total immersion in ultra-Orthodox Judaism—the Torah, Talmud, philosophy, teachings of Chabad, and commentary on the Torah, and the end of formal learning about the secular world outside. From the age of 12, I studied no more English, science, or mathematics.

One of the aspects of the Chabad lifestyle that school nurtured in all young boys was community outreach. It is no exaggeration to say I enjoyed this immensely. The philosophy follows the teachings of the Lubavitcher Rebbe, who encouraged his faithful to reach out to secular Jews and bring them back to the fold (Judaism is not a proselytising religion). Every Friday afternoon and on Jewish festivals, all around the world, Chabad Jews go around to shops, businesses, hospitals, old-age homes, and any place where Jews can be found, including street corners, and ask them: 'Excuse me sir/madam, are you Jewish?' If a male says 'Yes', he gets asked if he has put on *tefillin* that day. If he says 'No', he is offered the opportunity to do so. Such approaches could be made on the street, or in their shops, or their homes. If a female says, 'Yes', she is offered candles to light for Shabbat. (Tefillin are known in English as phylacteries, a set of small, black-leather boxes containing scrolls of parchment inscribed with verses from the Torah, which are worn regularly by observant Jews on the forehead and upper arm during most weekday morning prayers).

Led by a group of charismatic young Chabad leaders known as *shluchim*, emissaries sent out by Chabad in New York, the young boys would spend hours walking around the Yeshivah precinct and beyond—including walking hours away (due to the prohibition of driving on the Sabbath and some Jewish festivals), door-knocking randomly. I started doing this at around the age of 10. We would go in a whole group, split up, and proceed block by block. It didn't matter what the weather was. Hot or cold, sunshine or pouring rain, you did it. I used to love it. It was a hands-on education, and you walked away with great experience in engaging with people at an intellectual, emotional, and, of course, religious level.

Excuse me sir/madam, do you happen to be Jewish?

If it was a particular Jewish festival, we would bring with

us symbols of the festival—a *shofar,* or ram's horn, for the New Year, or a *lulav*, the frond of a date palm tree, for Succot, the Feast of Weeks.

We would ask them if we could demonstrate the festival ritual. Sometimes, they would take up our offer. *Sure, come in and have a drink.* Other times, it was 'No thanks'.

Occasionally, it was downright rude: *Get the fuck out of here.*

In hindsight, it was probably confronting for many to be asked a question they least expected—and didn't think was anybody else's business. Now I find it amusing when I walk past a Chabad stand and I get asked these questions. *If only they knew*, I think to myself.

After we finished, we would go back to the Yeshivah for a debrief, and we would be excited by our experience. 'Yes, we met someone who had not put on tefillin since his barmitzvah, or shaken the *lulav* in years,' we would report, and then sometimes drink a *L'Chaim* (usually a shot of whiskey or vodka) or even sing about it. The highest 'score' was always to put tefillin on someone who had never done so. Chabad even has a special label for such people.

I used to love it; all the boys did. The practice also developed important life skills. We became confident in meeting and talking to strangers, projecting a sense of enthusiasm, even charisma, around our special form of advocacy. The young boys watched and learned from the American emissaries who led our groups. After following them for a few years, by the age of 15 those same skills came naturally to us, and to me.

Underlying all the celebration, however, was an unshakeable message about the centrality of the Rebbe in our lives. This was a mission ordained by a Rebbe whose wisdom we had to accept unconditionally, and whose perfection was beyond question. When I was about 10 years old, the discussion at one of our weekly study sessions turned to the subject of sin. The emissary told us that the Rebbe had never sinned. I could not resist the challenge: 'You're telling me the Rebbe has never made an *aveira* (sinned)?' The next thing I knew, the New York emissary slapped me in the face at the impudence of my question, and responded, '*Chas v'Sholom*' ('Heaven forbid').

One aspect of the Yeshivah culture rarely discussed is racism. This would surprise the outsider. In a school full of Jews—a religious school, no less—what reason is there for kids, parents, and teachers to be racist? The answer, at least for my family, lay in skin colour. As noted, my mother's family came from Yemen. They were African and had darker skin, which was passed on, in varying degrees, to the children. When we moved from Sydney to Melbourne and joined a school composed almost exclusively of fair-skinned students from European backgrounds, the Waks boys stood out. We were taunted, harassed, and assaulted regularly—mainly by fellow children, but also by parents, and even teachers and others in positions of authority. On one occasion, the other boys took one of my brothers and chucked him into a rubbish bin. We located one of the main culprits and reciprocated. There were dozens of kids taunting us, and trying to fight with us, week in week out. Ironically, the main fights occurred on Shabbat during prayer services, and later in the afternoon, when we returned to the Yeshivah Centre for afternoon youth activities.

They wanted to hurt us, so we decided we had to fight back. And not just with our fists. As we were vastly outnumbered—it was often dozens against the five of us oldest Waks boys—we would get stones and bricks, and throw them back at the others. *So now you're Palestinians,* they would taunt us, referring to how we had resorted to the weapon of the weak—throwing stones. Another irony here is that simultaneously they used to taunt us by referring to us as DIBs, which was an acronym for Dirty Israeli Bastards. It was a battle we could never win so, sometimes, when we were more grown up, we resorted to diplomacy. One year, on the festival of Succot, half-a-dozen Waks brothers went to the home of an adult who habitually taunted us, and confronted him in a non-violent manner. We ended up having a few drinks at his home, and he stayed quiet after that. For many years, my mother used to wait for the boys to come home crying after such confrontations. In the broader scheme of things, the Waks boys were never fully accepted by Chabad—at least not by the Yeshivah community. Our skin colour meant we would be permanent outsiders. Although I could accept this—I was an outsider for so many other reasons—some of my siblings could not, and they bent over backwards to be accepted by their peers. In my opinion, some still do. But there's no doubt that this racism left an indelible mark on many of us.

The one value that did bind us all together, regardless of skin colour, was anti-Semitism, which was a regular feature of life on the streets of St Kilda and its surrounds. Even as young boys we were dressed in the traditional black pants, coat, and yarmulke—and a hat post-barmitzvah. We looked very Jewish, which made us targets. People would pass us on Carlisle Street, pretend to sneeze, then say *Ah-jew,* instead of *Achoo.* Sometimes people would throw eggs at us from moving cars—or more often just yell *Fucken Jews* from a speeding car. When I was 13, Shneur and I had a far more disturbing experience one afternoon as we walked from the Yeshivah Centre to another institution within the ultra-Orthodox neighbourhood for religious sessions.

Almost directly across the road from the Yeshivah was a new housing block, with a 7-11 convenience store adjacent on the ground floor. Suddenly we heard a whistle from across the road, next to 7-11. We turned around and saw a man with his arm in a sling. In his other hand, he held what looked like a gun and pointed it at us. He only held the gun in view for a few seconds before hiding it under the sling. We were shocked, but did not know what to do, so we continued to our religious-instruction session. Later we told the man in charge of security at Yeshivah, David Cyprys, who took our allegations very seriously. Cyprys asked us to show him where it happened, then went straight into the property to investigate it. We watched in awe. Although he never found anything or anybody, we were both impressed by his courage.

David Cyprys went on to figure prominently in my life for many reasons. This is the only positive thing I have to say about him. But it's what drew many young boys to him. In some ways, he was our hero. Countless times, we watched him take on people much larger than him, especially when he escorted non-Jews off the Yeshivah Centre basketball courts.

Chapter Five

Dark secrets

Police Report

September 5, 2011 — City Police Station, Canberra

My full name is Menachem Leib Waks, and I am thirty-five years old, with my date of birth being 10th of April, 1976. My personal details are known to police and I make this statement of my own accord.

On the 17th of September, 1996, I made a sworn statement to a Senior Constable WARNER, in relation to sexual assaults committed against me separately by both Velvel SEREBRYANSKI, and Shmuel David CYPRYS.

This statement is in addition to the statement I made to Police on the 17th of September, 1996.

Our family would often pray at the Russian Synagogue in East St Kilda, known as the FREE (Friends of Refugees of Eastern Europe). It was the Chabad House for members from the former Soviet Union, and there was more room there for our large family to participate more actively. Occasionally, some of us would lead the service or read from the Torah on the Sabbath and Jewish festivals.

One man who read from the Torah regularly was Velvel ('Zev') Serebryanski. Velvel's father was a prominent Chabad rabbi who taught me at school, and his grandfather was one of the founders of Yeshivah—a man I became close to towards the end of his life as he used to teach me private lessons. I still hold dear the special Hagaddah (the book from which we read on Passover) he gave me as a barmitzvah gift, which included a personal inscription. Grandfather, father, and son had all been in our house on several occasions during community and family celebrations. I have a photo of Velvel's father at the *bris* (circumcision ceremony) of one of my brothers. He was carrying the baby and holding its legs during the circumcision, which is a big honour, as it brings blessings to the person and also signifies closeness to the family. I have another photo of Velvel in our house, at the same ceremony, touching the baby's head. This photo was taken around the time he was abusing me. Although I did not have any personal friendship with Velvel, his face and his family were very familiar due to our association with Yeshivah.

In 1987, when I was in Year 6 and about 11 years old, Velvel sexually abused me over a period of several months. He would have been in his early twenties at the time. The first incident occurred at the Yeshivah Centre, inside the synagogue itself during the Jewish festival of Shavuot, when it is customary for men to remain awake all night to undertake religious studies.

Women did not stay up praying or studying, so the women's section was empty, and I went upstairs to rest there for a while on one of the wooden benches. I remember seeing someone following me. I caught a glimpse of the person and saw that it was Velvel, but I felt it was too late to do anything about it. I thought: *Oh shit! Why is he following me?* It felt wrong. As I walked into the women's section, I saw a kid a few years older than me fast asleep on one of the benches. I lay down on a bench near him. All I could do was pretend to be asleep when Velvel came in. I closed my eyes, wishing him away, but anxious that something was going to happen. I had no inkling of what was about to unfold; I only felt uncomfortable and that something wasn't right. Velvel came across and stood next to me, and then kneeled over with one leg next to me. He started to caress me and stroked my legs several times. His hand then moved up to my groin area.

I didn't know what to do, so I froze. A part of me thought if I did not respond, he might stop. I was so confused, so embarrassed. But Velvel did not stop. He undid my belt, then my fly while I was lying there, unable to move. I continued to pretend I was asleep. I knew it was clear that I wasn't. He started to move his hand around my underpants above my penis, and felt it. Then Velvel stopped and said quietly: 'This is not for a *shule* [synagogue] — let's go out of here.'

He led me to the adjoining bathrooms. I did not want to follow him, but in my confusion and shock at what was happening, I did not know what else to do. The abuse continued in the bathrooms. He pulled down my pants till they were around my ankles and did the same with his trousers. Then he put his hand on my penis and put my hand on his. He started rubbing it. Velvel then put his mouth on my penis and started to suck it. During this time he did not say anything, and nor did I. I don't know precisely what happened next, but it was as if I had blacked out briefly and suddenly awoke to see we were both on the floor.

Then, without anything being said, we both got up and went our separate ways. I don't remember anything that happened immediately after that, either in the synagogue or at home. It is a blank in my memory and my mind. Perhaps intentionally so.

Velvel abused me again in a similar way on at least two other occasions, each time on the Sabbath at the Russian Chabad House, which is virtually around the corner from the Yeshivah Centre. It happened over about a two-month period. I felt sick and confused, and I made it clear to him that I did not like what he was doing and I did not want him to continue. At some point I told him to stop, and he did.

These incidents did not happen out of the blue. As I reflect on them now, I can see there were several signs of Velvel's intentions that I simply did not have the capacity to understand. First, he was clearly infatuated with me, and expressed this non-verbally in synagogue. I remember him staring at me, with a sense of longing, even when he was in the middle of reading the Torah to the congregation. I would be sitting around the table with my family, and would catch him staring at me in a way that was very clearly a longing for me. It was creepy, but it was not physical.

Second, he behaved in a way that we now call 'grooming'. Velvel was around at our house often, as our family lived opposite Yeshivah, and one day on either a Sunday or the school holidays when I was over there playing sport—possibly with my brothers and/or others—he invited me to get in his car and drive it around the open Yeshivah grounds. I was around 11 years old. During the daytime there would not be many cars around, and on Sundays and school holidays not many people were around. I recall this then happened a number of times. I'd drive around the back freely, sometimes dangerously. He could see that I enjoyed the taboo nature of what I was doing. He didn't say anything specific or ask for anything in return. Velvel also took me to his small apartment on Carlisle St on several occasions. He didn't do anything to me, or say anything inappropriate. He just took me over there or invited me.

It wasn't until many years later that I learned that this sort of grooming is common in child sexual abuse. The abuser offers the victim gifts or experiences that they are missing—it fills a void. It may be tangible, such as money or a present, or it may be intangible, such as love or attention. This creates a unique relationship—there's a reliance, there's admiration or appreciation. It also creates a feeling of guilt (and other emotions) in the victim, and establishes a private bond that the victim is scared to break for fear of seeming ungrateful and disappointing the abuser, possibly leading to the severing of ties or other potential consequences. Thus the abuser gains and develops a secret control of the victim, before, during and/or after the abuse takes place.

My best friend at school was Yerachmiel Gorelik. We were in the same class and went to the same synagogue, because his father was head rabbi at the Russian Chabad House. So we would see each other every day at school, on Shabbat, and at our extracurricular activities. Yerachmiel had a sleepover at my house soon after the abuse by Velvel, and I told him what had happened. I didn't go into great detail, but I made it clear that Velvel had sexually abused me. Within a few days, it seemed to be common knowledge around the school that something had happened. All of a sudden, friends and classmates were teasing and bullying me, throwing around comments such as 'poofter', 'homo', and the like. At times, this taunting occurred in the presence of teachers at school and others in positions of authority within the Yeshivah Centre, but no one acted to stop it. I felt that many people, including adults and teachers at the school and centre, knew what had happened to me, and tolerated me being bullied about it. I thought this because no one intervened or helped me. I walked around feeling embarrassed, upset, and angry. No adult at the Yeshivah Centre ever asked me what was happening. Most of the time, I felt completely deserted and alone.

My saving grace was my ability in sport. For a period, I was class captain in basketball and soccer, which ensured I was not completely marginalised. This meant that kids always wanted me to be on their team, and allowed me to still participate with a sense of normality in school life. But you could not quarantine the taunts and jibes. If I accidentally touched someone near their genitalia—sometimes anywhere on their body—it would start again.

One Shabbat, there was a Chabad youth program for our class. We had two staff members looking after us while we played games, prayed, ate snacks, and so on. They were about 18 years old, emissaries from Chabad in New York, and uneducated in a secular sense. Despite having grown up in an English-speaking country, they arrived with no real ability to read and write in English—in fact, often their spoken English was limited as well. However, they were familiar with their national sports, so they got us to play gridiron. In the course of one of the games, I went to block and intercept a pass, and another guy fell into me and touched my groin. Suddenly, a few boys smiled, smirked, and laughed. Someone made a snide comment. I recoiled with embarrassment. I was angry.

I would go into school expecting something to be said. The bullying was often incessant, relentless. While it didn't happen every day, that didn't matter. The looks and comments were always there. I just did not want to be at school. I knew deep inside I hadn't done anything wrong. *Someone had done something wrong to me.* Yet through warped thinking, everyone jumped on the bandwagon, and I became a target.

There was another incident when we were playing wrestling, mimicking the guys who were on television. Our family didn't watch TV, but other boys did. As noted earlier, Yeshivah College took in students from across the spectrum, and most of the boys came from non-Orthodox families, so popular culture infiltrated my world through them. During our wrestling period, which transpired during a Year 8 Jewish studies class with Rabbi Dovid Rubinfeld, and which were often chaotic, I picked up another boy for a pretend body slam, and dropped him while I was holding him.

This classmate turned around and said angrily and loudly: 'If you want to fuck me so much, why don't you just do it already?'

This was in the middle of class. As I said, it was fairly chaotic, but I distinctly remember that the class became very quiet after that outburst. I was humiliated. I didn't know what to do with myself. Rabbi Rubinfeld didn't say very much, if anything. We just continued. But I'll never forget the embarrassment and the hurt.

I recoiled again, overwhelmed with the same combination of shame, embarrassment, and blind anger. I just wanted to hit someone, hard. But I didn't. I never did. Years later, in 2011, I wrote an email to this classmate about what he had said, and how much it had hurt me. He sent me a dry, bureaucratic reply. Clearly, it wasn't natural. To me, it felt as though he had either been told what to write or felt awkward about how to respond. But, as I wrote to him, we were just children at the time, and now, as an adult, I wasn't upset with him about it. Kids will be kids. I'm sure that, as a child, I hurt kids as well.

However, what Yerachmiel did, even though he was just a schoolboy, was the ultimate betrayal. I was devastated. Despite his father being a rabbi, he was somewhat of an outsider in the popular-class group as well, and he wanted to become more accepted. He thought that relaying the information about my abuse would give him some power, make him more popular with the other boys, who spread the news about me. He refused to admit that he had ratted on me, and I also never acknowledged it was him, until much later. As is the way of schoolboys, who are emotionally immature and tend to deny conflict, we stayed friends for a long time. It was too confronting for me to raise the subject, and too hard for him. To his credit, he did apologise, unilaterally and off his own initiative, a few years later when we had left school. At the time, I accepted his apology.

When, much later, I went public with my allegations, I asked Yerachmiel whether he would be prepared to make a statement that I had told him about Velvel at the time. Any such corroboration would support my case, I told him. Yerachmiel questioned whether my recollection was accurate, but he did acknowledge that I had told him about Velvel. Subsequently, he clarified to me that he hadn't really been questioning my memory, but was trying to make some order in his own mind—he had just used the wrong words to convey his thoughts and feelings. Later, he agreed to go to the police to give a statement to support my case. However, he initially said he wanted to think about it, as opposed to saying *Yes, of course*. I felt that he was still playing games with me. He ended up providing a police statement in July 2013, about 18 months after I first asked him to do so, and after much pressure from me. Consequently, I'm left questioning the sincerity of his apology. It's fairly easy to apologise to someone you hurt so much. But taking action—even seemingly simple action such as providing a statement to the police about what you remember—would have demonstrated where he really stood on this issue. And he left me bitterly disappointed. And surprised. But I try not to judge. Everyone has their own story. And this issue is confronting. So I've let the matter rest.

Yerachmiel's support was and remains academic at this stage, because Velvel is still in New York. Despite my statement to police about his sexual abuse of me, Australian police have not yet attempted to extradite him, because the level of proof that is required for extradition is high—even higher than what is required to simply charge someone. The resources required to undertake this exercise, when the police are unsure of the strength of their case, has held the cause of justice back. To date, I am the only victim who has lodged formal allegations about Velvel. I do know of two other alleged victims: one who went to my school, who I have spoken to, and a second person whose situation I heard about through another victim advocate, who has also yet to go to the police. At this stage, neither is ready to go to the police and endure a potentially lengthy court process. Of course, I fully understand them, as well as the police position on this matter. The police have made it clear to me that if Velvel comes to Australia, he will be 'arrested and interviewed'. Obviously, my hope is that justice will prevail.

I was never a model student. Although I was well behaved at home, I did not apply myself to my studies. After the abuse commenced, my behaviour at school and at home, as well as my studies, deteriorated. I was getting kicked out of class all the time, and also faltered academically. I got my lowest-ever mark in any subject, 13 per cent in Year 7 science, and when the science teacher, Mr Pinchas Henenberg, told us not to pour cold water over a test tube after we'd heated it on the Bunsen burner, that was exactly what I did. It shattered, and my reputation dropped another notch. I got dragged by my ear to the front of the class and placed in the corner. It got to the point that when I left general studies in the middle of Year 7, another teacher told me she thought I would become a garbage collector.

The only time I excelled during this period was when a group of us found an exam paper in a teacher's drawer. As I sat down to do the test, I said to myself: *I am not going to get them all right. I am going to get one wrong, just so they don't suspect anything.* The next day, the teacher, Rabbi Chaim Zvi Groner, handed out the marks, and I got just under 100 per cent. 'Well done,' he said, and smiled as he handed out the papers. I never got busted, but I never got a mark like that again. As the eldest boy, my underachievement was always compared with the brother born after me, Shneur, who was a keen and excellent student, and seen from an early stage as a prodigious talent capable of reaching great heights. Later, he was considered by many as a future potential Chabad leader. Similarly, the brother immediately under him, Shmaya—two years my junior—also featured prominently on many award and achievement boards. He was considered a child prodigy. It was even felt that he had a photographic memory—he was able to recite endless religious texts off by heart. At a young age, he even represented Australia in an international competition in Israel.

My father saw that I wasn't doing well. Before making any decision, as is common within Chabad, he consulted several rabbis and others (including, apparently, the then principal of Yeshivah College, Rabbi Avrohom Glick). The group made a decision that, halfway through Year 7, I would be sent to Israel, with Shneur, to spend six months studying at a religious school. *When in doubt, send them to a full-time religious-studies Yeshivah* is the default response of many in the ultra-Orthodox community. They thought that a change of environment might reset my focus, and that immersing me in full-time religious studies might spark my Jewish soul. I have no doubt that they felt they were doing what was in my best interest. So my mother chaperoned us, along with two of our younger siblings, to Israel, via a quick visit to New York to see the Lubavitcher Rebbe in Crown Heights.

Shneur and I stayed at my mother's sister's home in B'nei B'rak, widely regarded as the most ultra-Orthodox city in all of Israel. There has always been tension between the various Hasidic sects such as Chabad, Gur, Satmar, Belz, and others, as well as between all these Hasidic sects and non-Hasidic ultra-Orthodox Jews commonly referred to as Yeshivish, Litvish, or, as we mostly referred to them, 'Misnagdim' (the 'opposers', meaning that they oppose Hasidism). To the outside world, they all look the same. While they share certain values, beliefs, and traditions, each sect has its own individual, sometimes idiosyncratic, rituals and practices, ways of dressing, and codes of behaviour that, collectively, promote a powerful identification with the sect. It's tribalism with a black hat (or a fur one), and the most important value of tribalism is loyalty—to the community and, ultimately, their Rebbe. The need for control drives the heads of each sect to indoctrinate their followers into a blind and ritualised allegiance.

(For example, we grew up using the foulest language about our fellow ultra-Orthodox Jews. A common one was: 'They aren't even Jewish'. Ironically, many said this about us at Chabad—we were idol-worshippers, the idol being our revered Rebbe. We would also spit out the word 'Misnagdim' every time we walked past them. Back in Melbourne, some Chabadniks would not eat meat that had been certified kosher by an authority from Adass, a local conglomerate of all the other Hasidic groups, excluding Chabad. The sects also placed a taboo on intermarriage with other sects. The intrusion into everyday human relationships sometimes verged on the perverted. Even now, it's a common practice within the broader ultra-Orthodox community for a husband to give his wife's underpants to their rabbi for a verdict on whether she is menstruating (that is, if she finds spotting on her underpants and is unable to make a determination as to the cause—apparently, the rabbi is well placed to make such a determination), and whether it is appropriate for the couple to have sex.)

There was open tension between the sects in B'nei B'rak; Chabad's high profile and the media attention on our New York-based Rebbe made our group a target of disdain, made worse by the fact that we were a small minority—both in general terms and even more so in B'nei B'rak. (There's a town in Israel called Kfar Chabad [the village of Chabad], which has the largest concentration of Chabadniks). For some reason, members of the Chabad and Gur sects got along in a type of an informal alliance. The rest of them hated Chabad.

Two incidents stand out in my mind. One night after

dinner at my cousins' house, Shneur and I were home with some of our cousins—our uncle and auntie were away—and, with the legacy of an inter-sect argument still in my mind, I wrote a note: 'Rabbi Shach [their Rebbe-equivalent] is the dog of dogs, the lowest of the lowest', and threw it outside to a group of Misnagdim who were loitering nearby. They had previously made some derogatory comments regarding Chabad, including showing great disrespect to the Rebbe. Within a few minutes, there were what seemed to be dozens of kids outside screaming at us. They were raging with anger. When my aunt got home right in the middle of the turmoil, she filled up a pitcher of water, and walked outside and threw it towards them to disperse the mob. Even after that, they kept screaming at us. If I had been out in the street, it would have turned violent, no doubt. When my aunt came back inside, she was furious with me for writing the note.

The second incident occurred during municipal elections for B'nei B'rak. Gur and Chabad established a joint headquarters where they would organise how-to-vote cards and other electoral material. My cousins, my brother, and I went to the headquarters, and found the organisers sending out carloads full of supporters to help with voting cards. They also had taxis chartered, filled with young Orthodox men, around 20 years old, holding walkie-talkies.

Whenever a fight broke out between Chabad/Gur and the other Orthodox groups at a polling booth, a message would be sent via walkie-talkie. 'We need 20 men, send them over' was the cry. The chartered taxis would be despatched to the scene of the fight, and our guys would get out to support their group and fight the others. This happened all day long. We were shocked at the hatred between the groups. The fighting was physical. I recall one of the Misnagdim screaming

'*Chabad are murderers*' in Hebrew while the punch-ups were going on. It left a strong impression on me. But admittedly, as a 12-year-old, it was one of the highlights of my trip to Israel.

Although I enjoyed my six months in Israel, it did not produce any religious or academic revelation for me. Upon our return home, the B'nei B'rak Cheder [religious school] sent a note, which read something like the following: 'Shneur is an excellent student; we'll have him back any time. Keep Menachem [Manny] close to you.' These words referred to my studies, and to my general behaviour. Ironically, they turned out to be prophetic with regard to more important life experiences.

Shortly before I'd left for Israel, I'd been sexually abused by a second man, unrelated in any way to my first abuser. The incidents started just after I began high school, and then continued once I returned to Melbourne. The perpetrator's name was David Cyprys, and he was responsible for security at the Yeshivah Centre opposite my house. He also had a locksmith and security business, Shomer Security. Cyprys, who was about 20 years old, roamed around the Yeshivah grounds freely, thanks to his security role and the fact that everyone knew him. He had full access to every room on the Yeshivah premises. We would go across the road to play basketball at Yeshivah after school, and Cyprys would often be there. Sometimes non-Jews—big, blond, muscly guys—would wander in and try to play with us. Cyprys would kick them out. His self-confidence left an impression on me. Although he was short and scrawny (something I only realised recently), he seemed big and strong. He had a black belt in karate, and got rid of the intruders fearlessly.

Cyprys also taught karate classes for the boys at the back of the Elwood Synagogue, and would come and pick me and my brothers up in his Shomer Security van to take us to the lessons. Cyprys always made me sit in the front of the van, and the smaller boys would sit on the floor in the back. While we were driving, he would reach out and suddenly fondle my genitals. I knew it wasn't right, especially after my experience with Velvel, and I felt very uncomfortable. But as with Velvel, I just froze. Sometime Cyprys would even sit all three of us in the front and, as I sat down, he would touch me in a way that my brothers couldn't see. I kindof got used to it after a while; I steeled myself to expect it. It felt like it came with the territory.

The karate classes were once or twice a week, always in the evenings. Cyprys was the only instructor, and there were usually about six students in the class. After molesting me during the drive, he would strategically place me in the back of the class and suddenly come up behind me during class and pinch my backside. At that stage, I thought he was just being silly and that he was a bit crazy. Then it got worse.

One time, he dropped my brothers off first, parked the van nearby, and touched my penis and groin area over the top of my tracksuit pants. On at least one occasion, when he gave us a training exercise that required us to stand with our legs spread wide, he grabbed my crotch area from behind and squeezed my penis and testicles. Cyprys always put me at the back, and would walk around while we did training. 'Look at the front,' he would yell, and we all did as he commanded. Little did I realise at the time that it was to enable him to brazenly molest me during class. It was as if he enjoyed the thrill of possibly getting caught. While we stood there waiting for the next instruction, he would come up behind me and suddenly grab my genitals. This happened several times. After my experiences with Velvel, I knew exactly what he was doing, but I chose to ignore it, to pretend it wasn't happening. Cyprys continued to molest me on a number of occasions over a period of around two years.

Another time, Cyprys concocted a story that I had done something wrong in class, for which he needed to punish me. He took me outside while everyone else was told to continue practising, and gave me two options for my punishment. The first was something impossible for me to do. The other option was to drop my pants and run around the yard half naked. He effectively left me with only one choice, to run several laps around the yard with my pants around my ankles while he watched. Although I felt humiliated and distressed, I felt I had no choice but to comply, because I was relatively powerless compared to this grown man. Also, I was worried he might make me do something even worse. And ultimately that is what happened. When I was about 14 years old, Cyprys held a personal karate session for me and a classmate at the back of the Yeshivah Centre—the only time I can remember training with him on the Yeshivah grounds. After training, Cyprys asked me to accompany him while he dropped my friend off at his home, because he claimed he wanted to show me something afterwards. This was despite the fact that I lived across the road from the Yeshivah Centre. After we dropped off my classmate in East St Kilda, Cyprys drove me back to the Yeshivah Centre and took me to the male mikvah, or ritual bath.

The mikvah is a ritual bathing house, a sacred place. It is a tradition within the global Chabad movement, as well as within other ultra-Orthodox groups, for males from a young age to immerse themselves on a daily basis in the mikvah. On

Fridays, in honour of the Sabbath, and on other occasions, this ritual is repeated. It is meant to be a holy and purifying experience. There is a public change room where everyone removes all their clothes, and prior to immersing oneself in the mikvah, one is expected to have a shower at the facilities provided. Often, people also shower after immersing in it. Inside the mikvah itself, it is customary to dip your entire body three times under water — you rise above the water each time, and then fully immerse yourself. In my experience, most people also generally use the mikvah as a place to relax and socialise. Often, depending on how busy it is, there are numerous people there at the same time, just chatting and relaxing. Before my experience with Cyprys, I had never had any indication that it could be an unsafe place; on the contrary, I had always assumed the baths to be a very safe place, due to their religious significance. Never in my wildest dreams had I imagined that Cyprys would sexually abuse me in this holy place.

'Let's go in the water. I want to show you some floating techniques,' he said. We were both naked. He asked me to lie flat on my back over the water. Then he proceeded to touch me on my leg and groin. He then masturbated me. Simultaneously, he was noting that I was floating, and he asked me why my penis was erect. I can't remember if I had to touch him — but there was definitely some contact with his genitals. He may have simply been rubbing himself against me. Throughout the abuse, I was confused and distressed. I started getting very hot, the air burned like a sauna as the water was very hot, and I felt faint and dizzy. 'I don't feel well,' I whispered. I got out of the bath while holding the railing and wall, and sat down on the floor in the drying section and started blacking out. Cyprys came over to me, clearly concerned, and asked if I was alright. I remember he touched my body there as well—I couldn't tell if it was out of concern, or for his further gratification. But I felt repulsed by his touching. At some point, it felt like I blacked out completely. I'm not entirely sure if the abuse went further. When I felt I had the strength, I got up, dried and dressed myself, and went home.

I felt very confused about what was happening to me. At the time, I did not feel there was anything I could do about it. Due to my initial experience of having been bullied after disclosing the abuse by Velvel, I did not even consider sharing news of this abuse with anyone. This time, certainly more than before, I felt that it was somehow my fault. After all, why would two separate, well-known community members sexually abuse me? My shame and guilt was exacerbated by the fact that the issue of sex was never spoken about around me; certainly not by any responsible adults, including my family unit.

Despite the fact that I never spoke of my abuse by Cyprys, it seemed to me that people around me were aware that he was abusing me. I was very surprised by this, and to this day I am not sure how people came to know about it. No one ever explained it. I suspect that people saw us spending a significant amount of time together, and simply assumed that something was going on. I recall one particular incident that made me realise many people knew what I thought was my secret. A rumour started spreading that another schoolmate around my age, but one year below me in school, a boy from Brisbane who was alone in Melbourne, boarding within the community, had been abused by Cyprys. At one stage, the victim himself told me what had happened. I vividly recall the way he conveyed what had happened. He said that Cyprys had touched his privates, while pointing to his genitals. He mentioned that some weird urine came out of his penis. I can't remember what I said—I probably would have remained silent.

Soon after my schoolmate told me this, his mother flew from Brisbane and came to the Yeshivah Centre. I met her just outside my classroom in the college. When she saw me, she seemed to know exactly who I was, but I am not sure how. Perhaps her son, who was walking a bit behind her, identified me. In front of several people, she said that Cyprys had sexually abused her son and that she had heard that he had also abused me. I was so embarrassed and, again, I just froze. I had an overwhelming desire to run away. I probably just nodded and mumbled. All I wanted to do was get out of there and away from that confronting situation.

For my part, I kept Cyprys's abuse a secret for many years—mainly as a result of what had happened when I had told Yerachmiel about Velvel. The bullying that followed, and the lack of support from staff at Yeshivah, made me unwilling to share this new information with anyone. I did not want to suffer that secondary humiliation and bullying all over again.

Chapter Six

My world turned upside down

The combined effect of two periods of sexual abuse by two different men, over around three years, turned my inner and outer worlds upside down. I felt ashamed, guilty, and angry. I was taunted and teased at school. I felt alone, and became alienated from my family, friends, and community. The ultra-Orthodox way of life, and the institutions around it, had exposed me to incredible pain and humiliation, and I soon came to loathe religion, its practices, and its leaders. I began to rebel against the belief systems that had been instilled into me from infancy. The most obvious expression of this rebellion occurred with my barmitzvah, the milestone at the age of 13 when a Jewish boy comes of age and is permitted to participate in the full range of religious responsibilities. For Chabad boys, the barmitzvah involves spending up to a year learning a religious Chassidic text by heart, and reciting it in Yiddish in front of the congregation (as well as other commitments). It is a daunting challenge at the best of times, let alone for a boy traumatised by sexual abuse, and angry with his surroundings and religious elders.

My stay in Israel was in the year before my barmitzvah, and during that time I was expected to study my text and commit it to memory. As the eldest boy, I was under a lot of pressure from my parents to set a shining example to my brothers. I was very proud when, as was customary, two months beforehand, I started wearing the traditional black hat and tefillin.

However, I just wasn't interested in studying, so I did not learn the text by heart. On my barmitzvah day, the synagogue dining room was full of family and friends, and the Chabad congregation waited to hear me recite traditional texts. I read the text in Hebrew from a book in front of me, not by heart in Yiddish, as was common practice. I knew that I had disappointed both my parents; it was a big letdown for them. Nevertheless, I was excited at moving into manhood—Chabad style. I was also looking forward to the party that followed. There were about 250 guests at the reception, among them Velvel Serebryanski and his father, which didn't cause me any particular anxieties, as I had so much else on my mind that day—although there was the usual discomfort whenever I saw him. The party was held in our house and catered for by my mother, who had an amazing capacity to project manage and cook for large family and religious celebrations. My mother decorated my barmitzvah cake with a large tefillin. Although some of the guests (extended family and old friends) were secular, the overwhelming proportion were ultra-Orthodox. In turn, most of the presents I received were religious books and paraphernalia.

In the daily rhythm of life, the abuse hit me in ways I could never have imagined. For one thing, I began to regularly soil my pants. I know now that other victims wet their beds after being abused. This didn't happen to me—my problem was more difficult. Without warning, while walking around school, I would get an overwhelming urge to go to the toilet, and would have to race to the bathroom, but often wouldn't get there in time. It happened so many times that I almost thought it was normal. Although embarrassed, I managed to keep it a secret— even from my mother. I would go home, quickly change my clothes and have a shower, and put my undies into the dirty laundry wrapped in a pile of other clothes. With 17 children, my mother had massive washing loads every day, and never noticed my problem.

My disaffection with Judaism produced other emotional and physical pain. After my barmitzvah, I was supposed to 'lay tefillin' (wear the phylacteries) and pray with them every morning (excluding Shabbat and other occasions). But I started to skip a few mornings, and my father belted me for these acts of rebellion—literally. He took a belt, and hit me with it when I didn't lay tefillin. This was part of my rejection of everything I had been brought up to respect and love. At home I became a very difficult child, rebelling openly against my religion. I would often not wear tzitzit (the stringy adornments to our woollen underclothes that we wore on the outside to show our piety) or a yarmulke—a major snub not only to my parents, but to the community all around me. I stopped keeping the Sabbath, I began to eat non-kosher food, and I didn't always pray or fast on religious holidays.

My father would find other ways to combat my errant behaviour. These included having me mentored in traditional Orthodox skills, such as the kosher slaughtering of meat.

This highly valued role, known as a 'shochet', is learned by some rabbis as part of their suite of skills. In my mid-teenage years, my parents sent me off in the early mornings with Rabbi Meir Shlomo Kluwgant, later to become head of the Rabbinical Council of Victoria (RCV), the Organisation of Rabbis of Australasia (ORA), and a host of other senior roles (from which he was unceremoniously dumped years later over his behaviour towards me and my family), to watch him slaughtering chickens and livestock at the abattoirs. I would also help sell live chickens on the eve of Yom Kippur, the Jewish Day of Atonement, and swing them around my head and others'. According to this ancient ritual, known as *Kapparot*, you swing the chicken around your head three times to symbolically transfer your sins to a fowl.

My parents also arranged for me to learn from an expert to inscribe the Bible on parchment with a feather dipped in ink. It just so happened that our family knew a recognised 'scribe', Rabbi David Kramer, who would later be convicted of multiple sexual-abuse charges against two of my brothers and others. Around this time, I was also taught how to make tzitzit, and I became a 'chazan', or cantor, at the Russian Chabad synagogue. This involved leading the services. Some weeks, I also read from the Torah, and at some point even got paid for it. When I was 13 and 14, Rabbi Yossi Gordon from our local Chabad community—also a family friend and teacher—arranged for me and a few others to be flown to Hobart to be the cantor for the High Holydays, Rosh Hashanah and Yom Kippur. They had a very small congregation in one of Australia's oldest synagogues. For a young religious boy who needed some positive reinforcement, this would kill two birds with one stone. I was very excited—it was an adventure and a privilege. The second year, I flew over in an air force plane after the domestic carrier Ansett went bust. Being inside a military aircraft was an added thrill. In hindsight, it's clear to me that my parents were doing what they considered to be in my best interest.

However, despite the pleasure I took from this experience, my rebellion continued in other ways. I began regularly consuming large quantities of alcohol, which signalled the start of a long-term substance-abuse problem for me. Alcohol had been part of our life since I could remember. It was not only common, but almost mandatory, to have bottles of alcohol—often whiskey—at our family table during meals and religious celebrations. It was also easily accessible at the Yeshivah Centre, other Chabad synagogues, and at friends' homes. We were encouraged to participate in the drinking—it was considered to be an important part of the religious practice. It was spiritual, at least in theory. We spoke words of Torah and Chasidut (Chabad wisdom), and sang Chabad *niggunim* (songs and tunes) together. So having a bit more was both hard to detect and not such a big step for me. The first time I recall getting drunk was at Shneur's barmitzvah, a year after mine. Soon, at events outside the home, I was regularly the most drunken at the table. This didn't seem to raise any alarm bells. And my mother never seemed to notice the vomit-filled clothes in the dirty laundry.

I have a photo from my 14th birthday that encapsulates this beautifully. A group of children—some of my past and present classmates—is sitting around a table, but no adults are present in the photo. There is a large bottle of whiskey on the table. Two classmates are holding their hands together in a mock 'gay' scene. It is a reference to me. *You're so gay*, they are implying to my face—at my own birthday party. It is a response to the rumours already circulating at the time about me being abused, but that played out as me being gay, and thus 'wanting it'. It should be noted that, at the time, there was a misperception about sexuality among many within the ultra-Orthodox community, who conflated homosexuality with paedophilia. Today, this is less prevalent.

In school, my behaviour deteriorated, especially during religious studies, which invariably resulted in constant confrontations with and alienation from my parents, teachers, and friends. I reserved the worst behaviour and greatest grief for Rabbi Serebryanski, or Reb Arel as we called him, the teacher who was the father of my first abuser, Velvel. If another boy cracked a joke, I would start laughing, but couldn't stop. Or I would crack a joke to make other boys laugh and disrupt the class. The teacher would threaten me: *Stop laughing, or you're out.* Since I had a nervous laughter response, sometimes I just could not stop giggling, and I would be sent to see Rabbi Yitzchok Dovid Groner, or Big Chief, our spiritual leader, who looked the part with a big grey beard and severe expression. Rabbi Groner (who has since died) would give me an animated mouthful in his office, and I would always crack up, which didn't help.

In winter, before class began, I would hide in the pile of coats at the back. Reb Arel, with his long beard and serious face, would then come in and start teaching the class, who were tittering as they waited for me to do my thing. After five minutes, I would get up and shout: '*Surprise.*'

'Get out,' he boomed in a strong Russian-Yiddish accent. I responded by inviting him to play chasey. I dared him to chase me, which used to get him mad. One time, Rabbi Glick, the school principal, just happened to open the door and saw me. 'In my office,' he scowled.

News of my constant misbehaviour spread to my parents,

as it always does at school. In my case, the news was often delivered via a special courier—my brother Shmaya, who used to delight in dobbing me in to my father. If Shmaya saw me standing outside the classroom, or walking through the grounds, he would smile as soon as we made eye contact, and I knew I was done for. As soon as he could, he would run back across the road to our house to give them the news that his older brother had been kicked out of class yet again. All afternoon, I knew that I was going to cop a belting.

Around 1990, at the age of 14, I was placed in a full-time religious studies program called Mesivtah, which was solely about Torah, commentary, Chasidism, religious history, and philosophy through the words of rabbis and the holy scriptures. Given my errant behaviour, this seemed to them an effective way to help maintain my strict religious beliefs and practices. Lately, over the past few years, my parents have copped some criticism for having put me into this program, on the grounds that it left me ill-equipped to deal with life in the broader world when I grew up. However, their decision needs to be seen in context. First, I was already flunking secular subjects. Second, all such decisions were made in consultation with rabbis and other relevant leaders at Yeshivah. Ultimately, it was consistent with the Chabad philosophy, and several of the oldest Waks brothers were put in Mesivtah at varying but young ages.

Although I found the religious instruction unbelievably tedious, there were a few benefits to this new phase. First, we didn't have to wear school uniform. Rather, we wore the Chabad uniform; dark suit and black hat. We were also allowed to leave the premises during the day, so I mostly went home for lunch. Occasionally, a good friend at Mesivtah, Pini Althaus, took me out because he wanted company. His father

was on the Yeshivah executive, and somehow Pini used to
have contacts through his Chabad activities. We never knew
where he got the money to pay for his extravagant lifestyle. I
recall that he also used to turn up to Yeshivah, at the age of
16, in a BMW, despite not having his driver's licence. It just
didn't add up, but as young boys we were impressed by this
conspicuous display of wealth. There were rumours that he
managed to get money and cars from the wealthy people on
his weekly route when doing the Chabad outreach work.

When I was 14, Pini took me out to the movies—my first
time ever. Unfortunately, a Yeshivah teacher called Mrs Feiglin
saw us there. She was a former teacher of mine in secular
studies, and told my father, which landed me in massive
trouble. Pini pleaded with my father not to tell his father, as he
was due to go on a trip to New York—the annual pilgrimage
many in Chabad made to see the Rebbe for the Jewish High
Holydays. My father and I can't remember whether my father
told Pini's father in the end.

Mesivtah was, at one stage, a class of just six boys, and
the intensity of the education only heightened my lack of
interest and disrespect. When my cohort concluded the
year, as they were at least a year older than me, they went
to Yeshivah Gedolah in Melbourne—a full-time religious
program for older students (who had to be at least 16 years
old). This, together with the fact that my brother Shneur was
also joining Mesivtah, led to the decision to send me to the
Yeshiva Gedola in Sydney, to see if a change of environment
might help me. So in 1992, at the age of 15, I moved to
Sydney and made a fresh start. I was the youngest-ever
student to be welcomed there. This was at the behest of the
head of the institution (and distant relative) Rabbi Boruch
Lesches, who was informed of my behavioural problems and

predilections, and made some unorthodox concessions to make me feel at home. I lived in the institution's dormitory, across the school grounds in Flood Street in the heart of Bondi. I enjoyed the change of scene and sense of freedom. They let me watch TV and movies, and even go to bars and pubs, as long as I kept Rabbi Lesches in the loop about my whereabouts. I did not mind being away from my family, although I did miss my friends.

Even before this period, I was breaking the rules of Shabbat. To call this emotionally confronting is an understatement. All my life, I had been told that turning the lights on during Sabbath warranted the death penalty. I didn't rationally think anything physical would happen to me, but the scale of punishment had such a psychological hold that I had to force myself to do it. I remember recoiling when I flicked the light switch, half-expecting some invisible force to come and strike me down. Although this became progressively easier, I faced similar traumas with eating non-kosher food, especially meat. At the age of around 15, I bought a chicken schnitzel — one of my favourite dishes — to eat with some co-workers where I was briefly employed selling Kirby vacuum-cleaners. It tasted disgusting, and I felt like throwing up after the first bite; I had to force myself to finish it. Of course, it tasted fine, but because of my indoctrination regarding *traif* food, which is not only non-kosher but has a much more profound negative connotation, it tasted disgusting. To this day, I have problems eating some of these foods — for example, cheeseburgers (although, for some reason, I love meat on my pizza).

By this stage, I was drinking several times a week, in a pattern that had been promoted from my younger days through *farbrengens*. Away from the confined world of Chabad in Melbourne, I would go to the pub and get drunk.

I drank tequila —but I accepted anything on offer.

However, even with this lax arrangement, I managed to get kicked out of the Sydney Yeshiva Gedola—twice. The first time was over my decision to go to a good friend's birthday party *farbrengen* in Melbourne. As my parents were overseas at the time, they did not want me to return to Melbourne and exert a bad influence on the rest of the children. When I defied instructions and nevertheless went, the Sydney Yeshiva told me not to return. My father pleaded with the school to take me back. His only alternative would have been to send me overseas, and he preferred to keep the trouble closer to home, where it would be easier to manage. Some time after I returned, I was kicked out a second time, for lack of religiosity. I went back to Melbourne, at a loose end until I was accepted by Yeshivah Gedolah, and was then kicked out of Melburne a second time.

During this time, for a group of restless 16-year-old boys, what had been a one-off birthday party turned into a series of *farbrengens*, which became much more than religious celebrations. Often, after a few hours of drinking hard liquor, some of us would get drunk, and we would not feel like just going home to bed. Once we reached a certain age, and grew a bit of facial hair, my classmates and I started going to nightclubs. We scored fake ID cards from older Chabad guys and other contacts—for some reason, fake driver licences from Caracas, Venezuela, were popular—changed into regular clothes, and took off our kippahs or put on baseball caps, depending on our level of religiosity, and then headed out to get drunk and to party.

The Pulse, in Melbourne's CBD was a particular favourite on Thursday nights, and not just because of the $1 VB beer cans on offer. We enjoyed the dance music and party atmosphere. Some of the other boys were nervous about being discovered, but I was already a bad boy, and they knew they could count on me. If you wanted to get drunk and go to a club, I was always up for it. Sometimes we would try to pick up girls, but if we got any interest, there was nowhere to take them. I didn't have a car, and the idea of sneaking a girl into my parents' house or to the Yeshivah Gedolah premises was unthinkable. But there was enough to do in the clubs or outside. And, boys being boys, sometimes going to a nightclub was not the end of the evening. The combination of alcohol and testosterone occasionally led a few of us to the local brothels. I remember going into one establishment with three friends. When we all met up at the end in the lobby, and with the girls still around, the prostitute I'd been with started talking to my mates about how I came from an ultra-Orthodox family and was one of 17 kids. For some reason, that's what we'd discussed in the room.

Their jaws dropped. 'What the fuck did you say and do in there?' they whispered as we left. For once, I said nothing. The situation was too bizarre.

Fortunately, my earlier experiences with Velvel Serebryanski and David Cyprys did not regularly play on my mind. Alcohol led me into situations that I didn't think about too much. And if there was an occasion that made me think about the abuse, in any context, I tried to push the thought away—more often than not with the help of some substance. Around that time, I first tried smoking marijuana.

On one level, this sort of experimentation was part of a normal teenage rite of passage. However, combined with my yo-yoing between Sydney and Melbourne during these teenage years—being kicked out of schools in both cities twice—my behaviour reflected just how unsettled, even lost,

I felt. Where did I belong? I did not want to study, or stay a part of the Chabad community. In some ways I was already secular, although I looked the part (a Chabadnik). And what was the alternative? What other community could I feel comfortable in?

I was 17, I had the odd job but no real prospects, and nowhere and nothing to engage with. Suddenly, the alternative was staring me in the face. I decided to make Aliyah, or emigrate to Israel and join the Israeli Defence Force (IDF), something I had considered in previous years. One of my mother's brothers had served with the Paratroopers, an elite infantry brigade within the IDF, and was killed in action just after the Six-Day War in 1967 and before the Yom Kippur War in 1973—during the War of Attrition in 1970. This had left a huge impression on me as a younger boy, and now emerged as a way I could define myself as a man, a way of getting away from Chabad, and also as a mechanism for doing something meaningful. I started lifting weights and jogging to get fit, ahead of the physically demanding training ahead.

The Chabad movement is not Zionist, but it's not anti-Zionist either, so although my parents weren't thrilled about my decision, they didn't try to intervene. Not that they could have, as I was about to turn 18. I'm not even quite sure why I waited until that age; perhaps I needed my parents' permission to make Aliyah. The only real problem was that my mother was scared about my safety—really scared, especially due to her brother's death. But there wasn't much she could do. I was now an adult.

In the lead-up to my departure, I returned to Melbourne and tempered some of my behaviour, but used the symbolic power of dressing differently to snub my nose at my religion. Inside the family home, I wore tzitzit out of deference to my parents; but once outside, I took off my skullcap and tzitzit, which was noticed within the community and got back to my parents. There are photos of me with friends that show them wearing the traditional white shirts while I am in a T-shirt. It felt like an exciting time. I was getting away, forging my independence, getting ready to taste the richness of the wider world.

By contrast, my sisters had a broader secular education than the boys. 'Whereas for men, there is a concern of *Bittul Torah*, the prohibition of wasting time that could be spent in Torah, there is no such concern for women, who have no commandment to learn Torah,' *The Jewish Daily Forward* in New York noted in an article on the subject on 7 December 2015. 'On the contrary, [ultra-Orthodox] leaders believe it better that women should obtain secular skills, so they can support their husbands' learning [of the Talmud].' All my sisters finished their Year 12—most with top marks.

My understanding of the secular world was profoundly limited; I was not equipped to work in it. Until the age of 15, I didn't know what month of the Roman calendar my birthday was in. I had only ever known of it in the Jewish calendar, the month of Nissan. In fact, I wasn't able to recite all the months of the year by heart until well after I turned 18. As for science and evolution, I was raised to believe that the world had been created by God and was only a few thousand years old. Even though I have since moved on, I still struggle to accept the idea that the universe is older than six thousand years (the Orthodox view), that it is millions of years old, and that we humans have evolved from monkeys. I find all this implausible.

My concept of history was so blinkered that, until my early twenties, I did not know the difference between Jesus and

Hitler—I thought they were one and the same person. In my Chabad upbringing, both figures were only ever referred to in vague terms as an enemy of the Jews, without being discussed in specifics. With this intellectual and cultural ignorance of the wider world, the idea of going to fight for Israel was an attractive option, but one full of unimagined pitfalls.

Chapter Seven

Escape to the Promised Land

A tide of excitement flooded through me as I walked through the gates at Customs and set out into a new future. For the first time, I was off doing something by myself, for myself—taking my destiny into my own hands. This was 1994, just after I had turned 18 in April.

In my carry-on bag, I had brought a razor. As soon as the seatbelts lights were switched off after take-off, I went to the bathroom to shave off my beard (or the few facial hairs that I had on my face—mainly a moustache). There was just one problem. I had never shaved before, so I didn't know what to do. I had a razor blade but, amazing as it sounds, I didn't realise you need to use shaving cream to soften the skin. I butchered myself, and returned to my seat with tissues covering the various shaving cuts and blood all over my face. The passengers around me looked on with concern and bewilderment. I felt so embarrassed. Yet I was determined to modernise myself, so when the flight stopped over in Thailand, I got my second-ever 'proper' haircut—in a salon.

They sold me some gel and showed me how to apply it, but it never really quite worked out.

One of the first things I did in Israel was go to the draft office, who told me that first I had to do an army *Ulpan* (a set of Hebrew classes). While my Hebrew was OK, it was not at the required level. I had a command of religious but not vernacular language. Ironically, because of my dark skin I looked Israeli, and when I spoke Hebrew with an Australian accent, the locals thought I was taking the mickey out of them, especially once I had my uniform on.

However, the subject of skin colour and racism also turned ugly for me in Israel, as it had at Yeshivah in Melbourne. Several times when I went to a bar with friends, they were allowed in but I was refused because my skin was dark. The Ashkenazi–Sephardi divide is well documented in Israel.

Then I was involved in an incident that demonstrated how embedded racism was in Israeli society. One day I caught a bus with my brother Shneur, who was visiting me at my grandparents' home, from Kfar Saba to Jerusalem. The route required the bus to go through Ben Gurion Airport, and it stopped for a security check at the airport perimeter. A security guard of Ethiopian background came on to have a look around. (This was in the early 1990s, shortly after the Oslo peace accords had been announced, amid a period of optimism but uncertainty in Israel.) A passenger who was friends with the bus driver was clearly annoyed by the security guard, and when the guard stepped off, this man badmouthed him to the driver.

'Who does this Ethiopian think he is?' he sneered.

Standing next to where we were sitting on the bus was another passenger, a female soldier who was also Ethiopian. She was visibly offended, and walked off towards the back of the bus. That pressed a button; I stood up, and turned to the passenger near the driver.

'What does the fact he is Ethiopian have anything to do with it?' I said.

The guy was shocked, and started mumbling. Shneur looked around, embarrassed.

'There's a soldier on board who is offended, and so am I,' I continued. 'That was pure racism.'

No one else intervened. But when the man later got off, the driver turned to me. 'You're right,' he said.

I felt vindicated. Although this was a small incident, it made me see yet another division within Israeli society, and showed me how empowering it felt to stand up to prejudice and injustice. I later discovered that the racist streak was alive and well within the army, too. Soldiers with dark skin, such as Israeli Jews from Yemenite or Moroccan background, were often looked down on. My Australian background provided me with an element of protection.

During the first few months, I stayed with my maternal grandparents in K'far Saba. My grandfather had been warned about me, told that I was a firecracker, so he was prepared and able to handle my unorthodox behaviour—at least that's what he told me over the phone before I arrived. He thought my parents had been too strict with me, and indicated he'd be much more tolerant.

It didn't quite work out that way. There was one core transgression that he particularly could not overcome: I did not keep the Sabbath. When the family went to synagogue, often I would not go with them. He took this as an act of teenage rebellion and personal affront, unable to appreciate the wider context. Soon after, he kicked me out. I stayed with friends, other relatives, and at hostels.

I was trying to forge a new identity in a new country. In the lead-up to my departure from Melbourne, in a bid to scrape up money for the trip, I sold all the religious books that had been given to me for my barmitzvah; they no longer had any relevance. As soon as I arrived in Israel, I consciously tried to forget anything I knew about Jewish texts, months, and festivals. I wanted to push that part of my life as far away as I could. I felt genuinely disturbed by the approach of Rosh Hashanah (the Jewish New Year) and other major festivals on the calendar. I was fighting an internal battle to forget about all that, and the calendar landmarks were an uncomfortable reminder. The passing of the Lubavitcher Rebbe soon after my arrival (in June 1994) was another—it shocked me and the many formerly Chabad Hasidim I was now connecting and hanging out with. We were all in mourning. We had never imagined his death. He was meant to be the Messiah—or so we had been indoctrinated to believe.

I did not like being called Menachem, as it sounded too religious, and reminded me of a world I wanted to escape, and my English-speaking friends would call me Waxy. Once I even got a haircut that inscribed the word 'Waxy' into the back of my hair. I was so obsessed with the change of identity that when the commanding officer of my army unit called me Menachem once—we mostly referred to fellow soldiers by their last names, and everyone certainly referred to me by my last name—I snapped back, 'Your mum's Menachem', which was basically *Go fuck yourself* in army slang. It cost me a weekend of my normal fortnightly leave. My social life was soaked in similar rebellion. A lot of people I knew from Yeshivah in Melbourne had been sent over by their parents to spend the equivalent of a gap year studying in a religious seminary. We would party together.

In November 1994, within six months of arriving, I was accepted into the IDF, but during induction training, the instructors told me that my poor eyesight would prevent me from joining my preference of the Golani Brigade, which required a fitness-to-serve profile in the highest tier. I have worn glasses since childhood, to correct my minus-six level of nearsightedness, without which I'd be practically blind. My compromised eyesight meant I was put into the second tier, and thus ineligible for certain units. Instead of Golani, I was assigned to a tank unit, which was a bitter disappointment, as I'd been set on joining this unit. Golani had a reputation for being rebellious, a place for bad boys, so it seemed like the right fit for me.

After completing the Ulpan, which included basic training at the main recruitment base, I refused to accept assignment to the tank unit, and was put in the lock-up at the base for a couple of days, then sent to do basic training for about a month in a general, non-combat unit. During this time I kept agitating and asking to join Golani, but instead they assigned me to a non-combat unit in the West Bank. Our job was to implement the handover of the territory from the Israelis to the Palestinians. I was required to go through sensitive documents and to ensure these were forwarded to the right place. With my poor level of Hebrew, this was a bizarre placement. We were predominantly stationed in Nablus and Ramallah, from where we also undertook some jeep patrols. However, I would not give up on my Golani dream. Finally they relented, and let me join in March 1995, around five months after I had signed up.

'I came here all the way from Australia to join Golani, and

to defend Israel,' I told the recruitment officer who was doing his reserves duty, and was therefore more laid-back than the compulsory-duty recruitment officers I had previously encountered.

He laughed: 'How can I deny you this right? You're in.'

Just like that. I was stunned, but excited.

In the Golani Brigade, during the initial meeting with my new company commander, I saw a name on the board in one of the three platoons—David Benau—that I immediately recognised. David was a former classmate from Yeshivah in Melbourne. As he was secular, and had basically arrived around the time I ceased taking secular studies, we were never close at school. The commander confirmed to me that David was indeed Australian, and he decided to put us in the same platoon. We soon teamed up, and together did basic, intensive, and specialised training, served in the territories, made arrests, and partied hard. With David, I also tried taboo foods. I ate my first BLT (bacon, lettuce, and tomato) sandwich in the Riff-Raff café in Jerusalem. I felt sick shoving it into my mouth and had to force myself to swallow the bacon, bit by bit. But I did. It tasted disgusting, but I got used to it. On a trip to Thailand together when we had leave, he was with me when I tried pig's testicles from a street vendor. It tasted like chicken, but when I was told what it was, I didn't have any more.

The training in Golani was very hard—50km walks, often in atrocious conditions, with 50kg backpacks, sinking into mud up to my knees. But I was more bothered by the amount of kitchen duty they gave me. I had come over to fight, not to waste my time on menial tasks. I decided to fight fire with fire; on our days off, David and I went out to bars and nightclubs, and got wasted. At times I went with others, or others joined us. There were two nightclubs in central Jerusalem, the Underground and Arizona. The Rock Bar also featured prominently in our repertoire, especially mine. We had guns and uniforms, and cigarettes. On the strap of my M16 machine gun, I wrote in bold with a permanent marker: 'Fighting for peace is like fucking for virginity'. Tourists would stop and crane their heads and try to read it. This was the perfect combination for picking up girls, especially when combined with my unique Australian Marlboro Reds cigarette packets of 25. The locals hadn't seen anything like it, and it was a great conversation starter. It differentiated us, especially once we got talking and they heard our accents. We had a fairly solid strike rate with the girls. Often the narrow Jerusalem alleyways were turned into temporary bedrooms. We would get to the bars at the start of happy hour, at around 5.30 pm. For a period there was a special—all the beer and wine you could drink in 20 minutes. It cost around 20 shekels, not more than A$6.00 at the time. By closing time we almost rolled home. I got into this same routine with all my friends, and spent many a drunken night like this. At the time, I loved it.

Since our parents were from outside Israel, David and I were both designated as 'lone soldiers', which entitled us to certain privileges. Among other benefits, we could go overseas for a month a year to see our families, while in Israel we were allowed to stay in special soldiers' homes around the country for free. All soldiers had free use of public transport. On one occasion, our unit held a special weekend for Golani's lone soldiers—Russians, Ethiopians, Americans, and Australians—together with the Israeli girls of the brigade. David and I showed them how to party. The girls loved us, until we were completely out of control. David and I played up; we caused more trouble than other soldiers, and spurred each other on. I went with David to get both of my tattoos. He already had his, and I don't think I was particularly sober when I got mine. The first one was in Tel Aviv very soon after I arrived in Israel. I didn't care what the tattoo was—I just knew I had to have one. It was one of the worst things a religious boy could do to his body; apparently, you couldn't receive a Jewish burial with a tattoo, or so we were told. But I had to do it. The second one was in Eilat. I was definitely under the influence then, and the elephant-chain design around my forearm was David's idea. We stuck out, no question about it. We were cool, we were Australian, and we spoke English. For a lapsed Chabad boy, this was heaven.

We also ended up doing military prison together. One weekend, en route back to a pre-determined meeting spot with the rest of our unit, a few Australian girls were on our bus. We only knew where they'd come from because David and I were recovering that Sunday morning from another booze-fuelled weekend—often we still felt drunk while returning to base—and were singing aloud a crude Melbourne song. The girls cracked up, and soon revealed their identity to us, as only Melbournians would've known this song. They told us they were on their way to a kibbutz, and invited us to a party there that night. We took the details, but told them we were going to base, so unfortunately wouldn't be able to join them. Still, I told them, 'Don't be surprised if you see us.'

Once we got to the meeting point with the unit, we all got on the chartered bus to the base. On the way we stopped off for 20 minutes for some food. At this point, wild horses couldn't have stopped us. David and I decided to bolt. We tried to convince a fellow soldier, a Brit, to join us. I remember the pressure we put on him, but he refused. So we told him to let the commander know that we'd left so they wouldn't search for us and create an emergency situation. We hitched a ride, instructed the driver to take us to the central bus station, and caught a bus to the kibbutz. Needless to say, the girls were surprised to see us. My recollection of the party is vague—perhaps that's telling enough. The next morning, we made our way back to the base and found ourselves under military arrest. At our hearing, I explained the situation crudely but directly.

'We are away from home and family, and we met some Aussie girls. It reminded us of home.' I paused. 'You're a man—you know our needs.'

Then I burst into laughter, but no one else was amused. David gave me a dirty look. Apparently, I should've taken the matter more seriously. We were both sentenced to 10 days in a military jail. My parents knew nothing about this, because I did not speak to them for around 18 months while I was in the army. I was not estranged from them; it was just my way of making a complete break. Plus, communication then was very different—phone calls were expensive, and there was no Internet.

The prison was divided into three sections. *Aleph* was very low-key: this was for combat soldiers who had served for some time, where typically you would get guard duty around the jail as your punishment. *Bet* was for soldiers with less service, but also fairly relaxed (this is where we were put for our first offence). *Gimmel* was for more serious crimes. Conditions here were very strict, and you had to march aimlessly for many hours. If you caused trouble in *Gimmel*, you went to solitary confinement.

David and I were given maintenance work and manual

labour outside prison, but we couldn't take it seriously, and at one stage started throwing paint at each other. We returned to prison at the end of the day covered in paint. The guards asked us what had happened. We made something up—we claimed that we'd walked under each other's ladder, and that the paint fell down. Of course it was implausible, especially when we couldn't keep a straight face. They didn't know what to do with us. My situation was greatly helped by the fact that one of the female guards developed a major crush on me. This provided me with numerous benefits, not least an extra shower in the evening. On those very hot summer days, the usual practice of a mid-morning shower was useless—by the time you went to bed, you'd be sweating and smelling. My second shower was a great relief. My cellmates, including David, were jealous; he got them all to come and playfully beat me up. Some of my best army memories were from that time. Somehow we got released early as part of an amnesty for Yom Kippur.

Prior to the incident that landed us in jail, I also crossed another line—this time with my military superiors. I had got up to some minor mischief, for which I was punished by being assigned cleaning duties, and was taken to a room full of loose bricks and some dead birds. It was an awful scene, and the place stank. I took one look, and told the officer in charge: 'I'm not doing it.'

'What do you mean?' he said.

'I mean I am not going to clean that room.'

'I am giving you a few chances to change your mind. If not, I will put you in lock-up on base.'

I had been doing some heavy training, and the prospect of time alone seemed appealing. It would give me a chance to rest. I repeated my answer.

'I'll put you in solitary confinement,' he added.

I can catch up on sleep. 'OK,' I nodded.

I was placed in solitary for a week. There was no mattress, just a sleeping bag on a concrete floor. It was the height of summer, there were ants everywhere, and the light came on early. Food was passed to me in a bowl. I am a fussy eater, and I couldn't stomach half the muck they dished up—some of the humus often stuck to the other food, and I hated humus, and avocado, and so much more. The guards took me out mostly once a day for a few minutes to have a shower and go to the toilet. It was an awful experience. Sometimes I screamed at the top of my lungs: *Get me out of here.* Often I would talk or sing to myself. It certainly wasn't the holiday I'd been anticipating. Towards the end, my guard felt sorry for me and took me out for a bit of extra fresh air—he couldn't understand why I'd come to serve all the way from Australia. And he wanted to hear stories about Australia. I craved human contact and could not wait to talk to people again, and was never so relieved to return to normal, boring duties.

After finishing the initial six months' basic and then intensive training, there are two options for combat soldiers—either deployment or further training. It depends where your brigade is at the time. Our brigade was undertaking training, part of which was designed to focus on our next deployment, either to the Lebanese border or the Palestinian territories. After this training, we headed to Hebron for deployment. I did enjoy that, to some extent—it was, after all, what I had come from Australia to do. I did not encounter any systemic or systematic human-rights abuses by the IDF, although there were a few, relatively minor, incidents that left me uncomfortable.

I arrested a Palestinian boy who seemed around 14 years old, which meant tearing him away from his family. His mother was wailing. It was horrible. The boy also copped a few unnecessary punches at the base. I regret seeing that, and ignoring it.

Once we stopped a guy who had guns and grenades in his car. We tied him up with a wire brace, which one of the soldiers pulled as tightly as he could. The guy was writhing in pain. Some of the soldiers laughed, but I felt uncomfortable about the situation then, and I don't feel proud about it now. While this guy was clearly a terrorist, that type of behaviour is clearly unacceptable, and in hindsight I should've spoken out—although it would no doubt have made me very unpopular. There was also the theft of 20 shekels from a Palestinian car during a search. I did refer this matter to a commander, who addressed it. I was certainly criticised for it by some.

On a more positive note, another time on patrol, we told a driver to stop, and when he didn't, we fired some shots in the air. Any discharge of weapons required an investigation into the shooting. No one was charged, but the army's response impressed on me the seriousness with which they treated accountability and following protocols. Despite the international condemnations of the IDF, I can categorically state that my personal experience there indicated that it was a moral army, which took the issue of human rights seriously. Of course, there were some rogue soldiers—or just regular soldiers frustrated by numerous factors—but their misconduct was in no way a reflection of the training that we received. However, I agree that the continuing dehumanisation of the Palestinians that occurs to some degree both in the general Israeli population and within the IDF itself is a contributing factor to the misconduct of some.

Chapter Eight

Deaf ears

In 1996, the army gave me permission to return to Australia for a month to attend the wedding of my elder sister, Shlomit, at the age of 21. As she was the first-born of our tribe, this event was a major *simchah* (celebration) in the life of the Waks family. The entire family was gathered together for the first time in quite a while—the youngest girl, Sheiny, was only months old—and my parents were overjoyed at the occasion. There were around 500 guests. By that stage it was hard for everyone to keep up with family news. My brother Shneur, who was studying overseas, only heard about the birth a few weeks after Sheiny was born. If nothing else, the wedding allowed everyone to catch up on what everyone else was doing in their lives. The Waks family newsletter— *Waks Cracks*—which was to have a relatively high subscription rate outside the family, wasn't yet in publication.

The event was captured in Barbara Chobocky's 2002 documentary, *Welcome to the Waks Family*. When my mother was asked on camera how she managed to accommodate so many people, she beamed and gave a simple answer that will resonate with many Orthodox mothers: 'You just have to do it. I can't explain it.'

Although it is traditional in ultra-Orthodox families for children to be introduced to spouses via networks within the community—typically through a *shadchan*, a matchmaker—Shlomit did not meet her husband David in this way. Although my parents did try to find a husband for her, in Australia and overseas, the exercise proved fruitless. While the children can be introduced, the decision still primarily rests with them, at least in Chabad.

Shlomit went to university to study dentistry, and ironically that was where she met David, who was also studying to become a dentist. David was Jewish, but completely secular at the time, although he became Orthodox by their wedding date and even more so through their marriage. He is now fully Chabad.

In the SBS family documentary, my parents were asked how it would affect them if any of the children strayed from the Orthodox path. 'It will hurt me if they don't follow the way we believe. I would like them to keep Shabbat, keep kosher, and to be more than that. We are Chassidic, very religious, and if they won't follow that, it will be terrible,' my mother replied.

This was an indirect reference to me. The voiceover said: 'To his parents' dismay, Menachem [Manny] has turned away from a religious life. Also, he dresses differently from the others—not in the black suit and black hat.'

My parents voiced their disappointment openly.

My mother: 'I love him, but I'm not happy with him. It's a big problem.'

My father: 'Every parent knows teenagers go through a

silly phase, so if that happens because of peer pressure, it doesn't mean you've got to say amen, and agree with what he says. It's very disappointing to us, but we hope there will be a change … Teenage[hood] is as much a turning point as your first child, because that's when you're much less in control.'

When I arrived in Melbourne, my parents were nervous about how I might behave in front of the other children, and insisted that I stay in the attic — not a particularly comfortable space, and accessible only by using a long ladder. But it was practically five-star accommodation compared to the tents I had been used to in the IDF. Their concern was justified. The attic suited me; I smoked and drank up there. My friends were also able to come visit me without going through the main section of the house. One night I picked up a French girl who was working at the French consulate, and snuck her up to the attic after everyone had gone to bed. Early the next morning, I could hear my father praying aloud and approaching the attic, and I realised that I needed to get rid of her before he reached us. His home office was right beneath the attic. There was no time to be polite. 'You've got to get out of the house immediately,' I hissed, and got her down that precarious ladder and out, literally moments before my father came around. The poor girl had just woken up after a wild night, and didn't know what had hit her. She looked dishevelled, still holding her shoes in her hands. I never saw her again. I felt bad about it.

The attic became a base from which I could do what I wanted. My parents turned a blind eye, as long as it wasn't in front of the others. I went out drinking with friends, I smoked, and I listened to non-Jewish music, which was forbidden under the house rules. But it was here, in this tiny space of internal exile, that I heard a radio news report that would change the course of my life. The New South Wales police force had launched a campaign against child sexual abuse in Australia in 1990, and were appealing for victims to come forward. It was called Operation Paradox. The trauma of abuse was never far from the surface of my behaviour, as my substance abuse, episodes in military prison, and disregard for authority demonstrated. I was angry and confused. Throughout my time in Israel, from 1994 to 2000, I'd felt bitter about the injustice of what had been done to me at Yeshivah, and its destructive impact. When I heard about Operation Paradox, my anger boiled over. It felt so natural to make the decision to do something about it there and then. I'm still uncertain why I had never even considered going to the police until that day, but I immediately went down the long ladder to my father's office in our family home and told him that I had been sexually abused by Velvel Serebryanksi and David Cyprys.

Although my father was clearly shocked, he was also very supportive and never doubted a word of what I was telling him. In part, this may have been because by that stage we both knew that one of my brothers, Yanki, had also been abused around five years earlier in class, by someone else—Rabbi David Kramer, who was a teacher at the school. My father had told me about it soon after the incident occurred, when I was at the Yeshivah Gedolah in Sydney. That revelation shocked me to the core. I didn't know what to say or do. I under-reacted, and tried to ignore what he was telling me. I probably knew that if I showed any interest, asked him about details, and had to face up to Yanki's trauma, I would be confronted by my own. For the next four years I tried to push the memory of my own experience down and away, and move on with my life. Subliminally, I also thought that because there had been so much gossip about me at the time of my abuse, my father already knew what had happened to me. In any case, I did not have the stomach to test my suspicion.

Now I was ready. I told him about Operation Paradox and that I wanted to make a statement to the police. To his great credit, he called the police immediately and arranged for them to come to our family home. In September 1996, officers from St Kilda police visited me at my parents' home, and I gave them a statement about what had happened to me. My father also provided a statement. The police told me that they would interview Cyprys. By this time, Velvel was living in the United States, where he still lives. The police later told me that they had interviewed Cyprys and that he had denied everything. They said it was a case of my word against his, and they could not do anything further at that stage. However, they said they would not close the case but would wait to see if more evidence came to light. Having made such a huge decision to tell my father and then the police, their reaction came as a major slap in the face. They had asked for victims to come forward, and yet did not seem willing to do any hard work to establish a case on my behalf.

My anger at their reaction was aggravated by the fact that Cyprys was still working in a security role at the Yeshivah Centre. I often saw him on the premises, looking like a security official, which incensed me. I made a decision to speak with Rabbi Groner, the director of the centre. Rabbi Groner lived around the corner from us, and I took the opportunity to speak with him one day when we ran into each other in the street. Although I had geared myself up for an awkward exchange, the conversation was surprisingly brief. Rabbi Groner made it clear that he knew about Cyprys, so I didn't have to spell out any details. 'We're dealing with it,' he said.

'Don't do anything about it yourself.' It felt like he was trying to cut me off and that he wanted to bring our exchange to an end.

Rabbi Groner knew about Cyprys's activities before my allegations, and it seems that my father may have suspected something was amiss, which may explain why he believed everything I told him in his office in 1996, which is different to the common response for many within the ultra-Orthodox community. As he later told the royal commission:

> I first became aware of allegations of sexual abuse against Cyprys in late 1991 or early 1992, when Detective Donaghue from the Victoria Police child exploitation squad rang me. He told me that Manny's name had come up in relation to an investigation into Cyprys and he asked me to speak with Manny with a view to finding out if he knew anything about Cyprys and to let Manny know that the police were interested in speaking with him. I did speak with Manny, who said he was not interested in speaking to the police. I assumed that Manny was a witness in relation to an assault on another boy. I told Detective Donaghue that Manny did not want to speak with him and left it at that.
>
> Not long afterwards I became aware that Cyprys had been charged with indecently assaulting a boy who had been at school with Manny [found guilty in September 1992 in Prahran Magistrate's Court but no conviction recorded]. The charge and the fact that Cyprys received a good behaviour bond was widely known and talked about in the Yeshivah community.

The fact it was gossiped about was hardly surprising, because Yeshivah had received complaints against Cyprys from as far back as 1984. 'One victim and the father of another complained to the head of Chabad Youth,' wrote journalist David Marr in his coverage of the royal commission in *The Guardian* on 19 February 2015.

> The father also confronted Rabbi Groner, who promised to look after the matter and assured him his son was so young he wouldn't need counselling. Years later the father would give evidence that from that time he didn't hear another word from Rabbi Groner. Complaints about Cyprys kept coming. In 1986 Rabbi Groner told a 30-year-old mother whose son was being abused: 'Oh, no, I thought we cured him [Cyprys].' She trusted the rabbi's assurances that all would now be well. A long time later she discovered the abuse of her son continued for another two years.

I'm close with both of Cyprys's 1984 victims, who confirmed this to me.

My father later revealed that before he knew about my case, one of my brothers claimed that my other abuser, Velvel, had put his hand on his leg. Through our family friendship with Velvel and his father, my father had some insight into the younger Serebryanski's views about sexuality. He had an approach to paedophilia that was 'totally off the planet', according to my father. Apparently, Velvel believed there was no such thing as paedophilia in Jewish law, that there was no concept of a child being 'too young' to have sex. He conveyed to my father the idea that a child of any age could consent to sexual relations.

Armed with this information, well before any of Velvel's crimes came to light and even before my father knew about them, he went to a senior Melbourne Chabad leader to warn him about Velvel. 'This guy is dangerous,' he said.

The response was: 'No, this is all just talk.'

Also, only recently did my brother Shneur recall an incident with Velvel in the mikvah. Velvel and several other young boys were fully naked. Velvel lifted Shneur on his shoulders while he was jumping up and down and the boys around them were doing likewise.

I had approached two sources of authority, religious and secular, and both had given me the same message of a lack of interest in the subject: *Leave it with us, we will take care of it and let you know if there is any news.* There never was any news. As I later told the royal commission: 'I had gone to the police and to the Yeshivah Centre's leader, and effectively had the doors shut in my face. It was difficult to accept.'

Was it any wonder that I did not return to Israel as scheduled, after a month, to complete my military service? Instead, I stayed in Australia for around another five months, and embarked on a binge of substance abuse and other reckless behaviour. At the time, I could not work out why I overstayed my leave like this. I was technically AWOL, I knew there would be serious repercussions. I knew it made a mockery of my struggle to join the Golani Brigade. The system of law and order in Australia had let me down, I could not come to terms with it, and I was clearly unable to move on with my life, or return to the one I was trying to start in Israel.

The longer I stayed, the harder it became to return, and to face the punishment and my own shame at letting myself down. Somehow, eventually, I managed to board a return flight to Israel, though I am still not sure what pushed me to take myself to the airport. It could have been boredom, or a sense of guilt about either my unfinished military service or my parents' pushing me to return. It was a very different flight from the one I had taken two years earlier, when I was in such high spirits about starting a new life. I remember my close mates accompanied me to the airport. It made the departure more bearable, and entertaining.

I felt too vulnerable and scared to go back—both to the IDF itself and to the frontlines where I had previously served as an infantry soldier in Golani. Scared of being arrested, I stayed with friends and resumed the partying life I had lived in Melbourne and in Israel before that. Around three months into this period, my mother came to visit, and stayed with her parents in Kfar Saba. I went to visit them, and stayed with a relative across the road from my grandparents. At around 6.00 am after my first night there, there were loud knocks on the door. It sounded ominous. The military police were standing at the doorway, telling me to come with them. I needed to pack a few things, so we strolled across to my grandparents' house. It was humiliating. My heart was beating very fast.

I went to my temporary bedroom where my mum was staying—I had occasionally returned to visit, and had been able to leave some of my belongings there. I opened the cupboard to get some items, and right there was a large bong. 'Tell them you have a problem, and you need to smoke,' she advised me hurriedly in English. 'Maybe they'll go easy on you.' I reminded her that most people in Israel understood English. As it happened, the Military Police officers saw everything and heard this exchange, but just smiled and said nothing. They were very nice to me, and in the car we also had a nice chat. Had they taken this matter further, I would have received a hefty sentence—I knew that I faced a six-month jail term if illegal drugs were found in my urine or blood. It had been a lucky escape. My mother denied she had dobbed me in, and I believe her. But I'm certainly glad someone did.

I was taken to the military jail I'd been at with David, but this time in the bad section, Gimmel, which was reserved for the more allegedly serious criminals, as well as for those who were yet to face court, like me. There, I met a guy who had allegedly raped his female commanding officer while on drugs, and had then stolen a military vehicle and caused a road chase.

That experience was a bad one. I hated it. I looked forward to my day in court, as all I wanted to know was how much time I'd need to spend in this hellhole. When the day finally arrived, I explained to the military court that a police matter had kept me in Australia. I did not elaborate. Of course, this didn't adequately explain why I continued to be AWOL for another three months once I was back in in Israel. But, thankfully, they believed me, and reduced the sentence to a relatively meagre 45 days (for eight months of having been AWOL). With good behaviour and other considerations, I would have to spend around 40 days in the military prison. Upon being sentenced, I was relocated to the easiest part of the jail, where the combat soldiers who had served for some time guarded the jail in shifts. This was a great relief.

Once released, I couldn't bear the idea of fighting any more. My brigade was in Lebanon at the time, but I was over the whole idea of combat, and asked to be assigned to a non-combat unit guarding a base—a role that generally meant you remained on the base for around five days, followed by 10 days at home. I was granted this request, and served on a base in the Jordan Valley. Many got jobs during their 10 days off, but I just partied harder. Towards the end of my service I wanted to move to a base closer to the centre of the country—closer to where I was living—and this was granted in a different role, but under the same conditions. I concluded my military service in March 1998. This included the time I had to make up for jail and for being AWOL. All up, I spent around 15 months in Golani, which ensured I received the much-coveted brown beret and Golani pin. But after everything I had gone through to be accepted by it, I was deeply disappointed that I did not conclude my service in Golani. It remains one of the three great regrets of my life.

Now out of the army, I found work in security in East Jerusalem, for a company that provided security for Jewish people who were living in the area, mainly in the Muslim Quarter in the Old City. It was all paid for by the Israeli government, and we had to meet certain standards. All the staff were former combat soldiers, either straight out of the army or after their post-army trip while mainly studying. Whenever the local residents wanted to leave their house, they would call for guards to escort them to safer areas, including the Western Wall. It was shift work, and the hours suited me. I was renting a fairly run-down apartment in the centre of Jerusalem and about ten minutes' walk from the old city, so it was very convenient and also easy for me to respond to after-hours requests by colleagues to take over their shifts. I'd come and leave at all sorts of hours. I also had plenty of time to party. Often I'd go to work after not sleeping for a night, possibly more, and do a shift under the influence. It was utterly irresponsible. But at the time, I certainly didn't care.

At some point I was reassigned to a less flexible job, but one of great importance; I became one of the full-time government-funded bodyguards of Mati Dan, the head of Ateret Cohanim, a right-wing Jewish organisation that purchased houses from Arab residents in East Jerusalem and re-occupied them with Jews. Often the vendors weren't aware of whom they were selling to. Typically, the company would act as a broker or agent for the sale, and send a representative to a hotel to handle the transaction so the vendor would never know that he or she was selling to a company that was buying it specifically for Jewish residents. The job was often tense, because it was a controversial concept and the head of the organisation was seen as a potential target, warranting government-funded security. In addition, on one occasion I was given a backpack that I was told contained around US$250,000 in cash. I was not particularly comfortable with working for such an organisation, although back then I was much more sympathetic to their views. However, my job prospects were fairly limited. Having been raised as an ultra-Orthodox Jew, I did not have any life experience or work skills, apart from my training and time in the IDF. Mati was a lovely person to work with, although he was unpredictable, and we often had very long days. And the pay was relatively good.

Mati also liked to introduce me to people. Once, in the Kotel, the Western Wall, he bumped into someone he knew. It happened to be the Australian-born US ambassador to Israel, Martin Indyk. As Mati knew I was Australian, he introduced me to him. Martin asked for my name. As soon as he heard the word 'Waks', he asked: 'Do you know Steven or Nathan Waks?' I responded affirmatively: 'Steven is my dad, and Nathan is my uncle!' He told me that they'd all grown up together in Sydney. He asked how everyone was. I told him that Steven was now Zephaniah and had 17 children. We had a bit of a laugh, and that was the start of my relationship with Martin, whom I have come to greatly admire and respect.

Out in the real world, a new battlefront was developing. The ultra-Orthodox community in Jerusalem was becoming increasingly aggressive and intimidating to those people who did not live according to their rules. They famously threw stones at cars and people who desecrated Shabbat. They spat at those who dared to walk among them in immodest clothing. They picketed stores in the secular centre of Jerusalem that were being allowed to open on Shabbat for the first time. It made me very angry to see this intolerance and hypocrisy. In many ways, it reminded me of my past. My hatred of ultra-Orthodoxy was never greater. It was one of the main reasons that prompted me to leave Israel, in March 2000. I returned to Australia with my then-girlfriend, Elise, a European whom I had met in Israel.

Chapter Nine

A new lease of life

Due to the change in attitude by my parents—at least to some extent—I now felt more positive about being back in Melbourne, and this meant I was slightly more deferential about my parents' concerns about displays of respect. So, in my mid-twenties, I reached a compromise with them about dress codes. Whenever I turned into their street, I would put on a kippahh, and I agreed to never wear shorts into their house, even at the height of summer. I also agreed not to drive around their neighbourhood on Shabbat.

Elise and I got married in Melbourne in November 2000. It was a joyous event, and I was thrilled to have all my 16 siblings there—it was the last time we'd all been together, and may very well remain that way. It was also the first time since Shlomit's wedding four years beforehand that we were all together. The family documentary noted that at various times in between, seven of the children had travelled overseas for religious study.

The occasion was also tinged with sadness, which delivered

an insight into how ultra-Orthodox communities think and operate. During the wedding preparations, my father received word that my mother's father in Israel had suffered a massive stroke and had been put on life support. My father decided it would be better if my mother didn't know. He offered a candid explanation on the documentary: 'The guy's unconscious; there's nothing she can do. If she went to Israel, the wedding would be without her, which would change everything.'

When news came from Israel that my mother's father had died during the wedding, my father asked his rabbi for advice about whether to tell her. He was told he should say nothing to my mother until after the traditional seven days of celebrations, known as *Sheva brachot,* that start with the wedding festivities. Once my mother was informed, her response vindicated my father's behaviour. 'It was a shock and very upsetting. I had not seen my father for 10 years. As for Zephaniah not telling me ... I admire him for that. He suffered by himself and let me be happy with Menachem's wedding. Otherwise the whole wedding would have been a flop, which is not fair.'

My mother spent a week of mourning at home, then flew to Israel for a month with three of the youngest children. Beyond a grandchild's normal grief, his passing at this time held a special significance for me. We had been estranged since I had stayed with him in Israel, and he had thrown me out because I had disrespected him by not observing his rules. Now, when I was getting married, I was unable to share with him the change in my life that probably would have brought him joy. Not only that—ironically he passed away during my wedding. I used to feel close to him once, so it was sad.

Apart from this incident, there is one other matter I want to mention about my wedding. My parents sent invitations to my aunt Sheree and her husband, Bob, and their children, and my uncle Nathan and his wife, Candice. But not to their children, my cousins Sam and Mina, who, as I've said earlier, were not considered Jewish because Candice was not Jewish.

Nathan was offended, and told my father: 'Either we all come, or no one comes.' My father would not budge, so his brother and sister-in-law did not attend my wedding. Even though I had not seen them for a while, I had developed a solid bond with them over the years. For some reason, I didn't stand up to my parents on this issue. They had compromised on several other conflicts, and I think I was taking the path of least resistance at that stage.

Their absence, in those circumstances, is one of the enduring regrets of my life. They are some of the relatives I am closest to.

I would like to say there was no bad blood between Yeshivah and me at that point in my life, but it would not be strictly true. Often on Shabbat, we would walk to my parents' house for lunch or dinner, and invariably, while walking past the Yeshivah Centre, we would see David Cyprys standing guard as I walked the gauntlet past the gate. It was incredible that the Yeshivah still permitted him to perform responsible duties, and he would glare at me in contempt, as if to say *We both know what I've done—I've won, and there's nothing you can do about it.*

Before we were married, I had mentioned the abuse to Elise, but had not gone into any detail about it. Now, walking past Cyprys, I would feel the anger rise in my entire body. Slowly, I shared this with her.

The insult and injustice was too much. So was the fact

that the Yeshivah seemed to be continuing to put its children at risk from this paedophile. So I decided to approach Rabbi Groner again, specifically to ask him why Cyprys was still working there. Although it was always a daunting task to approach him, I had no anxiety this time. I met him in his small office on the Yeshivah premises. 'I can see David Cyprys is still standing here doing security,' I told him. 'How can you have this person here, providing him with access to children, when you know what you know?' Rabbi Groner said that he was personally dealing with it, and he was adamant that I should not raise it elsewhere. I recall that he practically pleaded with me not to pursue the matter.

Cyprys was getting professional help, he said, and the professionals claimed he was improving. I was not satisfied. 'Can you assure me that Cyprys is not currently reoffending, or that he will not reoffend in the future?' I asked.

Rabbi Groner: 'No.'

At this point I said I had to go, and I left. The conversation left me with the clear understanding that Rabbi Groner did not wish me to go to the secular authorities regarding what Cyprys had done to me. It was also clear that nothing was going to change.

Despite my best efforts to stay civil, my anger boiled over in a way I could have never imagined. My brother Shmaya, a fervent Chabadnik based in the US, returned to Melbourne for a visit over the High Holydays. Each year, Chabad held a major youth event at Luna Park in St Kilda, renting out the whole of the premises for the occasion. While the singing and dancing was strictly segregated, as is usual for Chabad festivities, Shmaya noticed a girl who looked Chabad dancing on the side by herself. He considered this inappropriate in public, as it allowed men to see her moving rhythmically, and might get them aroused—something forbidden in Chabad. He claimed he warned her a few times to stop, and when she did not, he went over and grabbed her hair to pull her away. Shmaya pulled her hair hard, and although he was sure she was young, it was not real hair. It was a wig, which meant she was married, and it came flying off. As it turned out, the woman was the sister of Rabbi Moshe Kahn, the Chabad rabbi in charge of the entire event and of Chabad Youth more broadly, and Shmaya's actions spread through the community like wildfire. I felt that his action was deplorable.

A few days later, when Shmaya was inside the Yeshivah synagogue, a Chabad member called Eli Marcus came up to Shmaya and flicked his Chabad hat off in an act of retribution. 'How does that feel?' he sneered at my brother, who did not retaliate.

When I heard what Marcus had done to my brother, I was furious. 'What you did was wrong, stupid, and unacceptable,' I told Shmaya, 'but what Marcus did wasn't justified in any way.' I was also concerned that things might spiral out of control. I knew how this community worked—(relatively mild) violence wasn't uncommon, and we had experienced plenty of hate from within it as kids.

I vowed to tell Rabbi Groner to make sure there would be no further retaliation, and dragged Shmaya to the annual feast for the festival of Succot being hosted by the rabbi. It was just before we all commenced the meals in our respective homes. The rabbi, by that stage an elderly man, was sitting with his guests in the temporary hut, topped with branches, that Jews sit in by custom during the festival.

I went straight up to him, and talked right over the guests around him. 'Rabbi Groner, what my brother did was wrong. But now it's turning to violence. You, as head of the Yeshivah

Centre, need to take action.'

Rabbi Gróner replied: 'I'm a sick man. There's nothing I can do.'

'If you're sick and can't handle the situation,' I said, 'tell someone else to deal with it.'

'It's not so simple,' Rabbi Groner replied weakly, and blathered on with explanations.

The guests were stunned at my aggressive behaviour and challenge to his authority.

I was obviously emotional, but I was not finished. I leaned forward. 'Rabbi Groner, you've already let me down regarding another matter,' I said. 'You cannot continue doing this. You need to take action—you're the leader. You need to show leadership, and take responsibility for what happened. And if you personally can't, ensure it's handled by someone else.'

Shmaya, like all the people around us, did not understand what I meant. We turned and walked out, and I told him later what lay behind my outburst. I was talking about Rabbi Groner's response to my own experiences. He didn't do anything, but I felt empowered calling him out, on his own turf.

The next morning, on my father's way to synagogue, he passed Marcus on the street and knocked his hat off, too. As it says in the Bible, 'An eye for an eye, a tooth for a tooth.' Though I do prefer the Chabad version: 'A hat for a hat.'

Chapter Ten

An education from left field

For the first time in my life, the real world loomed large. True, I had served in the Israeli army, but that, too, was a form of escape. Now, as a married man living in secular society (although close to my former community), I had to take stock of my assets and skills. My secular education had ended in mid-Year 7, when I was 12. For the next five years I pursued nothing but religious studies, firstly in Mesivtah. then at the Yeshivah Gedolah in Melbourne and Sydney, until I flew off to Israel and the IDF. Beyond my military experience, I had no professional training or courses behind me.

I was offered a job as an integration aide at Leibler Yavneh College, a Modern Orthodox Jewish primary school in Elsternwick. I didn't really need formal qualifications. The fact that I came from a very large family stood me in good stead; my prospective employers assumed that I had to be good with kids because I grew up in that sort of environment. Together with my Chabad background and army experience, which signalled that I was a Zionist, the college thought I ticked all the right boxes.

I was mainly tasked with looking after three children with diverse learning difficulties — ADHD, deafness, and Asperger's. My job was to integrate them into the classroom, keep far away while they were working, but be on hand to offer help if they needed support. It seemed to go well, and after six months of working casually I was offered a full-time position the following year. It was an eye-opener for me, and I enjoyed the opportunity to help, use my social skills, and develop empathy and patience for those who needed it. The following year, I was offered an identical job at another Jewish school, Bialik College, a secular Jewish day school that was more relaxed about religious observance. I was pleased to not need to wear a kippah and be so immersed in a religious environment.

The job was a start. I also needed an education, so in 2001 I enrolled in VCE (Victorian Certificate of Education), the equivalent of Year 12 matriculation, in a class for mature-age students at Swinburne University in Prahran. My intention was not to get a high mark but to become 'normal', and at least to have the bare minimum educational qualification every child should have. I took four evening subjects, which was the minimum needed to qualify for the VCE: two subjects in 2001 and another two in 2002.

Secular learning made me nervous, so for my first two subjects I chose Hebrew and Health and Human Development, because it sounded easy. Hebrew was fine, but the other subject proved to be harder than I expected. I had never learned about biology and how the body works. My level and comprehension of English was far from what it should have been. Since returning to Australia, at times I had been struggling to properly understand some of what people were saying. So at the end of a conversation, a TV show, or similar, I would list on a sheet of paper all the words I didn't understand, and every couple of days I would look them up in a dictionary and write down their meanings. Somehow I was able to mask my ignorance. However, I would sometimes get caught out in the classroom when kids asked me for assistance. Once a Year 5 boy asked me what the word 'indifferent' meant. Grateful for this apparently easy question, I replied, 'Not different'. It took a few years for me to realise the mistake I'd made.

Now, having to study at the age of 25, was the first time I needed to read a secular book. I had never read a novel—or any other book, for that matter. Indeed, I did not read my first book for enjoyment until a few years later. And it was all a big struggle—not just the actual reading, but even much later when it became easier, I never enjoyed it. The only books I was familiar with were religious ones. So, in many ways, books were a major burden to me. (It's interesting to note that during the past few years, families in North America, the UK, and Israel who sent their children to ultra-Orthodox schools have begun suing the state for not providing their children with adequate secular education.)

English was compulsory, but it took me till the second year to get more confident with the language. Naturally, it was a nightmare. Sometimes I had difficulty expressing what I wanted to say, because my vocabulary was very limited. I continued to write down all the words whose meanings I did not understand and to look them up later. When I was given an English essay to write, I remember tensing up and having an overwhelming feeling of fear. It was so foreign to how I had been brought up. Fortunately, the English teacher happened to be Jewish, and had taught one or two of my siblings earlier in her career. She knew about my background, and was very supportive.

My fourth subject was Information Technology. As I was unsure about going on to university, either in terms of my marks or my interest, I thought this was, if nothing else, a strong, practical subject. I was also weak in computer skills, which made the course more attractive. I toyed with taking psychology, but felt it would be too challenging. In the end, I found IT hard, and hated it.

My bosses at Bialik were happy with me, and I was enjoying the challenge of studying. Being in Israel had whetted my appetite for learning about politics and international relations, so I decided to apply for university, and got accepted at La Trobe. In 2003, I became a full-time university student there.

For reasons that are still unclear, I also developed a gambling problem during this period. Whether it was an unconscious urge to get hold of some extra money to help cover my fees and living expenses, or the result of my earlier abuse, I opened an account with an online betting agency and began wagering on the results of Australian Football League matches. I must admit that by this stage, my childhood passion for Carlton had mushroomed into a full-blown football obsession. After having been denied permission as a child to watch football on TV, I now watched pretty much all eight games every weekend. I knew the teams and their form, and followed the odds on the matches. I did a couple of dry runs and got the odds pretty right, so I decided to bet. Crazily, the first time I bet I put down $7,000 and walked away with over $3,000, feeling pleased with myself over the easy money I had just made. Admittedly, I had been nervous and excited all week between the time I put down the bet and until I won it—a real adrenalin rush. In the first year, I was always winning. I saw an opportunity for me to make some easy money. *OK. Go for it*, I told myself (and no one else). So I went for it.

From footy odds, I moved to sports that I knew nothing about, betting on best and fairest in rugby league, or tennis tournaments and soccer games in various parts of the world. I was seduced by the odds, assuming that my knowledge of footy would steer me through my ignorance of other sports.

At one point, I was ahead by $35,000 until I placed two bets of $10,000 each on a weekend—and lost. I was gutted, and the hollowness was sufficient to make me go cold turkey. *That's enough,* I vowed. It was little consolation that I was still up by $15,000 after two to three years of indulging in my private vice. It did pay for my university fees, and in hindsight was a lesson in how easy it is to slip into weakness—not that I needed reminding. I have never bet since.

Like most first-year Arts students, I chose a range of humanities subjects, such as sociology and history, to give myself a broad sampling of what was on offer. Campus life appealed to me; I enjoyed the challenge of academia, and did well enough to switch, in my second year, into the prestigious Bachelor of International Relations program at La Trobe University, which was more suited to my interests. The course was taught by some prominent academics, including distinguished professors Robert Manne and Joe Camilleri. Both of them were distinctly left of centre in their politics, and both were excellent teachers who offered me a genuine challenge. It was a unique opportunity, and it took some getting used to.

Coming from a conservative religious and extremely pro-Israeli background, I found that most students and academics in my subjects were at stark odds with my views and beliefs. Although I did join AUJS, the Australasian Union of Jewish Students, I stuck mostly to the cultural and social events, and did not become politically active with them. This was partly due to the fact that I was much older than my peers, most of whom were 19 or 20 years old. I was in my late 20s.

In truth, my activism started in class. Much of the time I felt like it was me against the rest of the other 20–25 students, as well as my teachers. There was a dedicated sprinkling of pro-Palestinian students in my courses, and almost every day I clashed with them. The exchanges were always respectful, which I really appreciated. Occasionally, one or two others would take my side. Typically, they would be students whose background was from the Balkans. One student in particular totally supported my more conservative views. He and I both came from conflict zones, and had first-hand knowledge of the toll that war could inflict on civilian populations.

One day, Robert Manne asked us whether torture could ever be justified to use against prisoners. The year was 2004, with September 11 still fresh in the memory. My argument was that if you had credible information that a suspect had placed a bomb somewhere and you couldn't get the information from him using normal means, it was justifiable to torture him to try to save the lives of many innocent people. I invoked the principle of utilitarianism, hurting one person in the interests of protecting many, and the greater good. On the other hand, what was credible information, given the flawed evidence used to justify invading Iraq?

I had absorbed many intellectual and academic ideas from my brother Shneur, who had been at university for a number of

years, studying mainly philosophy. Shneur had gone through
the whole Chabad system and became an ordained rabbi, but
in his mid-twenties he also started asking bigger questions.
He shocked many when he went to university. He started
trimming his beard, and then stopped wearing his kippahh,
and effectively stopped being religious altogether. Effectively,
he became a teenager in his late 20s, sampling sex, drugs, and
rock n' roll, and ideas way beyond Chabad, which he had not
experienced at the age of 18. Many were shocked; others were
disappointed. To them, Shneur was destined for great things
within Chabad—he was much liked, and considered a great
intellectual. It was Shneur who told me about the philosophy
of Machiavellianism. When he explained the exact meaning,
that the end justifies the means, a light turned on in my head.
I felt like that principle described me pretty well at the time.

Robert Manne would counter: 'How can it be justified to
hurt another human?'

I returned fire with fire. In another context, I asked:
'Why are there so many resolutions against Israel, when
there are so many other countries that commit human-rights
abuses—why is the UN obsessed with Israel?'

I loved learning about these ideas and developing the skills
to debate them, as opposed to simply argue about them. But
my shortcomings with the English language occasionally
reared up to remind me of how much there still was to learn.
In one exam, there was a question asking if Israel's victory in
the Six-Day War was a pyrrhic victory. I did not know what
the word meant, and had to ask the examiner. (There is a joke
about the level of English at the premier Chabad Yeshivah in
New York. A boy asks his friend: 'Can you borrow me a slice
of paper?' when he really wants him to 'lend me a piece of
paper.' Until quite late in my twenties, when someone told me

something I didn't believe, I would reply: 'I will take that with a salt of grain.') Nevertheless, this period was an intellectual flowering for me, and led me to the view that all professionals, in particular doctors and lawyers, should be forced to take humanities subjects outside their narrow field of learning. My mind was broadened by history, politics, and other subjects. It was also enriched through a couple of internships, one with the Jewish federal ALP member for Melbourne Ports, where we lived, Michael Danby (I also went to Canberra briefly to work for him), and another at the prestigious Lowy Institute for International Policy in Sydney, where I was mentored by former Australian diplomat and their Middle East expert, Anthony Bubalo. I helped Anthony write a paper about Australia's economic relationship with Israel.

I finished the degree with an average just under a High Distinction, which was a source of immense satisfaction, given my standing start. Beyond the enrichment for its own sake, university instilled confidence in me for the activism and advocacy skills I would need a few years later. This transition was reflected in another symbolic change. When I started university, I was called Menachem. Fellow students could not pronounce the name, so I decided to change it. Immediately after I graduated, my name became Manny: it was simpler and less religious-sounding, and was close to what many of my Israeli relatives had been calling me for years (Meny). That's how I started introducing myself. There was another major change during my last year. I became a father, when the first of our three children was born.

In retrospect, my politics were decidedly right wing at the time, and over the years I have moved to the centre-right, and then to the centre. Today, if people ask me to describe my political stance, I would see myself as more pragmatic than ideological. I am happier to concede arguments and positions in the interests of a fair and positive outcome. For instance, if I felt that formally dividing Jerusalem would bring genuine peace between the Israelis and Palestinians, I would support it. However, I can't see it happening, so at this stage I would not endorse the idea.

Similarly, I don't believe in the moral or practical arguments for Israel's policy of destroying the homes of the families of terrorists. This collective punishment, which is based on instilling fear about the consequences of a terrorist action, works to punish many for the actions of the individual. It is wrong morally, and it has not been demonstrated to work as a deterrent in practice. If firm, unequivocal evidence emerged that showed it did work, I might review my position. And, of course, if there was evidence that the family was involved in a specific terrorist action in any way, my position would be different. It's the guilt by association that I oppose.

However, the 'security fence' that prime minister Ariel Sharon built in response to the wave of suicide bombings in the early 2000s is a different matter. The fence—in a small area, a wall—was a non-violent, low-temperature mechanism to stop terrorists and suicide bombings. Without doubt, it has succeeded. The criticism that it is an 'apartheid wall' is ludicrous, and a cynical view of its purpose. It was built as a security barrier. That is a separate issue from the land it was built on. Parts of the fence were on Palestinian land, which effectively took that land from them, and has occasionally been addressed in court. I am not justifying the unofficial borders it redefined. But as a security response, it has been an obvious success.

On the subject of apartheid, I think the allegation that Israeli society is a de facto apartheid state is nonsense. If you want to call Israel apartheid, then Australia is also apartheid, through its separate communities for Aborigines, and other policies that have effectively caused massive discrimination against them, and in fact marginalised them. Like all states, Israel is imperfect. Racism does exist—against Arabs, and even against Jews from Middle East backgrounds and Ethiopia. And some of the policies against various groups, especially against Arab Israelis, may be somewhat racist—I use 'somewhat' only because it's not always quite so black and white. There are security factors, not made easy by that sector's frequent support of attacks against Jews—so Israeli actions against them may be fuelled by revenge and in some cases by legitimate security concerns. It's important to remember that many terrorists have come from this sector. But apartheid Israel? Like in South Africa, where blacks were completely discriminated against from every perspective—when they couldn't vote or stand for election, and had to use different buses? Really? Nevertheless, I wouldn't jump to refer to all those who accuse Israel of being an apartheid state as anti-Semites. Too many within the Jewish community do so, and it's to our detriment. Misguided? Sure. Influenced by an effective global campaign? Certainly. Well-meaning? Often. But anti-Semites? Rarely. Sadly, we have cheapened its meaning.

When I finished my degree in 2005, a job opportunity arose through my brother Yosef (Yossi/Joseph), who was working as the head of a European student body in Brussels, Belgium, which had a pro-Israeli focus and was funded through a Chabad entity. This broader organisation wanted to establish a pro-Israel think tank, and they needed someone to work as an advocate for Israel. Although my experience in the army, my internship with a politician, and my studies provided a reasonable CV, ultimately I missed out on the job because they wanted someone who spoke decent French in order to lobby in the European Union. They flew me there to meet with the board, so they were seriously considering my nomination.

Another brother loomed into view. Yanki (Jacob) had recently moved to New York, where he had established a thriving real-estate business. He needed someone to help manage a part of the business. It wasn't exactly the direction my studies had taken me, but I needed a job. He asked me to fly over and have a look. I liked what I saw—it seemed there was great potential for many opportunities—and we agreed that I would start working there. However, just before I flew over to New York, I saw an ad for the position of Executive Officer in the B'nai B'rith Anti-Defamation Commission (ADC), an organisation established to mainly combat anti-Semitism. Although the role was senior and looked way beyond my experience, I thought it was worth applying for, if for no other reason than to get some practice with such tasks, and to see where I could improve next time. To my great surprise, I got an interview, which went well, and I flew off to see Yanki, buoyed by my performance but really not expecting much of it. However, upon my return from New York, when I started preparing to relocate there, I received a phone call out of the blue from Dr Paul Gardner, who was chairman of the ADC, to offer me the job. Yanki would have to make his fortune without me.

Chapter Eleven

A real job

I had to pinch myself. I thought I had set myself an over-ambitious goal— to have a 'real job' before I turned 30. And yet, in the previous five years I had earned my VCE, then acquired an undergraduate degree, and now I was going to be a leader in the Jewish community. A steep learning curve lay ahead of me. Fresh from student life, I was suddenly running an organisation with around five staff, and was responsible for another 100 volunteers or so through our various activities. I was also tasked with organising the annual Gandel Oration, a public lecture given by a prominent global figure in the area of human rights. There was so much to learn. I had never organised an event before; I had no idea how to develop strategy or policy, at least not in a practical sense. Except for my brief stint with Mr Danby, I had never dealt with politicians, bureaucrats, or the media.

I worked closely with the chair, Paul Gardner, and was asked to deliver a monthly report to the board about our activities. It soon became clear that my natural strengths were media relations, advocacy, marketing, PR, and branding. I changed the logo, issued lots of media releases, and wrote letters to the editor and opinion pieces. I had numerous successes early on, which seemed to impress Paul, the board, and others who were involved at the time. I spoke at an academic conference in Brisbane, and brought out the Australian-born former US ambassador to Israel, Martin Indyk, to present the Gandel Oration—I reconnected with him years after our 1999 encounter at the Western Wall in Jerusalem.

I relished the opportunity to be able to apply my skills, ideas, and enthusiasm to the job. The ADC's profile had been low when I arrived. This changed soon after my arrival. I also significantly increased our budget through fundraising. Still, some things took longer to master than others. Public speaking scared me, seriously. I used to get incredibly nervous speaking before any audience. My heart would beat super-fast, and my stomach would turn. I remember asking Indyk about it when we drove together to the oration.

'Martin, you look so relaxed,' I said to him. 'Before I speak, I am so nervous. And you don't even have notes.'

Indyk was reassuring: 'I have done this so many times. I know what I am going to say. I organise it in my mind as best as I can.'

'I look forward to that day,' I replied.

Some of my most memorable encounters had nothing to do directly with the job. During a meeting with Senator Steve Fielding from the conservative Family First party, he casually noted that he was one of 16 kids. He scanned my face, waiting for the look of amazement that I imagined usually greeted his revelation. 'Senator Fielding, I am one of 17 kids,' I said. He was taken aback. 'Any twins or multiple births?' he replied, trying to find out whose mother had more individual births. I smiled. 'Sorry. None.'

The ADC also showed me the sensitivities involved in working within the Jewish community. I spent at least half of my time dealing with bickering and infighting. Typically, other organisations would complain about us stepping on their turf—geographically and/or to do with a particular subject matter—which led to untold petty arguments and disagreements. When these could not be resolved, the situation would be escalated, and the chairmen would enter the fray. It was such a waste of time and resources, and not what I had signed up for. Some of the professional leaders of other Jewish organisations felt the same way.

I learned the hard way about the overlapping and blurred identities of the two main bodies, the Executive Council of Australian Jewry (ECAJ) and the Zionist Federation of Australia (ZFA). I came to see that they work in parallel, with the respective state bodies reporting to them. Although the ADC is national, it does not operate under the ECAJ but acts as an affiliate—a structure that creates many opportunities for turf wars. Often, the ECAJ and ZFA are indistinguishable. While the ECAJ is a Zionist body, and some focus by it on Israel is appropriate, it does so, in my opinion, at the expense of domestic issues such as poverty, aged care, abuse, education, and social justice—subjects affecting the Jewish community, as well as Israel. It spends an inordinate amount of time focusing on pro-Israel advocacy and on countering the Boycott, Delegitimisation and Sanctions (BDS) movement. In my view, these responsibilities should predominantly rest with the ZFA. However, I understand some of the reasons why the ECAJ would not want to give up its Israel obsession. Ideologically, it's at the forefront of the mainstream community's identity. On a practical level, it also relies on donations from wealthy individuals and foundations who are openly and overwhelmingly devoted to pro-Israel advocacy. Israel is also a 'sexy' topic. It ensures significant media coverage and other opportunities, such as political engagement and relevance, for the organisation.

The blurring of roles between Jewish organisations—and not just between the ECAJ and the ZFA—is exacerbated by the rotation of chairs between them. The same names crop up in the Jewish Community Council of Victoria, the NSW Jewish Board of Deputies (NSWJBD), and state and federal Zionist councils. While the public spirit of community leaders is admirable, and they have given many years of service, there is a sense in which they are resistant to new blood or, at the very least, are unable to nurture it. Worse, often they treat the organisations they lead as their personal fiefdoms—this, despite the fact they employ senior staff to run the place.

The Australian Jewish News summed up the problem elegantly in an editorial in November 2013:

> The fact that there are only three names mentioned in this editorial raises cause for concern. A quick recap of the recent leadership of [the ECAJ and ZFA] may highlight the issue at hand: From 2008 to 2010, Robert Goot was president of the ECAJ; in 2010 Danny Lamm became president; in 2013 Danny Lamm stepped down … and was replaced by Robert Goot. Since 2006, Philip Chester has been president of the ZFA; in 2014 Philip Chester is set to step down … and is tipped to be replaced by Danny Lamm.
>
> … Are we so lacking in qualified and credible leaders within our community that we have to keep falling back on the same people to fill these positions? The answer … is surely not. After all, each week in these pages we write

about dynamic, intelligent and erudite individuals who are all incredibly well versed in communal and international affairs, and who would be more than capable of holding their own with the nation's decision-makers.

Which then begs the question, why aren't these individuals seeking office? Why does our communal leadership instead take the form of a merry-go-round or a game of musical chairs?

What is being done to encourage new leaders from within our ranks, to bring fresh blood to the fore of our community, to educate and inspire activists who are not only able but also willing to take on these roles?

What the *AJN* did not say was that many of the community leaders are barristers, which means that they bring an adversarial perspective to their roles, and see public affairs as a zero-sum game. In my experience, their modus operandi favours competition over co-operation. *It's either you or me—only one of us can win.* So individuals end up being attacked more by people within the organisations than by the anti-Semites outside.

Beyond that, there is a deeper problem arising from the limited talent pool. The people elected to boards of the diverse community groups bring specific, parochial skills and interests—for example, to do with disability, aged care, and sport. Yet, from this limited platform, they can get elected to larger umbrella organisations that make influential policy about issues way outside their personal knowledge or experience. For example, a person may be interested in joining the Maccabi Victoria board, an organisation that deals with sport in our community. This individual will then have a say on a range of other matters through their membership of the Jewish Community Council of Victoria (JCCV). And the decisions that are made at the JCCV work their way into the ECAJ. They have no direct mandate from the Jewish community—in most cases, community members don't have a vote—to make these decisions. Some of them hide and become invisible, leaving the decisions to those who are used to talking a lot. The community is the loser, and instead of vigorous, informed debate, we get predictable positions and a merry-go-round of leaders.

Looking back, three highlights stand out from my time at the ADC. The first, and by far the most significant, was developing an interfaith leadership program, called Multi-Faith Future Leaders, which is still running today. We wanted to identify future leaders within the various faiths and build a program with community leaders, media figures, politicians, and professional trainers to develop their leadership skills in the context of interfaith. I am proud to say that I scoped this out and secured funding for it, although I didn't get the opportunity to implement it before my departure.

The second highlight was meeting the Dalai Lama backstage at a youth conference and getting the chance to ask him a question in front of the 10,000 participants. I had never met such a prominent leader from any faith outside the Jewish community. The actual meeting was memorable. In my new secular outlook on life, I was reluctant to wear a kippah to any public functions, but would keep one in my pocket just in case—especially as my role at the ADC at times required me to go into a synagogue or to meet a rabbi. I disagree with those in the Jewish community who don't usually wear a kippah but who do so just because they are participating at an interfaith event—to me, it sends out the message that to be Jewish you must wear a kippah. However, on this occasion, while reluctant, I just decided at the last minute to put it on. I'm not sure why, but it just felt appropriate. When I was introduced to the Dalai Lama backstage as 'Manny Waks from the Jewish community', he grabbed my head with both of his hands and brought it towards him to check if I was indeed wearing a kippah. 'Yes, you're wearing a yarmulke. You *are* Jewish,' he confirmed with his usual laughter. What a strange vindication that turned out to be. I still have a photo of the Dalai Lama checking my head.

The third highlight was persuading Martin Indyk to deliver the Gandel Oration. A figure of his prominence lifted the whole stature of the lecture, and built an important platform for the ADC's future mission. I also look back at some of my other accomplishments there with great satisfaction. And I credit my time there with providing the basis for some of my success in the future.

On the other side of the ledger, I found it difficult to deal with the political agendas and egos of the various people involved there. One of the leaders wanted to identify young potential leaders who were going to join the political parties. I could not see what direct relevance that had to do with fighting anti-Semitism. I was also directed to put the name of one of the leaders on every media release for a period of a few months in the lead-up to elections completely unrelated to the ADC. 'I need some visibility,' he said. In my experience, he and at least one other tried to turn the ADC into their personal fiefdom. This sort of behaviour also reduced my role into one of standing back and making them look good.

Another frustration of the job was balancing the various political sympathies of stakeholders. As part of our pro-Israel advocacy, we issued several media releases that were critical of Australian Labor Party policy in relation to Israel. In due course, Michael Danby, with whom I had done an internship a few years earlier, would be on the phone, wanting to talk with the chairman. I told the chairman repeatedly that Danby wanted to speak to him, but he was a staunch Liberal and seemed reluctant to call him back. That is, until we were in a meeting and had a few minutes free. 'Let's call Danby now,' he said. We tried once, but there was no answer. 'Well, we tried,' he said. From that time on, Danby has practically ignored me. Before that time, I'd say we were on very friendly terms.

When that chairman fell out with the board, he was replaced by his deputy, another lawyer with whom I had repeatedly clashed. As the new chairman, he wanted to put himself forward as the public face, and get me to raise money behind the scenes and stay out of the spotlight. That is, he wanted me to become his and the board's *shlepper*. It was not in my DNA to accept that sort of demotion—and besides, it wasn't what I had been employed to do, nor what I had been doing for quite some time. I refused to accept his instructions, and that was the beginning of the end of my work there.

In hindsight, I now know much more about the personal ambitions that drive people into community-leadership positions. But at the time, in my first job, these lessons stung. The chairman wanted to change my role dramatically, and I felt I needed to stick to my guns. The ADC was a great experience for me, but at the end of my tenure in early 2008, I was ready to move on, and felt a certain vindication when the *Australian Jewish News* published an editorial in March 2008, headlined 'Bring Back Manny':

We'd like to think that there is a continued role for Manny Waks in some capacity. Until recently, he was the executive director of the B'nai B'rith Anti-Defamation Commission, and yes at times, he was particularly outspoken and needlessly provocative. He might argue that as a loyal employee, he was merely trumpeting the views of those who paid his wage.

Perhaps so, but Waks is one of the more media-savvy members of our community. He is a master of the 15-second sound byte, as well as lengthier responses, and has a knack for getting himself heard. More importantly, journalists know him and like him and have his number on their speed dial.

We don't know whether Waks' next job will be inside or outside the community. But irrespective of where he ends up, our community would be well served to enlist his services in some shape or form as an advocate for both Australian Jewry and for Israel.

Where do you go after such an intense initiation into community advocacy and politics? In my case, I got back on the horse, as the saying goes, but took a few short rides in different directions. The following year was spent in a series of consulting roles. I enjoyed the variety, and the chance to see more of the big world that lay outside ultra-Orthodoxy. My first project was to scope out a feasibility study for creating a new Jewish community think tank, a non-partisan body that would be a hothouse of ideas and fresh perspectives. Although the think tank did not eventuate, I still believe it is something that needs to be pursued.

Next, I was asked by one of my predecessors at the ADC, Professor Danny Ben-Moshe, to undertake some research at

Victoria University on interfaith activities within government and health organisations. I spent quite a bit of time touring regional Victoria and talking to, for example, hospital staff about their cultural diversity. It was also somewhat liberating to step out of the Jewish community. Danny and I stayed in touch after this project and, as many readers know, as a filmmaker, he went on to direct two documentaries about my struggle for justice regarding child sex abuse, *Code of Silence* and *Breaking The Silence*.

I was then lucky enough to work on a short project at Foxtel, through Kim Williams, who was CEO at the time. Kim's sister Candice is married to my uncle Nathan, and through this family connection he had acted as one of my mentors over the years after I met him at their house and we hit it off. I had been in the army, and worked in the not-for-profit sector, and Kim wanted to give me some exposure to the corporate world. Obviously he also believed that I'd be able to contribute to Foxtel. I was grateful for the opportunity, but realised fairly quickly that the corporate world was not for me, at least not then. Perhaps it will be later, if the stars align, but as a young man starting out, I found the emphasis on numbers and procedures unfulfilling and stifling.

My short stint at Foxtel also sticks in the memory on a personal level. My upbringing forbade me to listen to non-Jewish music, let alone go to a concert. I had been to a fun rave event in Israel with the Chemical Brothers and Run DMC, but at the age of 33, had never gone to a conventional concert featuring a big act. The closest I came was during my teenage years when I almost went to see my favourite group at the time, Roxette.

Foxtel is a multi-media company, and through its commercial links with other entertainment groups is able to run competitions with giveaways to major touring acts as prizes. As a staff member, I entered a few, and won two tickets to see Leonard Cohen, in intimate mode in a small arena. I knew a little of his music, especially his signature song *Hallelujah*, and could hardly contain my excitement. But I was also nervous, as I didn't know what to expect. If people sang along, I'd probably be the only one who didn't know the words. A group of us, including my close mate Tony, were going to the concert, which was on a Saturday evening, and we had to get going around 4.00 pm. As it turned out, for family reasons, it became difficult for me to go. I was torn. This was a bucket-list item for me, but if I went, my wife would not have been able to come with me. Whether it was out of solidarity with her, or guilt, I gave away my two tickets — one to my brother Shneur, and the other to a female friend of Tony's. Afterwards, I was so angry with myself: *What the fuck was I thinking?* To this day, my friends keep bringing it up. I can honestly say it is one of the regrets of my life. At the time of writing, I've still never been to a concert. There's something holding me back.

Chapter Twelve

Manny goes to Canberra

When I applied for the ADC position back in 2005, I also applied for a few government jobs in the area of transport security. I got invited to attend an interview, but by then I had already secured the ADC role. I felt I had some genuine insights into this area through my army experience—ensuring checkpoints were safe, and monitoring transport access—and then by having worked in private security afterwards. When I realised Foxtel wasn't for me, I saw a few vacancies being advertised in the federal government's Office of Transport Security (OTS), applied for them, and was lucky enough to be offered a job. It was an executive-level position, but it was in Canberra. In early 2009, we moved from the town house we had purchased in Caulfield to the national capital so I could take up a position as assistant director within the OTS. It was a counter-terrorism organisation that had responsibility for the security of four key areas: airports, aircraft, ports, and ships. It worked closely with the Australian Federal Police (AFP) and other security agencies.

I had never encountered public-service thinking or procedures before, and the job interview offered me a stark introduction. At the end of what had been a fluent interview, I was asked to do a written exercise. My task was to fill in a document called a New Policy Proposal, which is something every government department needs to fill in to apply for new government funding for any proposal. You make your case by detailing how you propose to allocate resources for the funding, and outlining the concrete benefits of the program you want to implement, among other things.

I had never seen anything like it, and my heart sank. *OK, that's it*, I thought. *I've got no chance.* I gave it a go and later, when I was in the job, admitted to one of my interviewers: 'I had no idea what the hell that was about. I'm sure I handled it pretty badly.'

'We knew you had never seen anything like it,' she replied, 'but we were most impressed that you had a go at it. That's what we were looking for.'

The role was much more policy oriented than I was used to, but I was very excited at landing my first government job, and threw myself into the challenge with customary enthusiasm.

The job focussed on two areas. One was developing policy responses to new security concerns, which was not my strong point, and the other was managing stakeholder engagement, which I knew a lot about from the ADC. Initially, I sensed some jealousy from colleagues who had worked their way up within the public service to my level and resented how that I'd been parachuted into a relatively senior job. I could see their thought bubbles. *Who are you, coming from the outside into an executive level straightaway?* I hadn't met anyone who'd taken my path—they were all career public servants. Despite these teething troubles, the first six months were challenging and satisfying. I had a great boss, and some good colleagues. The warnings I had received about public-service procedures and protocol seemed baseless, at least in my part of the world.

But within a few months, I was eating my words. The job imploded in a series of five restructures, all within the first year. Five! I had not experienced anything like this in my brief working life, and it was bewildering. Two sections were amalgamated, then the new section was merged into another entity. Before that had a chance to be bedded down, the whole branch was restructured. Of course, with every change, the project we were working on was often frozen and then moved to another manager's line of responsibility. I had no real ownership of anything. This bureaucratic paralysis was very dispiriting, and after a while I started to understand the mentality of the career public servants around me: *Just do your job, don't do anything stupid, and don't get overly attached to your work, because your managers don't really care about it. Even if they did, they are just as likely to be moved on and to leave you behind.*

There is classic public-service gallows humour about firing staff that sums up the mindless focus on protocol. To sack you, your boss has to prove you've breached a public-service code of conduct. This means that, if you murder someone, that's not enough; but if it can be proved that you bullied the victim as well, your boss can get rid of you. This was the workplace wisdom I gained from chatting in the corridor. I went to countless morning and afternoon teas, where I learnt to somehow stomach the pork sausage rolls they invariably served at birthday parties, and to welcome and farewell staff—which, as noted above, was a regular occurrence.

Sometimes there were five parties a week, plus the cards we

had to sign and for some reason hide from the relevant staff member—as if they didn't know it was coming. For someone of my temperament and background, it was unbearable, a form of living death.

It was time to reassess. I had a secure, well-paid job for the first time in my life, I had three young kids, and I lived in a child-friendly city. I would get into work at 9.01 am and leave at 4.59 pm. But what's the point of security if your daily life is mind-numbing boredom? I needed to break out of the stagnation, and use my passion and entrepreneurial disposition to find a more meaningful way of spending my time, without throwing away the security.

It dawned on me that I was in the capital city, I had a lot of time on my hands, and I had access to many influential decision-makers, local politicians, senior bureaucrats, and foreign diplomats. Here was an opportunity to create something, so I established the Capital Jewish Forum (CJF), a non-partisan, independent organisation to host a program of lectures and talks by the influential leaders in our backyard. My aim was to create a new space for public discussion and debate within the Jewish community that was free from the rigid politics that typically accompanies such events in Australia. It would also provide the opportunity for community members to hear directly from these leaders and to try to influence them—both roles thus far reserved for the very few mainstream leaders.

My motivation for the CJF came from what I had learned at the ADC. People had complained to me that the Jewish community leadership was obsessed with Israel, leaving ordinary Jews with limited opportunities to engage on a broader range of issues such as education, aged care, and culture. Also, the leadership promulgated a certain perspective on Israel—a staunchly right-wing one. I saw first-hand the marginalisation that resulted within the community. This was one of the things that bothered me about being Jewish in Australia. Unless you sent your kids to a Jewish day school, went to synagogue regularly, or advocated for Israel, there weren't sufficient opportunities to engage regularly with the organised Jewish community. Even the pro-Israel sphere had become increasingly contested. Many younger people were now more questioning, less accepting and comfortable with the actions of Israel than their parents ever had been. That had made them less comfortable with how Jewish organisations always placed Israel front and centre of their agendas.

I saw that no one was engaging with the ambassadors, senior public servants, and politicians who could bring fresh perspectives to familiar issues. That was the gap I set out to fill. My policy was that anyone was fair game to be invited to speak—apart from Holocaust deniers and anti-Semites. If someone had anti-Israel views, that was OK with me, as long as he or she articulated the argument. That was the point: I wanted open and frank discussions.

About six months after moving to Canberra, I launched the CJF with a speech by Mark Dreyfus QC MP, the federal member for the Victorian seat of Isaacs in the House of Representatives. Dreyfus, who is Jewish, spoke on a range of issues of interest to the Jewish community, and the event was attended by around 30 people—a significant number for the Canberra Jewish community, which only comprised around 2,000 unofficial members.

We were off and running, and I decided to turn up the temperature. My next guest was the Israeli ambassador, Yuval Rotem, who spoke frankly about a range of Israeli issues and perspectives. In fact, he spoke a little too frankly, prompting a left-wing Israeli-born academic in the audience to write an opinion piece that made its way into the mainstream media within a few days. Sure enough, I got a robust phone call from the ambassador, and he was entitled to be upset. There was an expectation that the events would operate under Chatham House rules—that everything said would stay within the room and could not be publicly reported. Unfortunately, I had neglected to make this protocol clear to the guests. It was an oversight I remedied for subsequent speakers.

Whether it was my persistence, or the fact that diplomats liked the idea of appearing in a less formal speaking environment, the monthly events quickly filled with a list of genuinely interesting speakers. Ambassadors from the United States, Jordan, Turkey, Egypt, the head of the Palestinian delegation, and politicians were among those who spoke in the first year. On average, we got about 30 people turning up. As I wanted anyone within the Jewish community to be able to attend and feel comfortable, I felt it was appropriate to offer kosher food. This was a challenge in Canberra—so Elise prepared gourmet sandwiches and other delicacies, which were always a hit. The Pakistani high commissioner went one better than speaking. She offered to host a full Pakistani dinner at the High Commission, and later told me she had only met a Jew once before. Several other ambassadors told me the same thing.

It was personally satisfying for me to have created something new in public discussion, and it also helped compensate for the disappointment of my day job. Although my experience at the ADC certainly gave me the confidence to approach these officials, it didn't necessarily open the doors or get them to answer my messages. That was down to plain hard work and lots of time on the phone and pre-event meetings. Soon I was a regular guest on the diplomatic corps events-circuit—cocktail parties, luncheons, and other events. Eventually, my public-service bosses caught on that I was on the phone too often about non-work matters, or that I'd disappear for long periods of time, and I had to rein it in during the day.

About 80–100 people turned up to hear a talk by the Jewish US ambassador, Jeffrey Bleich, and I then held a similar event in Melbourne with a similar attendance. I had developed a personal friendship with Bleich, and his wife Becky. When his appointment was announced, I had emailed him in America to congratulate him, and had decided to bring something to welcome him to Australia. Elise baked two challahs, and, on his first Shabbat in Canberra, I dropped them off on Friday afternoon at his residence. The ambassador later told me that the security guards didn't know what to make of them, and scanned the loaves through their machines in case they contained guns or explosives. The Bleichs were appreciative, and this cemented an ongoing personal friendship between us. In fact, the ambassador mentioned this story at both CJF events.

I also wanted to ask the Iranian ambassador to speak, and sounded him out about the idea; however, after taking advice from a senior member of the Jewish community, who was also my mentor, I decided against it. I would not have minded if the ambassador were to speak critically of Israel, as long as he explained his views rationally, but further private advice made me see how antagonistically such an event might be perceived by more conservative people. I was concerned that it could be used against me, and might spell the end of the CJF and my involvement in the Jewish community. I wasn't ready to take the risk at that point. But frankly, I thought this opportunity should have been afforded to the Jewish community. Had he come and repeated any of the Holocaust denial his then-president was espousing, or engaged in any other anti-Semitism, I would have had no hesitation in criticising him in front of everyone. In fact, I would've been prepared to ask him to leave, or I would've walked out.

Surprisingly, the Cuban ambassador was a challenge to secure. While he was keen to participate, his Foreign Office prevented him from doing so. It was a case of a 'holier than thou' mentality at work—he explained that their rejection related to the Palestinian issue. I explained to him that Canberra's Palestinian representative had attended—a couple of times, and that I was close friends with him. And that many of the other Arab representatives had also attended. After more than a year, he received permission. It turned out to be an interesting event.

Soon after I arrived in Canberra, I was invited to become involved with the organised Canberra Jewish community. They were aware of me from my time at the ADC. After a few months, I was invited to join their board. In quick time, I became vice-president and was then asked to stand for president, and was then appointed a vice-president of ECAJ, a role automatically given to the presidents of each peak state Jewish organisation. The president of ECAJ at the time was Robert Goot, who, together with some of the others there, liked what I was doing through the CJF. At one point, there were proposals about me going to work as a paid employee of the ECAJ, possibly on a part-time basis as its representative in various engagements. With my public-service job stagnant, I was genuinely interested, and a contract was even drafted—I had brought in a potential donor who was willing to consider such an arrangement. The ECAJ wanted to fold the CJF into its organisation, and we discussed how that reporting structure would work. But, as is my nature, I really wanted to keep it independent, to retain its credibility and the calibre of speakers. For one thing, I was keen on holding more CJF events in Sydney and Melbourne.

I tried to organise a CJF event with the Turkish ambassador in Sydney, but the NSWJBD was against it. 'There are local sensitivities you aren't aware of,' I was told. Relations between Israel and Turkey were strained at the time, due to the Mavi Marmara (Turkish protest ship) affair. 'We are already working with the local Turkish community.' The message was clear: *Stay out of it.* Even though I thought this was a smokescreen for them retaining control, I agreed to postpone the event as a show of good faith. I later regretted that decision, because soon after, I agreed to work with the NSWJBD and the ECAJ to get the ambassador to speak at a joint event, and found that, under their auspices, they were very happy to have him speak.

The resistance was even stronger in Melbourne when I made moves to hold an event there with the head of the Palestinian delegation, Izzat Abdulhadi, following a successful event with him in Canberra. This was just prior to a proposed UN vote on Palestinian statehood. Dr Ghassan Khatib, the spokesman for the Palestinian Authority's president, Mahmoud Abbas, was travelling around the world to try to garner support. He happened to be in Australia at the time, and Abdulhadi offered Khatib as a speaker at a CJF event. I thought this was a wonderful opportunity to engage directly with the spokesman for a critical world player involving Israel. Rather than relying on the media, here we had the opportunity to hear the Palestinian perspective directly from them, and at the same time, to share our views with them. The president of the State Zionist Council of Victoria at the time, Sam Tatarka—another barrister—was soon on the phone. 'You need to cancel this event,' he said. 'You need to tell me when you're having an event like this down here. This is my turf. You need to let me know and discuss it with me first before you announce such things.'

I have never liked being told what to do, and told him that, 'I can do whatever I want. I am happy to have a civil discussion with you, but I will do whatever I think is appropriate.' I did not have any more trouble from him, although some within the ECAJ told me the event was giving the Palestinians a free platform for their views. 'With all due respect,' I replied, 'they don't need the CJF as a platform.' We held the event, and it was very successful.

The rigidity of the ECAJ world-view was best demonstrated by its pro-Israel advocacy. When I got appointed as a vice-president of the ECAJ, I suggested to a very senior official there that I wanted to raise the issue at a board meeting, to open a discussion about the ECAJ's role vis-à-vis Israel. I was not suggesting any substantial change to its pro-Israel advocacy. Rather, I wanted to explore whether there might be need for a recalibration of its agendas. The response has stayed in my mind: 'I would strongly advise you not to even raise this.'

In hindsight, I may have asked for this too early in my appointment. However, I think the rigidity of their mindset also explains why someone like dissident political commentator Antony Loewenstein gained traction outside the mainstream Jewish community. I did not agree with a lot of what Loewenstein said, but he did open up a space for different perspectives on Israeli policy and government action. Regrettably, I never pursued this matter within the ECAJ—not because I didn't want to, but rather because I relocated prematurely back to Melbourne and was no longer on the ECAJ board.

After a year of running the CJF, I could see it would require a full-time commitment to keep it going and expand. As it happened, around that time I heard about an eight-week PresenTense Fellowship in Israel designed to incubate social initiatives within Jewish communities globally. Those who are accepted get the chance to meet professional experts and receive mentoring to help develop their projects. The CJF met the selection criteria, so off I went to explore ways to develop the CJF into a potential full-time job. I took roughly two months off work as unpaid leave, but was able to cover most of my expenses through fundraising.

Chapter Thirteen

The decision that changed my life

A year later, in 2011, I found myself back in Israel on another mentoring program, the Nahum Goldmann Fellowship for young or emerging Jewish leaders, which brought together some 50 people from around the world for lectures, workshops, and networking and other unique experiences. The course was for 10 days in the northern city of Tiberias, but I wanted to attend another event beforehand in Jerusalem that I had been invited to, the annual Israeli Presidential Conference, which brought together world leaders in various fields. It was a great networking opportunity. The names were A-list, and it also gave me an excuse to visit Jerusalem again.

After the last session at the conference, I went to a bar in the German Colony with some friends, and checked my mobile phone for news from Australia. Suddenly I was struck by an article in *The Age* about Rabbi David Kramer, who had abused two of my brothers (the second of whom was never publicly disclosed) and many other students at the Yeshivah Centre in 1990–91. It was not until 2015 that we learned exactly what my father had had to endure from the Yeshivah leadership in relation to the allegations against Kramer. This is how he described those events to the royal commission:

On a Friday night in 1993, as our family was sitting down to Shabbat dinner, I overheard two of my sons arguing. 'What are you fighting about?' The elder of the two other sons said that my younger son 'is saying that Rabbi Kramer touched him' ... At this time my sons were aged approximately eight years and nine years old. This argument occured as the family were about to sit down for our Sabbath meal. I was in a state of shock.

We did not discuss the disclosure of the abuse any further at this time. Kramer was loved and respected by all members of the community. He was probably the most popular teacher in the school at the time. Kramer's wife was from Israel, as is my wife, and our family were quite close to his family. Kramer and his family would visit my home many times for Sabbath, festival meals, et cetera. The closeness of the families made this disclosure all the more shocking.

I later found out a few weeks prior to my son's disclosure to me that he had made the same disclosure to my wife. My wife told me this, but said that the 'words went in one ear and out the other' because it seemed so odd and so unusual to us at the time.

When I say [I was in] a state of shock, it was shock not in the way that I was shocked to hear that this had happened ... The first advice we sought was whether to believe it even, because it was just so unbelievable.

On the Saturday night we were still in this state of shock whether to believe [it]. I spoke to two very good friends [psychologists] whether to believe or not. They said, 'Look, we don't know either, but you should definitely speak to Rabbi Glick [the school principal of Yeshivah College at the time] about it.' Because the question was even whether to do anything.

On Sunday morning I spoke to Rabbi Abraham Glick. I told him what my sons had said. Rabbi Glick told me that he would speak to Kramer. A few hours later, Rabbi Glick told me that Kramer had partly admitted to what had happened.

This admission was a huge shock to me, especially given my initial concerns as to whether I or anyone else believed my sons' account. The following day on the Monday I noticed that Kramer was still teaching at the school. I confronted Rabbi Glick and said to him, 'What's going on? How is it possible that he's still here?'

I just meant, 'Why is he still teaching at the school after you know this?' Rabbi Glick responded with words to the effect that, 'The psychiatrist has concluded that Kramer allowed himself to be caught because he wanted to be stopped. There is danger of self-harm. So we can't fire him.'

Shortly after Kramer's abuse was confirmed, apparently a community member was at the house of Rabbi Groner when the then chairman of the Yeshivah board of management, Hirsch Cooper, burst in and announced that the board had carried out its own investigation and had found 53 victims in Yeshivah.

If they were conceding 53 victims, we can be certain the total was even higher. After all, Kramer taught several classes and also led a number of extra-curricular activities. He was everyone's favourite teacher.

My father and another parent decided to tell the school that they would go to the police if the management didn't fire Kramer immediately, and set about calling a meeting of the parents. They started ringing other parents on the Sunday afternoon, splitting up a list of 15–20 names between them, and organised the meeting for seven o'clock on Monday night at my parents' home.

Apparently, when the police later began their investigation, they called on the other father who, in concert with my father, had rung up parents, to get evidence from him. He told them he did not remember anything about the incident. This was incredible. You don't forget something like that, not when you have been a prime mover in responding to it. Could anything highlight more clearly the power that the ultra-Orthodox community—in this case, Yeshivah—exerted over its members? Even when they had undeniable proof of a crime—allegedly from the mouth of the principal, Rabbi Glick—the congregation lost their voice.

Kramer was spirited out of the country a few days after the complaints came to light. In an article in *The Australian*, Cooper confirmed that Yeshivah paid for Kramer to leave. Others within the Yeshivah community helped out, such as by helping the Kramers to sell some of their belongings. Kramer was now somebody else's problem. It was revealed at the royal commission that not one piece of written evidence could be found at the Yeshivah Centre of the allegations against Kramer, nor of his escape to Israel.

As I've written above, my father had told me about Kramer's abuse of my brother Yanki soon after the incident occurred, when I was in Sydney. It was little wonder, then, that when I went to Israel in 1994 to join the army, my father would periodically send me messages asking me if I heard any news about Kramer, or to track him down. He was militant about it. And he was not the only person asking me to keep tabs on Kramer. Stories of his abusive behaviour were well known within the school community, especially among old schoolmates and friends. They also knew I was over there in the same country as him, and in the IDF. 'You're in Israel. What's Kramer doing? Keep an eye on him.' Some suggested I track him down and give him a beating. I didn't find out anything useful about him—admittedly, I didn't even try—but I carried his deeds around with me forever, alongside those of my own abusers.

After I returned to Australia, my father would occasionally refer to Kramer or my own experience when reports of child sexual abuse in other countries surfaced. I never discussed this with my mother. The subject hovered permanently in the background of our personal interactions. My father and I both felt it, and silently agreed not to bring it out into the open, especially since I had tried to do so in 1996 and been given short shrift by the police.

Ever since the mid-2000s, when I had started interacting with the media, I had wanted to go public. I knew this would be the most likely way to achieve justice and to get this dangerous man off our streets—and out of Yeshivah. But I always decided against it due to family and privacy concerns. There was also my extended family to consider, the very young siblings still at school and vulnerable, both in terms of their social status and potential marriageability. I had heard stories of young ultra-Orthodox boys and girls being blackballed by community marriage-brokers when someone broke ranks. My parents and siblings were deeply enmeshed within the community, and I knew the ramifications would be profound.

In many ways, I had tried to move on with my life. I felt

I had done everything I could, and had made no progress. Although it was in my mind often—consciously and subconsciously—I just did not want to talk about it.

However, something changed within me when I was in Jerusalem and read *The Age* article in June 2011, by a journalist called Jewel Topsfield, which described moves by the Victorian police to extradite David Kramer to Australia from the United States to face charges of child sexual abuse. After fleeing to Israel in 1993, Kramer had moved to the US, where he had reoffended against another boy and had been jailed in 2008 for around five years.

It wasn't just Kramer the police were after. My father also emailed me that the police wanted to re-open old investigations into allegations of sexual abuse within the Yeshivah Centre, and wanted to get in touch with me. He gave me the email address of Detective Scott Dwyer from the local Sexual Offences and Child Abuse Investigation Team, and encouraged me to send him a message.

I felt like a massive boulder had suddenly been placed on my head, provoking a surge of excitement, fear, and outrage. After all these years, was this the moment I had been waiting for? But why was it happening like this? I was staying in a room in the Jerusalem apartment of a friend, Marla Gamoran, someone I had befriended at the PresenTense Fellowship a year earlier. I was emotionally isolated, on the other side of the world from my wife and family, in Jerusalem, where there was no one close to share my burden with. Elise and I had long, difficult conversations about these developments and their implications.

Waves of anxiety ran through me as I typed up a message to the police. My finger hovered above the Send button for minutes, and I had to force myself to press down on it. *There,*

I've done it! Within 24 hours, I was on the phone with the senior detective, and bawling my eyes out as I shared my story. They were tears of raw emotion. I could not believe the police were actually re-opening the case after decades of rejection and silence. It was overwhelming. After years of nothing, not a word, all of a sudden they made it clear they were going to re-visit old wounds — involving Kramer, Cyprys, and possibly others.

At the conference in Tiberias, my life split in two. By day, I absorbed the wisdom of expert speakers, networking and chatting with friends, and then socialising with them afterwards. True to form, I became the party organiser. Late at night, I scoured my emails, and spoke to my wife and police about what to do, and how to proceed. I felt so alone and isolated; it was hard to sleep or function properly. I desperately needed to talk to someone in person, and ended up telling a colleague I connected with whom I had met at the conference.

The impact of the article in *The Age* finally convinced me that talking to the media was the best way for me to pursue justice. When I told the police about my intentions, they tried to talk me out of it. 'It will be counterproductive,' they insisted. 'It may interfere with the investigation.' I was adamant. 'There is no doubt this will help your investigations,' I told them. 'Mark my words.' I also remembered that in 1996 I had done it their way, and where that had got me? Leaving everything to the police wasn't a risk I was going to take yet again.

I phoned *The Age* journalist from Jerusalem, outlining my story, initially in confidence. I knew *The Age* had been more critical of Israel than News Ltd papers, but that wasn't relevant in my story. Ultimately, I chose it because Topsfield had written the Kramer article, and after communicating with her over an extended period of time, I developed confidence in her skill and sensitivity.

It was an exciting but confusing period, the prospect of getting justice balanced by the likely ramifications within the community. Although I knew that once the story was published I would become a target, my chief concern was the impact on my family.

Several weeks later, back in Australia, once Topsfield had finished her formal interviews with me, a photographer was sent to my office in Canberra. I was taken to a park in the centre of town and asked to look serious. Later, the same photographer came to my house to take a photo of my Year 6 or Year 7 school photo. I gave my managers at work the heads-up about my story coming out. Prior to this, I also rang my father in Melbourne to tell him I was thinking of going public with my story. 'How would you feel?' I asked him. 'Obviously, it will have an impact on the family.' He was OK with the plan and supportive, as usual. However, it later emerged that he thought 'going public' meant I wanted to share it with family and friends—within the Jewish community. I had never spoken publicly up till then, so that was his understanding of the term. He didn't realise that I meant I was going to the media, to *The Age,* and that it would be on the front page.

In my mind, there were many reasons for making this decision. In addition to being a release for me, as a Jewish leader, I felt someone had to show leadership on this issue. No one else was really talking about it—if not me, with my experience, then who would? The allegations against David Kramer were already out there, I knew of other cases within the community, and I hoped that others might follow my lead. In relation to one of my abusers, Cyprys, I also knew there were other victims, and I knew it could only help my case to share it publicly. And it wasn't even a consideration to share my story anonymously. I was sick of hiding. Besides, I knew the impact would be much greater if there was a name and a face rather than just the word 'victim' or 'survivor'.

At this point, I got a surprising foretaste of the minefields that lay in my path. A person who wanted to write an article on this issue for an online publication that focuses on Jewish life in Australia contacted me for a comment in relation to an article she was writing about David Cyprys. The writer, Malki Rose, told me she was a friend of Cyprys, and adopted an aggressive and intimidating tone, warning me that if I did not make a public response, she would write in the article that she had approached me and that I had refused to comment.

Rose claimed she was hearing rumours about Cyprys, mainly surrounding me, and that Cyprys was denying everything. She claimed she was trying to make sense of it all—who was lying and who was telling the truth? Although this was fairly standard behaviour by journalists—not that Rose was a journalist—the surprise timing of her call, in the last few days of my preparing for *The Age* article, added another layer of stress.

I referred the matter to Detective Dwyer, who later told me he'd been in contact with Rose to emphasise the moral and legal sensitivities over publishing anything about Cyprys, and in particular regarding her involvement with me. As it turned out, she did write an article, published on 5 June 2011 under the headline, 'Nowhere Left To Hide'. It was a broad feature about child sexual abuse within the Jewish community and our obligations to report it. The article mentioned David Kramer several times, but did not mention Cyprys or me. While Rose and I had met a few times over the years since around 2008, we had been on friendly terms, but not much more than that. Some time after her aggressive phone call and published article, she came to understand that I wanted nothing more to do with her. She contacted me to try to clarify the issues, and denied trying to intimidate me, but did reluctantly apologise.

In the week leading up to publication, I sent out two emails about the upcoming article, one to my close family and friends:

> The main purpose of this email is to ensure that those closest to me are aware of this predicament before it may become public. I do not seek sympathy but rather your understanding and support. I appreciate the support many of you have shown this far.
>
> This email also plays a role in my attempt to gain closure—I feel that it is making the process significantly easier by sharing something that I have been keeping inside for over two decades with people I am close to. I hope you do not mind!

After his initial confusion about what my 'going public' meant, my father voiced his support for the path I was taking. He was openly comfortable about the story going into the public domain. My mother was ambivalent. She had been much more formally involved within the community, having served for a number of years as president of *N'shei Chabad*, the Women of Chabad organisation. She was very nervous, tense, and uncertain about how the revelation would play out. Deep down, she felt it was not right, and would have preferred I did not go to the media. But she respected my right to do so.

I sent another email to my former classmates, urging them to come forward if they had any relevant information:

> In light of recent developments in relation to the sexual abuse cases at Yeshivah, I would like to take this opportunity to encourage all of you to share any information you may have with Victoria Police—irrespective of how important you believe your information to be.
>
> As you will see [from story links], the emphasis is currently on David Kramer. However, significant work is being done in relation to other perpetrators, including David Cypres [sic]. Please note that subsequent to the Age article and the attached document new victims have come forward. It is my understanding that there are many more out there.
>
> For the sake of justice and closure for the victims, I again urge you all to come forward with any information that you may have.

The article was due to be published on Friday, 8 July 2011, and the deadline was around six o'clock the night before. I asked Jewel Topsfield if I could see the story before it went to print. While it's standard practice for journalists to let people see the quotes that are being attributed to them in a story in advance of publication, it's not usual to let them see the story in its entirety, as this gives them some potential influence over the article. However, given the sensitive nature of this story, Jewel agreed, and I received the final draft an hour or so prior to it going to print. I suggested a few last-minute changes, which she accepted. That night, I hardly slept at all.

Chapter Fourteen

Genie out of the bottle

I normally get up early, as parents—especially of young boys—always do. But this morning I didn't even make it to five o'clock. And that was after a very late one the night before. I jumped out of bed, adrenalin pumping, and switched on the computer to check *The Age*'s website. There it was. My face—as a 35-year-old and as an 11- or 12-year-old—and my name and my story, on the front page, below a headline that read, 'Jewish community leader tells of sex abuse':

> 'This is about justice and closure, both for myself and other victims,' says Mr Waks, a vice-president of the Executive Council of Australian Jewry and president of the ACT Jewish Community, among other senior roles. He wants to hold to account the alleged perpetrators of the crimes and the Yeshivah Centre, which runs the college and which he says betrayed victims by persuading them to remain silent.

I had crossed the line. There was no turning back now.

My phone, email, and Facebook page were inundated with messages of support and goodwill from Australia and overseas: from family and friends in Melbourne, and from Chabad and ex-Chabad members in New York and elsewhere. The fact that we lived in Canberra—away from the hub of the Jewish community in Melbourne—made it easier. Most of the people we were interacting with on a daily basis weren't even aware of the story. Indeed, this had contributed to my decision to pursue the option of public disclosure through the media.

Although there would be consequences, I felt they would be directed more at my parents and siblings than at me and my family, which is why I had discussed it with my father first. They lived in Melbourne, in the heart of the Chabad community. Yet we were in Canberra. Who was going to give us trouble up here? In the back of my mind, I actually believed there would be a period of sound and fury, after which life would soon return to business as usual.

And whatever heat came my way, I felt I would know how to deal with it. My roles in public life had taught me how to deal with the cut and thrust of public debate and conflict. In the lead-up to publication, I took strength from my senior positions to date; they lent me credibility as a person of some stature, and would help rebut any claims that I was another victim merely looking for attention. I was, after all, a 'Jewish community leader'.

The first call came around six o'clock. If I needed confirmation about the power of the media, here it was. The caller was a prominent Jewish Australian, who congratulated me for having the courage to go public and then proceeded to tell me his own story. When this man was preparing for his barmitzvah at a major Melbourne Orthodox synagogue, he was given private lessons by its prominent senior rabbi, a towering figure in the Australian Orthodox rabbinate. My caller told me that the rabbi had masturbated in front of him during those lessons. Some time after this revelation, another prominent and respected figure within the Jewish community told me that he had been approached by another former community leader, who had shared with him precisely the same story. So here I had two independent allegations about one of the biggest names in the Orthodox rabbinate. Ironically, the rabbi had been uncompromising about the issue of homosexuality within the Jewish community.

The news relayed in the early-morning phone call caught me completely off-guard. It was not what I expected to hear, and I was shocked at his revelation. When I regained my composure, I encouraged him to disclose the information publicly, but at that point he couldn't bring himself to do it for personal reasons.

I should add that, while these are serious allegations, we must observe the key legal principle of a presumption of innocence, especially as the rabbi is not alive and is not in a position to defend himself.

My own story was quickly picked up by other media, and over the next few days a wave of goodwill poured forth, enveloping me. The police called to convey their gratitude. 'Thank you, you were 100 per cent right to do what you did,' they told me, in an admission that their earlier scepticism had been misplaced. Apparently, they'd been inundated with calls from members of the Jewish community after the exposé. Coincidentally, my parents and family were planning to come up to Canberra for a family celebration the day the article was published, on the Friday.

Also on the Friday, I received a call from Rabbi Yitzchok

Jedwab, who had taught me at the Yeshivah Centre when I was studying at mesivtah. Rabbi Jedwab would often throw me out of the classroom for disrupting the class—at one point, almost daily—which caused me considerable embarrassment and trauma. He called me now to offer his heartfelt apology for his actions, and for not having picked up the signs that I was experiencing significant pain and suffering. Rabbi Jedwab became emotional. So did I. I thanked him, but told him he had nothing to apologise for; he had no idea of what had happened to me. His phone call has stayed with me, for several reasons. It made me feel more comfortable about my decision, and it was the first recognition from within the Yeshivah Centre that I had been the victim of a crime carried out by someone from its community. It was powerful.

For over three years, at least until the royal commission in February 2015, his apology was the only personal one I received from anyone connected with the Yeshivah Centre. It was telling —a reflection on both Rabbi Jedwab and the Yeshivah Centre.

However, within a few days, the messages of support started to be accompanied by criticism. Two people stand out in my memory—Rabbi Sholom Mendel Kluwgant, the father of Rabbi Meir Kluwgant, and a major fundraiser (and a board member) at Yeshivah, and the late Harry ('Chaim') New, also a board member at Yeshivah. The gist of their criticisms could be summed up as follows: *Why didn't you come to the Centre before going to the media, and if you did have to go the media, why go to that anti-Semitic paper?* They seemed to have ignored *The Age*'s stature as one of Australia's leading newspapers. And then, after other media picked up the story, plenty of others chimed in: *Why do you have to keep talking to the media about your story, instead of going back to the Yeshivah Centre?* It then got personal. One of my former classmates, Pini Althaus, claimed that from an early age I was anti-Orthodox; that I had brought the sexual abuse on myself, as we all knew of Cyprys's paedophilic tendencies; and that I had nevertheless chosen 'to walk into the lion's den'. Of course, these allegations were false, and it was strange that he was acknowledging that everyone knew about Cyprys's behaviour (although it was true that, at some point, people indeed became aware of the allegations against him). Essentially, they wanted to keep the story inside the community, to keep control of it, to keep it as quiet as possible. In fact, they just wanted it to go away — and me to go away. In addition, many people within Yeshivah were very upset that, when I was quoted in *The Age* article, I had smeared the reputation of Rabbi Groner, the spiritual leader of the centre:

> Mr Waks made his first statement to police in 1996. He also told Rabbi Yitzchok Dovid Groner, Yeshivah Centre director. In 2000, after returning to Australia, Mr Waks was shocked to see his alleged abuser was still in a position of authority at the Yeshivah Centre.
>
> 'I said to Rabbi Groner: "How can you give this person access to children?" Rabbi Groner pleaded with me not to take it further. He said to me that [the alleged perpetrator] was getting help from a psychiatrist. I said: "Can you guarantee he will not re-offend?" Rabbi Groner said no and that's when I walked out. In my attempt to seek justice and closure I felt like I was working against an entrenched culture and system of covering up these crimes at any cost.'

Rabbi Groner (who passed away in 2008) had been a giant in the community. He was a larger-than-life figure — physically and metaphorically. He had been there for over 40 years, and created a dynastic network during that time. His stature was akin to a mini-Lubavitcher Rebbe—an Australian version. My allegations were seen as a massive insult to the community, as well as to its leaders. Foremost among these was his personally appointed and groomed replacement, his son-in-law, Rabbi Zvi Telsner, the leader of the Yeshivah Centre at the time. And as Althaus had made it clear, he was attacking me not for the sake of criticism, but to 'ensure that the great name of Rabbi Groner … does not become sullied'.

The trouble started for my parents as soon as they returned to Melbourne after the weekend with us in Canberra. Friends stopped saying good morning, while others threw dark looks at my father on the street. 'As soon as I walked into the synagogue the first time, I could just feel arrows aimed at me, and it just went on from there until the first Sabbath when I was back,' he told the royal commission. During that week, he was attacked verbally in the Yeshivah Centre by a prominent community member. When he asked what he had done wrong, the man said, 'You know', and then walked off. Apparently, my father's crime was that he hadn't publicly repudiated my actions.

In the Shabbat service at Yeshivah Synagogue the next weekend, Rabbi Telsner made an accusation in his regular weekly sermon that became infamous. In a question directed to my father, Rabbi Telsner spoke rhetorically to the congregation: 'Who gave you permission to speak to anybody?'

It was a dagger to his heart. My father walked out, and so did my mother and more than half a dozen of her friends. This act of intimidation was also clearly directed at me and my family. While I was less concerned about it than my parents were—after all, I was no longer a part of the Chabad-Yeshivah community—the attack made it clear that I was now regarded as fair game, and so was my family. Rabbi Telsner legitimised criticism of me and any acts of ostracism towards my family; in fact, he seemed to be leading the charge. In an act seemingly designed to silence me, by putting pressure on my family, he was accusing us all of the crime of *mesirah*, of reporting on another Jew to the outside, civic authorities instead of keeping the complaint within the community. My parents were guilty because, it was implied, they had not stopped me from going to the police, or to the media—as if it was in their power to do so. To be sure, during his sermon, Rabbi Telsner apparently outlined the various excommunication options available—seemingly a threat he'd be willing to use if members of the community didn't heed his warnings.

Not once did Rabbi Telsner try to rectify the situation, or try to speak to me. Not once did he try to teach me with the compassion and understanding that we had been taught at Yeshivah to show when dealing with people in trouble. Nor for that matter, did he show the love you're meant to show your fellow Jew, regardless of the circumstances, which was supposedly at the heart of the Chabad belief system. It was hypocritical at every level. Indeed, it was mind-boggling.

This toxic mix of cold shoulders, snubs, and indirect accusations against my parents intensified. In June 2012, in the week of his Jewish birthday, my father was told he would not be invited to bless the Torah (receive an Aliyah), as he had done every year up till then, and which every other Yeshivah member was honoured with. When the media asked why this was the case, Rabbi Telsner was quoted as saying: 'There is no obligation to grant someone an Aliyah. The decision is made in our congregation by the rabbi and [those in charge of the call-ups]. To give Mr Waks an Aliyah was not deemed appropriate.' He did not elaborate. He certainly didn't deny that it was connected to the continuing child sexual-abuse scandal plaguing his institution.

It seemed to many of us a deliberate step towards excommunicating my parents, which caused immense emotional pain and trauma for them, and indirectly for me and many others. It signalled that we were effectively *personae non gratae*. This intimidation continued and escalated. In May and August 2013, my father was physically assaulted in synagogue by a fellow congregant—someone he'd been sitting near at the Yeshivah synagogue for years.

It is hard to overstate the sense of betrayal being felt by my parents. Their whole life had been intertwined with the Chabad community, and now everything they held dear was being withdrawn from them by edict. All around them, others fell into line, averted their gaze, and stopped engaging with them, leaving my parents feeling isolated, tainted, and unwanted. They stopped being invited to friends' homes. Even long-time religious study partners stopped their daily and weekly sessions with my father.

The tension spread right through the family, demonstrated by another incident that occurred in the synagogue the day before my father was assaulted. At the end of the Tuesday evening service, Rabbi Telsner offered my much younger brother Chaim a 'Good Yontov'—a seasonal greeting for the festival of Shavuot. Chaim is secular, and rarely attended synagogue. He did so on this occasion, he says, purely to support my father in the face of the continuing onslaught on him. Chaim growled at Rabbi Telsner: 'How dare you fucking wish me a "Good Yontov"?' and slapped Telsner, causing the rabbi's glasses to fall to the floor. Telsner was shocked, but did not say anything about the incident, at the time or later.

I felt compelled to put out a statement condemning my brother's actions. 'I have informed Chaim that this type of behaviour is completely unacceptable. It makes no difference what an individual has done—in this case the ongoing attacks by Rabbi Telsner and some within his community against my family. The use of violence is never an option and needs to be unequivocally condemned.'

My punishment was delivered in greater variety. I received a torrent of hate mail and vilification via email, Facebook, and on blogs. They called me a 'media whore', accused me of going public for the money, and claimed that my family and I were all damaged. From a segment of the community came loud complaints; from the rabbis, only silence. Apparently, until this time, we had been fine in our various leadership roles in the community, but suddenly we were crazy. The common denominator of the attacks was an unthinking allegiance to the reputation of Chabad over its dereliction of the very human values it espouses.

Through all this, I had a full-time job in Canberra, and my other community roles to fulfil. And every day I waited for news from the police that Cyprys was going to be arrested. Deadlines came and went. It was stressful. Sometimes they had to ring and calm me, and other victims, while their negotiations came to a dead end. After the public disclosure, my interaction with police increased as other victims or people with information came forward. I became a conduit to the police. It was a time of great stress, but also of anticipation, of progress, and also of disbelief. Often I had to pinch myself. *Is this real? After so many years ... is it actually happening, or am I living a dream?*

At the back of my mind lay a nagging doubt that grew

larger the longer that Cyprys was not charged: *What if the case falls apart?* This anxiety was compounded by a letter I received from Cyprys's lawyer a few days after I sent an email to various friends about the police investigations. The letter said I had defamed Cyprys in my email, and demanded that I offer him redress. I couldn't believe the chutzpah. The longer he remained unarrested, the more this played on my mind. But, on the other hand, I felt comfortable that if he indeed took me to court, it would be my opportunity to prove that he had sexually abused me. It was unsurprising that I never heard back from Cyprys or his lawyer regarding this matter. But it did highlight how unrepentant and manipulative Cyprys was.

Cyprys, 43 years old at the time, was arrested on 6 September 2011, and was charged with 16 counts of indecent assault and 13 counts of gross indecency that took place from 1984–91 against young boys, most of them at the Yeshivah Centre. The Melbourne County Court heard that five victims were in Victoria, five now lived in New South Wales, and two lived in the US. He was granted bail on the condition that he did not go within 100 metres of a school and was not in contact with any child under 16 unless supervised by child-protection authorities. That order included his own children and stepchildren. Asked for a comment, my overwhelming feeling was one of relief: 'I am relieved that finally justice will be done for the crimes this person has committed, and that this dangerous individual will not be in a position to hurt other children. I am also hopeful that the handful of sceptics out there will now try to begin to comprehend what has transpired over so many years to so many people.' I also emphasised the need to treat Cyprys's family, especially his children, with dignity and respect.

With Cyprys charged, the police now moved on David Kramer, still in the US. In December 2011, police charged him over historical child sexual assaults, and a year later, they finally extradited him, and he appeared in a Melbourne court, charged with 10 counts of indecent assault and two counts of indecent acts with a minor. The charges related to four boys at Yeshivah College from 1990–92. As I've written above, two of the boys Kramer sexually assaulted were my brothers. Unfortunately, most of his alleged victims have not come forward.

The day before his appearance in the Melbourne Magistrates Court on 3 December 2012, I was chatting about the case with my two brothers, and they asked me to 'welcome Kramer back to Australia for us'. They were speaking ironically and only half-seriously. But their words stayed in my head as I sat at the back of the courtroom and watched Kramer face the music. He looked so different from how I remembered him in my youth. In the old days, Kramer was lively and smiling, always the centre of attention. I guess he still was, but now for all the wrong reasons. Now he looked like an injured bird in a cage. Although I felt a twinge of compassion for what he had become, it was quickly replaced by thinking of the anger and pain felt by all his victims.

As the hearing wound down towards the end of the first day, I quietly made my way from the back of the court to sit near him, facing the dock. My heart raced. *Am I going to do this? Yes, I am.* Around 10–20 metres from him, I said loudly: 'Welcome back to Australia, Rabbi Kramer.' He looked at me, clearly uncomfortable. I seemed to catch the judge off-guard, who quickly reminded the public not to call out anymore. And that was the end of it. I did not want to make a big scene. But I did it, not just for my brothers—I wanted to send a message, to all abusers, that they now faced their victims, as well as the law. *We're watching you, we haven't forgotten, and we're not going away*. Being the first of the numerous subsequent court hearings, I felt this was of particular importance. When I told my brothers about what I'd said, they had a good laugh and were clearly happy about the gesture, which was reported in the media the next day. However, that was not why I did it. My small act provided me with an element of empowerment, making me feel a little more in control of what was a very turbulent period of my life.

The arrests of Cyprys and Kramer, so soon after my public disclosure, rippled out into the broader community. Up till then, the Catholic Church had been the main public focus of institutional child sexual abuse, with a few cases from the Anglican Church and other institutions. The Victorian government had resisted sustained pressure by victims' advocates to hold an inquiry into the issue, but the publicity and arrests within the Jewish community made it politically easier for them to justify such an inquiry, which it announced in April 2012. It was not a royal commission but a parliamentary inquiry, with more limited terms of reference. It would investigate 'the processes by which religious and other non-government organisations respond to the criminal abuse of children by personnel within their organisations'. It did not have the power to compel people to give evidence, as a royal commission would have. Still, this was better than no inquiry.

By that stage, in late 2011–early 2012, I had returned to live in Melbourne, along with my family, having been granted a transfer within my government department to a non-executive role that was more concerned with auditing and compliance than with policy. It was the only available departmental job in Melbourne that I was suited to. Despite my initial judgement that being away from the spotlight would make life easier for us, it had become clear that we needed to return to Melbourne to keep on top of events as they unfolded. In Canberra we had neither family nor our closest friends for support. Also, with the avalanche of referrals, media reports, and police liaison, it was impossible to keep living in Canberra and dedicate the time and energy to the genie I had unleashed.

Then there was the task of preparing a submission for the parliamentary inquiry. Until you prepare such a submission, it is hard to imagine how much work it involves. There were several people involved in helping me—including a highly experienced lawyer, a friend and Yeshivah member, on behalf of more than a dozen Yeshivah victims and survivors. They all considered and approved the final version, a feat in itself. As it turned out, the effort we all put in was vindicated. There were several submissions to the inquiry from the Jewish community—from me, the ECAJ, the Jewish Community Council of Victoria (JCCV), and a few others. The inquiry decided to hold hearings into my submission and that from the JCCV.

I deal more specifically with these umbrella leadership organisations' actions in response to, and attitudes towards, child sexual abuse below (see 'Unfinished Business'). Here, I would emphasise that both initially showed a repeated failure of leadership, and an inability to grasp the seriousness of the problem within the Jewish community—although the JCCV, to its credit, turned its position around remarkably. In my view, it is one of the genuine success stories of this continuing scandal.

I was blunt in my submission:

No action was taken by these leadership bodies to protect endangered children ... remove suspected offenders from positions of authority or responsibility, or report the matters to the Police. The reality is that some offenders are currently utilising the protection of these leadership bodies to shield them from the possibility of prosecution—in some cases ... While some of the peak bodies have undertaken some steps since the Yeshivah Centre cases became public, we believe that these have been insufficient, especially when compared with their responses to other matters of importance to the community (e.g. Israel, school funding/security, alcohol abuse and green light automation for pedestrian crossings on the Sabbath).

The ECAJ, in its submission, rebutted my criticism vigorously, on the grounds that it was an umbrella organisation and did not have responsibility for institutions that fell under state jurisdictions:

The ECAJ, while a roof body, exercises no control over other organisations or members of the community. Its role is co-ordination by consensus ... It is on this basis that the ECAJ offers the community leadership and advice which is generally followed.

No allegations have been made of criminal abuse of children by 'personnel within the ECAJ'. It follows that Mr Waks' statements to the Inquiry concerning the ECAJ in addition to being scandalous, are outside the terms of reference and for both these reasons should be disregarded by the Inquiry.

The worth of this statement could be measured by comparing it against an interview given by ECAJ president Danny Lamm a month earlier on the ABC, when—after everything that had been exposed—he accepted the Yeshivah's claims that it was not covering up any alleged abuses and was fully cooperating with the investigation. (The interview is published in full in 'Unfinished Business'.)

As if this was not enough, the JCCV's executive director, until the last week of August 2012, was Michelle Coleman, who was Cyprys's partner. It was the second marriage for both; they had started dating in mid-2011, just when this scandal became very public, and tied the knot after he was charged. This scarcely believable conflict of interest, which lasted nearly a year after Cyprys's arrest, was aggravated by the fact that Ms Coleman was listed as the contact person in the JCCV's initial media statement on the issue. In various forums, sexual-abuse victims were repeatedly encouraged to contact her if they required assistance and/or advice.

As the leadership groups were forced to address their failures to act, ugly skirmishes erupted on the sidelines. One prominent example occurred in September 2012, when Sam Tatarka, a lawyer and then president of the Zionist Council of Victoria, verbally abused Bruce Cooke, a long-time Yeshivah member and donor, and a public supporter of Yeshivah victims, inside synagogue—another Chabad House, led by Rabbi Chaim Zvi Groner, son of the Big Chief—during a Shabbat service. The incident took place in full view of other congregants, and was so aggressive that Cooke was afraid that Tatarka might repeat his assault. I understand Tatarka's behaviour was along the following lines: He leant over to where Cooke was sitting, and yelled in his face to 'Fuck off' and to 'Go fuck yourself long and hard', and the tirade continued as he walked out of the synagogue. It was incredible to hear.

Cooke applied for an intervention order against Tatarka. A summons was issued, but, at the last minute, Tatarka apologised to Cooke over his outburst, who accepted the apology and withdrew his complaint. *J-Wire* reported that the altercation 'related to the fallout from the child sex abuse scandal at Yeshivah College. Cooke has been critical of the way the management and board of Yeshivah College has handled the scandal and conducted themselves throughout the investigation.' It should be noted that Tatarka's brother Reuven, or Ronnie, was head of Chabad Youth at the time some of the child sexual abuse occurred at Yeshivah. Indeed, Ronnie was involved because a victim and another victim's father—together—had reported the allegations to him back in 1984. The assault against these two boys occurred during a Chabad Youth Saturday afternoon program. In a meeting with me, Ronnie claimed that he shared this information with the late Rabbi Groner. Perhaps this episode had had an impact on his brother Sam.

I publicly called for Sam Tatarka's resignation after his tirade against Bruce Cooke. Predictably, Tatarka stood firm. We had a history going back just over a year, when I organised the Palestinian Authority-related CJF event in Melbourne, which he tried to pressure me to cancel. I did not expect him to roll over now, but I felt obliged to make the call. Once again, the community leadership was silently protective on this issue. But, then again, by now I knew they wouldn't criticise their mate.

Chapter Fifteen

Trials and tribulations

As the trial of Cyprys loomed, I began the task of sifting through files of documents and reports that might contain relevant information for what was to come. In the bottom of a drawer I came across the first psychological report ever written about me, prepared some years earlier by a psychiatrist for the Victorian Victims of Crime Assistance Tribunal (VOCAT). Although I had requested the report in the lead-up to the trial, I had never read it, and now—sitting there in my pyjamas on a quiet Saturday morning in Caulfield—I was interested to see what it revealed about my state of mind. I suspect I had an intuition about what it contained, which is probably why I had left it. Until now.

I will never forget what happened next. My eyes digested the assessment, and I was completely overcome by emotion, transported instantly to being that 11-year-old Yeshivah boy. I burst into tears, sobbing uncontrollably and unable to sit still, gripped by a suffocating sense of claustrophobia. I had to get out of the house. Immediately. In a flash, I was out on the street, wandering aimlessly at 10.00 am in clothes I had quickly thrown on. With tears streaming down my face, I walked towards my closest friend, Tony. I didn't call him. I was struggling to remain composed—it would've been too difficult to explain. I just walked up there and knocked on the door, and when he answered, I couldn't talk. I burst into uncontrollable sobbing. His close friend, Jodi, was also there. I cried like a baby. They were on their way out, but they stuck around for a while. They ensured I was relatively fine, and left. I was alone there. I couldn't return home, and I didn't want to go anywhere. All I could do was wait until they returned.

Until that point, I had never really understood the concept of a 'trigger'—an incident that leads to a traumatic response. It took me three or four days to recover from this experience, as if I had come down from a drug-induced high. Although I was profoundly traumatised, at least now I had some insight into what victims meant when they said an incident had this effect on them. Over the years since then, I have had a few more 'triggers', but none as intense.

In July 2013, Kramer became the first member of a Jewish institution in Australia to be convicted of child sex crimes. The former Yeshivah teacher was sentenced to three years and four months in prison, with a non-parole period of 18 months, after pleading guilty to five counts of indecent assault and an indecent act with a child under the age of 16. However, given the time he had already served, Kramer was eligible for release in as little as three months.

Although he described Kramer's offences as 'serious and unforgivable', Justice Michael Bourke noted that Kramer had himself been a victim of child sexual abuse. He also said that in passing sentence he had taken into account the fact that Kramer had participated in a rehabilitation program for sexual offenders while in prison for serious child-sex offences in Missouri, where he served four-and-a-half years of a seven-year sentence.

The judge said it wasn't his role to pass judgement on the conduct of Yeshivah, which had spirited Kramer away to Israel before he could be investigated and brought to justice.

I had mixed feelings about the sentence and the judge's comments. Although the sentence was a step in the right direction for victims, it was not long enough, and hardly reflected the severity and number of crimes Kramer had committed. Worse, the school had still not been brought to account. Many of us believed that Yeshivah had blood on its hands. Yeshivah issued a statement after the sentence was announced, in which they apologised for having failed to tell police about the child sexual-abuse complaints against Kramer. 'We would like to reiterate once again our unreserved apology for any historical wrongs that have occurred,' the college's principal, Rabbi Yehoshua Smukler, said. At least this was an improvement on the previous apology, which had only referred to 'historical wrongs that may have occurred'. Still, 'historical wrongs' was an attempt to minimise the rampant child sexual abuse that was going on there. And besides, actions speak louder than words. Yeshivah's actions were abysmal.

In reality, Yeshivah's statement was weak and meek. The school leaders should have issued an immediate and unequivocal apology to Kramer's victims, and voluntarily explained why it had allowed Kramer to go overseas—where he reoffended. There were no specifics, and certainly no mention of making good for these apparent 'historical wrongs', such as the ramifications of sending Kramer to

Israel, or of Rabbi Glick allegedly refusing to suspend him when his behaviour was first reported. Kramer served just 14 months of his 18-month sentence. He was released in September 2014, and deported back to the United States soon after. Neither the length of his sentence nor his deportation came as a surprise. Kramer was not an Australian citizen, so, upon his release, the government sent him back, as a foreign criminal, to where he'd come from.

In August 2013, one month after Kramer's conviction, Cyprys was found guilty of five charges of rape of a victim known as AVR—our old friend from Brisbane many of us remembered, from 1990–91, when he was 15 or 16 years old. At the time, this young boy dreamed of becoming a rabbi. I've always had guilty feelings regarding this case: had I spoken out after I was abused by Cyprys, perhaps AVR would have been spared. As I was a boy under the age of 14 at the time, I know I'm being harsh on myself. But that's just how I feel.

Following the jury's decision, Cyprys pleaded guilty to five more charges of indecent assault, four charges of procuring an act of indecency, one charge of attempted indecent assault, and two charges of gross indecency. Several of the additional offences are what is known as representative charges, where the police lay a single charge that is representative of several similar ones. Those further offences were committed between 1982–90, when Cyprys was between 14 and 22 years old, and they involved eight different young children, excluding the rape victim. One of them was me. As the only one of those victims to identify himself, I felt it was crucial that my name continue to be mentioned in the media. While most victims do not want their identity revealed, let alone repeated, I felt the opposite. But I had to fight for that right, to the extent that I lodged an affidavit with the Victorian County Court:

> I have given very careful thought to this present application to permit my name to be publicised as a victim of David Samuel Cyprys, and believe that it would not only be helpful to me personally in dealing with my own experience, but it would be of great assistance to others in my position to know that I do not feel any shame in coming forward.

On 16 September 2013, Cyprys was convicted on all charges to a total sentence of eight years in prison with a non-parole period of five years and six months, which he is currently serving. His story encapsulates everything that is rotten within the Chabad community—the historical unaccountability of its leadership, its insular mentality, its indifference to human rights, and the tragic consequences of a culture of denial. Cyprys's long history of abusive behaviour was known—in some cases, ought to have been known—by generations of Yeshivah leaders, and they did nothing. At one stage, he was on the boards of the Council of Orthodox Synagogues of Victoria and Elwood Shule, the synagogue where much of the abuse against me occurred. It was also the synagogue whose leader, Rabbi Mordechai Gutnick, also president of the Rabbinical Council of Victoria and the past/present holder of numerous other senior positions, told the royal commission that he 'was afraid to approach [me] personally' regarding this matter. This was a shame, because I would have welcomed such an approach. It was also strange that I was apparently able to intimidate such a senior rabbinic official without even engaging or meeting with him.

When Cyprys was finally charged, his second wife—the executive director of the JCCV—was, as we've seen, the person designated for other victims to contact for help. What is not known publicly is that when Cyprys was introduced to his first wife, her family made inquiries within the Yeshivah community about his character and suitability. Despite several approaches to prominent figures within the community, no one mentioned Cyprys's history to them. A former Yeshivah community member later told me that when she heard the couple was engaged, she contacted a prominent Yeshivah member to ask how this could be allowed to happen. The reply was that Cyprys had received counselling and was on the road to recovery. As a result, his wife only became aware of her husband's paedophilic tendencies after he had fathered two children with her. If someone had told them the truth at the start, they would have been spared a family trauma that continues to haunt their lives.

The tragedy of this story is compounded by the following information, which was disclosed to me by a reliable source. Cyprys was abused himself as a young boy, on multiple occasions, by grown men in the Orthodox Jewish community. When Cyprys first became an abuser, his crimes were allegedly reported to the Yeshivah leadership. The victims' parents reported him to Rabbi Groner senior, and Cyprys was removed from his position as a youth leader, but his own parents were never told that he was an abuser. This deprived them of the chance to have him treated and rehabilitated, and condemned other young boys to become his victims.

In the same month that Cyprys was convicted, another Jewish sexual-abuse scandal came to light. Although it was outside the ultra-Orthodox community, the case was significant for the similarities it revealed in the way that Jewish institutions handle their dirty laundry. A former basketball coach with the Victorian branch of the Australian national Jewish sports organisation Maccabi was convicted in August 2013 of sexual-abuse offences with four female basketballers, two of them while they were on a tour of the US for a Maccabi competition around 2000. The coach, Shannon Francis, was sentenced to eight years after pleading guilty to two counts of maintaining a sexual relationship with a child under 16, and single counts of sexual penetration of a child under 16 and attempted sexual penetration of a child aged 16. One of the victims was 14. Francis was in his early twenties at the time.

I had become involved in the case nearly a year earlier, when one of the victims contacted me for advice after attending a presentation I had given, titled *Airing Our Dirty Laundry*. In the following year, I took a close interest in the case, and spoke to both the Maccabi victims, a witness, and representatives of Maccabi.

According to one of the victims, the offences came to light once the girls discovered that Francis had been having relationships with multiple girls at the same time. Their parents met with Maccabi management, who fired the coach from all coaching jobs within the organisation. Maccabi contacted another other club, Waverley, where he coached, and informed them of the situation, and he was banned from the stadium where the girls all played. Francis signed a document which outlined that he would not go near the girls again, and that he would not appear at stadiums while they were playing.

The victims asked for privacy at the time, which was respected. When Francis was charged, the court imposed a suppression order to protect the identities of the victims.

However, as one of the victims then wrote in a private document, although the suppression order prevented Maccabi Australia from making any public media statement, it did not forbid them from reaching out to the victims and offering support as the case progressed.

The victims' feelings in this regard were perhaps best expressed in a letter they sent to Maccabi Australia in December 2012:

> Since the case was opened in 2011, we have had to tirelessly negotiate a continuing suppression order so that Maccabi's name and reputation would not be tarnished. These negotiations have been difficult and distressing, and we feel somewhat betrayed that while we have been protecting Maccabi's name, nobody from Maccabi has bothered to help protect or support us.

However, that has not been the end of the story. While the victims have to get on with their lives, Maccabi has refused to acknowledge any responsibility for the official who was in charge of the team delegation at the time the offences occurred. The victims remain angry at this denial. There is also a second alleged abuser, another former Maccabi basketball coach, whose case has not yet been brought before the courts, nor into the public domain. And Maccabi's response to these allegations also seems to have been mishandled. While the alleged abuser is no longer there, I can only hope that justice will be delivered in relation to his alleged offences as well.

The Maccabi basketball saga was not the only Jewish sexual-abuse case outside of Melbourne's Yeshivah. In 2013, the welfare organisation Jewish Care Victoria conducted an investigation into allegations of child sexual abuse at children's homes in the 1960s, run by its predecessor, the Australian Jewish Welfare and Relief Society. Several people alleged that they were abused at the society's cottages. But there were other cases, outside of Victoria. In the late 1980s, a Jewish man who I can only identify as AVB (the witness name assigned to him by the royal commission) was a student at the Chabad-run Yeshivah College in Bondi in Sydney's eastern suburbs. In the mid-year holiday break in 1984–85, AVB attended a religious learning program, along with students from Melbourne who would come and stay in the Yeshivah classrooms. One of those students was Cyprys, who befriended AVB and sexually assaulted him. At the time of the assault, the Melbourne Yeshivah had already received reports from victims and their families that Cyprys had sexually assaulted young boys.

A few years later, in 1987–88, AVB attended a Sydney Yeshivah youth camp, Camp Gan Israel, at Stanwell Tops near Wollongong, about an hour south of Sydney. Yeshivah teachers and volunteers attended the camp as chaperones or house parents. Among them was Daniel 'Gug' Hayman, aged 24, who used force to sexually assault AVB, who was 14 at the time. Hayman allegedly had previously been reported to the leaders at Yeshivah in Sydney for sexually assaulting a number of children.

In 1988, AVB moved to Melbourne and has lived there ever since. In June 2011, before I went public with my complaint, AVB approached Victoria Police to outline his complaints about Cyprys and Hayman. Police soon launched an investigation into various offenders, and wrote to members of the Yeshivah community seeking their assistance with their investigations. According to documents tendered to the royal commission:

On 17 June 2011, following the police letter to members, AVB sent an email to contacts within the community attaching the letter from Victoria Police that requested public assistance in relation to investigations that were conducted in relation to sexual assaults at Yeshivah College in Melbourne. He also attached to that letter, a resolution from the Rabbinical Council of Victoria that stated that the prohibition against mesirah did not apply in cases of sexual abuse.

In 2013, Hayman by then living in Los Angeles, returned to Australia for his mother's funeral. AVB says he heard about his return, but did not think it was the right time to arrest Hayman at the time of his mother's funeral, and thus did not inform police. He believed that the opportunity for an arrest would present itself after the traditional seven days of mourning, and intended to contact police then. However, when I heard Hayman was back—from a senior rabbinic figure who was comfortable with me notifying the police—I did not indulge in such courtesies for someone who was alleged to have sexually abused a number of children. I tipped off the police, who proceeded to arrest Hayman. Admittedly, I was surprised they were unaware of his entry into Australia.

On 10 June 2014, in the Downing Centre Local Court in Sydney, Hayman was given a suspended sentence of 19 months, subject to a good-behaviour bond, because the judge had to apply the laws operating at the time of his offence, in the 1980s, rather than in the present day. He got off on a technicality in relation to one of the complainants. The *Australian Jewish News* reported it on 12 June, noting the significance of Hayman's religious upbringing:

Magistrate David Williams laid part of the blame on Hayman's religious Jewish upbringing, stating that he accepted the submission of Hayman's lawyer that his client was immature, naïve and had limited sexual experience at the time of the indecent assault.

[Due to] the offender's strict religious upbringing, the opportunity for sexual understanding, experience and development was heavily restrained and may have led to distortions in his perception as to what was appropriate and what was not,' Williams said.

The evidence demonstrates that the offender's sexual naïvety did play an important part.

The magistrate said that in other circumstances, Hayman would be sent to jail. 'This is a relatively serious example of an offence of this type. Skin-to-skin contact under the victim's clothes, it lasted minutes instead of seconds, was not consensual and was in an isolated location,' Williams said.

According to documents tendered to the royal commission in February 2015, there had been several claims of abuse by Hayman in the 1980s made to Rabbi Baruch Lesches, who ran the Yeshivah Rabbinical College in Sydney in the 1980s. Lesches was my former teacher.

During this hearing, the commission then heard an extraordinary admission from Rabbi Pinchus Feldman, chief Chabad emissary for New South Wales since 1968. Rabbi Feldman told the hearing that in 2002, when a case of child sexual abuse was brought to his attention, he suspected the alleged perpetrator was planning to leave the country, but he did not see it as his responsibility to inform police.

On 24 July 2002, Rabbi Feldman and other senior leaders at Yeshivah, Bill Conway and Zev Simons, informed the alleged perpetrator, AVL, whose identity has been withheld from the public, that a child claimed he was sexually assaulted by AVL. That afternoon, AVL told Rabbi Feldman that he planned to leave the country. Rabbi Feldman did not tell the police, and by 25 July, AVL had already left the country.

Counsel assisting the royal commission engaged in the following exchange with Rabbi Pinchus Feldman, as the *Australian Jewish News* reported on 6 February:

> **Counsel:** What do you say to the suggestion that you might not have told anyone about the information from AVL so that you could allow him to take that course to leave the country?

> **Rabbi Feldman:** I did not know there was any such obligation. I was not taught of any protocol. If there would have been such a protocol, this is something I would have done.

> **Counsel:** But leaving aside protocol, Rabbi, I am asking you from a moral position as well what do you think about the fact that a person against whom an allegation had been made —

> **Rabbi Feldman:** Who is claiming his total innocence.

> **Counsel:** Quite often, those accused of crimes do?

> **Rabbi Feldman:** That's fine.

> **Counsel:** But in any event —

> **Rabbi Feldman:** I'm just putting this into perspective.

> **Counsel:** And the process is about to unfold whereby authorities are to be notified of that complaint, and that

same person says to you, 'Well, I might leave the country,' and you don't tell anyone?

Rabbi Feldman: As is said, I did not know there was a protocol or responsibility to do so. If I would have known that, I certainly would have followed that protocol.

Counsel: Leaving aside the protocol, was my question to you. What about morally, because the allegation did involve the sexual abuse of a child? What do you think morally about the fact that you had information that the person against whom the complaint was made is telling you that he might leave the country?

Rabbi Feldman: I thought if it would be established, police would be able to extradite him.

Counsel: It causes you no moral concern that you didn't act to notify anyone that a potential perpetrator was about to leave the country because, if it had been proved, he could have been extradited some other time?

Rabbi Feldman: The point you are making has validity.

Rabbi Feldman could not bring himself to say the word 'Yes', or 'I'm sorry', or 'I regret my inaction.' It was typical of the lack of accountability and responsibility we had witnessed.

Nor was sexual abuse within the ultra-Orthodox system confined to boys' schools. During a five-year period in the mid-2000s, Malka Leifer, the headmistress at the Adass Israel School in Melbourne—Adass is a Chasidic community made up of various Chasidic sects, excluding Chabad—is alleged to have sexually abused young female students at the school she was in charge of. Within hours of learning of the allegations, the school arranged for Leifer to be flown out of Australia to Israel.

One of the victims sued Leifer in a civil suit, and in September 2015, a judge awarded the woman, by that time 28 years old, more than $1 million in compensation for sexual abuse she had suffered. 'Justice Jack Rush said the victim had suffered fear, uncertainty, and major lifelong mental injury, including self-harm, and awarded her $1.27 million in damages,' the ABC reported on 16 September. (At least one other civil suit against Leifer is currently underway.)

The woman was abused, along with two of her sisters at school, on camp, and at the home of Leifer, who is herself a mother of eight children. The judge said Leifer's conduct as headmistress went unchecked by the school, and the fact that the abuse occurred under the guise of Jewish education by the headmistress made the breach of trust monstrous. He slammed as 'deplorable' and 'disgraceful' the school's response when the abuse came to light in March 2008, which involved the calling of a committee meeting to arrange to fly Mrs Leifer out of the country.

At the time of writing, Leifer is still in Israel, wanted by the Australian authorities to face over 70 charges of indecent assault and rape. She had been under house arrest in Israel since September 2014, was required to wear a GPS tracking device, and was subject to 24-hour supervision, but was resisting attempts to extradite her.

In mid-2016, she failed to appear at a court hearing for almost the tenth time, citing stress and a psychiatric condition. Her lawyers claimed the stress of appearing in court brought on psychiatric episodes that prevented her from attending the hearings, and asked Israel's attorney-general to block attempts to have her extradited. Her defence even had the chutzpah to demand 'justice' for Leifer, which was an insult to her alleged victims still awaiting justice back in Australia.

In June 2016, the presiding judge accepted the appeal to drop the extradition case, at least for a further six months until her psychiatric condition had been re-assessed after her monthly psychiatric sessions. This process could last for the next ten years or so. The fact that Leifer continues to avoid extradition is troubling, both for her alleged victims and for the credibility of the Israeli justice system. To me (and many others), the judge avoided the only two real-life options available to him—either Leifer was so psychiatrically unwell that she needed to be hospitalised until she had sufficiently recuperated to attend court, or she was well enough to face court. Many of us regard the judge's decision as a major travesty of justice.

While this theatre played out in Israel, an even grander spectacle unfolded in Rome, where Cardinal George Pell, the head of Vatican finances and formerly the Archbishop of Sydney and Melbourne, gave evidence—by video link, because he was apparently too unwell to fly home—to the royal commission about what he knew about allegations of child sexual abuse in the Victorian town of Ballarat in the 1970s and 1980s. Cardinal Pell's situation reminded me a lot of Rabbi Glick's. If he did know and failed to act, he should have resigned; and if he didn't know, he was out of touch, and should have resigned as an acknowledgement of his incompetence and responsibility.

I had been watching the live stream from Rome on my laptop at home in Israel (where we had moved in late 2015) for the first three nights. But I was regretting not attending in person. I knew some of those involved in the process—after an extraordinary fundraising campaign, they'd flown to Rome to be in the same room as Cardinal Pell while he gave evidence. I felt they should be supported, in particular by the Jewish community. It felt like the right thing to do, and I couldn't get my mind off it. With just one more evening session to go, I thought I had missed my opportunity, but suddenly I decided I had to try. The problem was, I had only a few hours to get there. I changed into a suit, quickly packed a bag, and ran towards the taxi rank near my home. I was in the taxi just after 4.00 pm—just when peak hour started.

I saw there was a 6.00 pm flight, which was practically impossible to get. The next flight was around 8.00 pm. I'd arrive in Rome late, even if I miraculously caught the first flight; I'd arrive very late if I caught the second one. In the taxi, we came to a complete halt. Traffic was crazy. My taxi driver also thought I was crazy when I explained that this ride was one big gamble. He definitely did his bit—cutting in where he could. I called on my mobile phone to try to purchase a ticket, but was refused. 'It's too late—you need to purchase it at the airport, if they'll even sell it to you,' the operator said. It seemed that my luck was running out. I considered asking the driver to turn back, to cut my losses, but I persevered. Using all my chutzpah with El Al, I managed to scramble onto the 6.00 pm flight. During the taxi ride, I had sent an email to my friends in Rome—the victims and their families—and informed them I was on the way to the airport, and that I hoped to join them.

Anthony Foster seemed pleased to hear this. I'd met him and his wife, Chrissie, in Australia, and we'd caught up in the Loire Valley as well. I have a special place in my heart for them. Two of their daughters were raped by a Catholic priest: one committed suicide, and the other is completely incapacitated after having been hit by a car while she was crossing the road after another night of binge drinking. So they effectively lost two daughters. I couldn't believe their strength, courage, and dignity. They were some of my new role models. I was really hoping to see them, and stand by them in their pursuit of justice. They'd been there for me at the public hearing into Yeshivah in Melbourne.

We landed in Rome around 8:30 pm local time, and I headed straight to the hearing. When I got there, I was honoured and humbled by how this courageous group welcomed me. They seemed genuinely pleased that I had come. They included me in their group, and in their activities.

I laughed with them; I cried with them. And we did plenty of both. I heard first hand some of their shocking stories, which moved me. But what also moved me was to see the bond between them, and the support they gave each other. Here they were, grown men, hugging each other freely. Sharing the hurt, sharing the tears. It was incredibly powerful. I was envious of them, as the Jewish community is so far behind in this area. I recalled that back in my Tzedek days, the idea of group sessions, which I raised, was dismissed outright by the victims/survivors. No one seemed ready for it. I also wasn't keen. But seeing the incredibly positive impact of it before my eyes changed my views.

The hearing concluded at close to 3.00 am. As they did every night, the group spoke to the media outside, and then went to regroup and debrief. One of the survivors asked me to accompany them to speak to the media. He spoke, and then asked me to say a few words. I said that I was proud to represent the Jewish community there and to stand in support of those courageous survivors. The group also told me that they wanted to turn the town of Ballarat into a centre of excellence in terms of addressing child sexual abuse, which struck a chord. In effect, this was one of the things I had been trying to achieve for years at Yeshivah. I noted that this issue transcended boundaries. I also repeated my view that Cardinal Pell should resign. The evening concluded around 6.00 am — after plenty of alcohol, hugs, and tears. I already felt that the trip was well worth it. The prominent survivor and advocate David Ridsdale kindly offered me his hotel room, and he went to sleep in his cousin's room. The next morning, everyone was up early for another busy day. I was up at around nine o'clock., and decided to walk around the streets of Rome for a few hours. When I returned, the group had just concluded a private meeting with Cardinal Pell. They met in the secluded area in the hotel, and the emotions on display were incredible. It was incredibly powerful. We had lunch, after which some rested, and others returned to the booze — some had already been back on it in the morning. I hung out with some of them, and then did some work. A donor from Ballarat paid for the group's farewell dinner that night, to which they kindly invited me. It was lovely.

My flight was at ten o'clock the next morning. I was trying to save money, so I went straight to the airport after dinner. I arrived at midnight, with 10 hours to burn. It was extremely uncomfortable, and I didn't get more than an hour's sleep. I was exhausted. I somewhat regretted not having paid for a hotel room, but, due to my financial predicament, I'd become used to cutting corners. I knew I'd survive. It was only when I arrived home that afternoon, and over the next few days, that I realised the profound impact this 30-plus-hours trip had on me. But despite the personal cost, from several perspectives, I was glad I went.

The practice of child sexual abuse chronicled above in the ultra-Orthodox Jewish community runs across schools, states, and genders. The repeated pattern of denial by community and school leaders, aimed at protecting the institution and helping perpetrators avoid justice, is as astonishing as it is sickening. While Australian society has already become familiar with these stories from other faiths and institutions, I have included them in detail for two reasons.

The first is to encapsulate the breadth of the problem in my community; the second is to highlight the fact that none of these other victims, despite their bravery in coming forward to the police and the courts, have publicly identified themselves. This stands out in stronger relief when compared with other religions and institutions where widespread sexual abuse has occurred. Victims' support groups are common, and the names of survivors can be found in some numbers. Admittedly, the total numbers within these other faiths and institutions are larger than for the ultra-Orthodox community, but the sheer lack of public faces needs to be remedied.

As I write this book, my brother Yanki and I, and Yaakov Wolf—another Cyprys survivor who lives in Los Angeles—are the only victims of sexual abuse within the ultra-Orthodox Jewish community in the whole of Australia who have revealed their names, faces, and experiences in public. That makes three names out of probably hundreds. In addition, the victim known publicly as AVB has appeared on television and spoken in detail about his experiences. Although his identity is widely known within the Jewish community, it remains off the public record.

The significance of this state of affairs needs to be highlighted. While other people have pressed charges, they remain out of the glare of the media, and the court of public opinion, and avoid what would otherwise be constant whispers and stares from within their own community. This is understandable. They are entitled to their anonymity, and I do not begrudge them their privacy. They want the freedom to get on with their lives as best they can.

However, their anonymity intensifies the blame, hostility, and ill-will directed towards me and my family. We have paid a heavy price for going public, and the longer that Waks remains the only name in the public memory, the longer this will continue. There is another crucial message wrapped up in their privacy: the almost unshakeable authority and power that the Chabad and Yeshivah leaders exert over their community. This control has forged a culture of fear and blind obedience that continues to drive my advocacy—not just within Chabad or the ultra-Orthodox community, but in the broader community.

Chapter Sixteen

Tzedek

In December 2012, I gave evidence to the Victorian parliamentary inquiry—a massive milestone. The hearing allowed me to share my story in the public domain, with an official government entity, and to have it validated and acknowledged. From a communal perspective, it guided me to take my public-advocacy campaign to a new level. My work was no longer just about me, but about the wider community. Since the initial article in *The Age* I had effectively become the voice of many victims, survivors, and their families; now, through the substantial submission I prepared, I was *formally* representing victims. In many senses, this acted as a practice run for the broadening of my commitment to speak up on behalf of other victims.

The inquiry led to several important reforms in Victoria, which came into effect on 1 July 2015. The key one was removing the limitation period for all relevant child-abuse civil claims, regardless of the time or context of the alleged abuse. This new law would be applied retroactively as well.

The Victorian government also made it a criminal offence for failing to protect a child under the age of 16 from a risk of sexual abuse. The new law required organisations responsible for supervising children to actively manage the risks of sexual offences being committed against children in their care. Under the changes, people in authority could go to jail for up to five years if they knew of a risk of abuse to a child in their care, but failed to reduce or remove the risk.

On a personal level, the Victorian inquiry had a much more dynamic impact. It acted as a catalyst for me to establish a public-advocacy organisation, which I called Tzedek (Hebrew for justice). After the arrests of Cyprys and Kramer, I had been inundated by people coming out of the woodwork asking for support and strategic advice. It's important to acknowledge the role of social media in this process. While victims 20 years ago could go either to the police or traditional media, both of which involved approaching an institution and having to be interviewed in person by at least one person, victims today can use a variety of digital tools to speak out on their own terms—Facebook, blogs, email—using either their own names, or anonymously. This has allowed advocacy to become more personal and for it to build momentum—and virtual communities—faster than in previous generations. It has also provided a new platform for other types of activism. Websites such as the original *Failed Messiah* have shown considerable courage in highlighting the failings of Jewish—in particular, religious—leadership. This has been of enormous value to me, personally, as an advocate.

It wasn't just victims who approached me, but also counsellors and psychologists, members of the ultra-Orthodox community, and ordinary people from other religions who had also encountered child sexual-abuse victims. I just couldn't handle and address all of their concerns on my own. With a full-time day job, and the responsibility of providing for my family, as well as other commitments, there was no time for me to do this properly. So, after the Victorian inquiry was announced in April 2012, I made a decision to establish an organisation, find the right people to work with me, secure proper funding to allow me to focus on advocacy full-time, and outline a mission. By the time I gave evidence to the inquiry in December, Tzedek was up and running—although it was officially established on 31 December 2012, the date on the Certificate of Incorporation.

From my past experience, I knew that one of the most challenging tasks was going to be establishing an appropriate board. One of my guiding principles in creating the board was to find people who were not part of the mainstream Jewish community network and did not have positions on other community boards. That way, we would avoid the potential conflicts of interest that I had seen cripple independent thinking during my days at the Anti-Defamation Commission. I knew we might have to tackle the peak bodies at some point, and if my board members wore other hats, or used to, it would get messy.

This wasn't going to be easy. The first person I approached was Josh Bornstein, a prominent lawyer at Maurice Blackburn, whom I had met as a result of us being interviewed on the same ABC *Lateline* story. Josh was cautious when I approached him, and made it clear he was not involved in any way in the Jewish community. In fact, he lived on the other side of town. That only increased my interest. But another issue he raised was the lack of time he had to carry out a board role properly. To my eventual regret, we both put that issue to the side. He eventually agreed to join—initially as my deputy president, and when I took on the full-time CEO role several months later, he became president. He was meant to be the figurehead, a wise and prominent elder, complementing me as a more confrontational CEO and spokesperson.

The original board comprised me as president; Josh as vice-president; another lawyer, Joel Vernon, as secretary; and Shawn Goldberg, an experienced therapist, to act as a sounding board and go-to person for the counselling arm of our responsibilities. Shawn was specifically recruited to manage a team of psychologists for a range of projects such as debriefing, drafting documents, and anything else that was necessary in his field. In the ensuing months, several others joined the board.

Our agenda and mission was set out in the initial Strategic Plan:

> Tzedek is an Australian-based advocacy group for Jewish victims of child sexual abuse—promoting their needs and interests and offering them and other relevant stakeholders a range of services. Tzedek's primary role is to work closely with victims and assist them, as appropriate, by developing and providing resources and services in accordance with their respective needs and wishes.

The advocacy would include issuing public statements to raise awareness of the issue, and helping people who wanted to go to the police, and outlining the options available to them. Although we were focussed on the Jewish community, we did find common cause with other survivor groups such as SNAP and Broken Rites, and a group we ended up working closely with, the In Good Faith Foundation.

Not surprisingly, the early months were intense. For a start,

I was working two jobs as I tried to bed down the structures and responsibilities. Josh suggested I stay in my day job until Tzedek gained financial security, so I took two one-month periods of unpaid leave to deal with the increasing workload and to get some momentum going. By March 2013, prior to having raised any substantial funding, I felt I had to leave my job in the public service. It was becoming impossible for me to focus on both roles, and I was confident of securing funding for Tzedek. Josh wasn't convinced, and preferred that I stay in my paid employment role. I made it clear that it was a gamble I personally was willing to take. This was mainly based on conversations I was having with potential funders. Eventually, for the first six months at Tzedek, I didn't get paid a cent, on the understanding I would be paid retrospectively when the funding came through. Various documents and discussions made it clear what my role was going to be, the way I was going to go about it, and other matters such as my salary. At no point were any of these matters raised as an issue by anyone on the board, including Josh.

However, in these early months, the larger challenge was on operations and governance. Community members and victims thought Tzedek was a one-man show, and expected me to be on call for them 24/7. This was aggravated by the passiveness of other board members, who were not nearly as hands-on as I had hoped, or in some cases, as they had promised—a problem reinforced at our board meetings, where my decision to bring in inexperienced board members proved to be a huge mistake. Josh was the only member who had had experience on a board, yet he also provided less leadership than I had hoped for or expected. Although I tried to lighten his load by arranging for board meetings to be held at his office, I was left to do just about everything on a day-to-day basis. At the early stages, there is probably only one board member I can think of who contributed in any meaningful way—and he was outstanding.

At the same time, my personal disputes with community members and leaders also became intertwined with the activities of the organisation, as was demonstrated by an incident in March 2103 that involved Rebbetzin Pnina Feldman—the wife of the chief Chabad emissary in New South Wales. In early March, I had posted a notice on Tzedek's website, which reported that the Rebbetzin had referred publicly to myself and my family as 'Massers' (a Hebrew term for collaborators with the secular authorities, in a clear reference to our work in combating child sexual abuse). Rebbetzin Feldman then issued a statement in reply, which included the following:

> In response to media requests for comment, I do not intend to publicly explain details of a private conversation that may embarrass or cause pain to certain individuals, including some who may have tragically been the victims of child abuse.
>
> I unequivocally stand by the Halachic rulings that reporting child sexual abuse and in fact any form of physical violence to the relevant government authorities is not Mesirah. I have personally reported such incidents to the Police in the past and have encouraged others to do so.

I responded that the Rebbetzin had neither confirmed nor denied my report of what she had said. As a result:

> Tzedek has made the difficult decision to sever ties with the Sydney Yeshiva Centre and its representatives until a

full retraction and public apology is issued by Rebbetzin Feldman. Of course this would not mean that the Rebbetzin's repugnant views have altered but at least it would provide a context in which a way forward may be achieved.

This was one of many occasions where my three hats—private citizen, public victim, and professional advocate—became conflated in public debate. Yet the Feldman dispute was small beer compared to a subsequent incident.

Within several months, I became involved in an allegation that Rabbi Abraham Glick, at that time the head of religious studies and in charge of student welfare (and a former principal) of Yeshivah College, had committed an act of sexual abuse. In December 2013, a person I'd never met before approached me, as head of Tzedek, with an allegation that Rabbi Glick had raped him while he was on the *bimah* (the raised area for reading from the Torah) in synagogue. As he told me his story, I thought he was serious and believable, but I also thought he would be widely disbelieved due to the identity of the person he was accusing, and the allegations he was making—not least that the rape had occurred in the middle of the day in the middle of the synagogue. I knew the story sounded unlikely, but by this stage I had heard so many stories of abuse that I could not dismiss anything out of hand. I know that many people within the ultra-Orthodox community believe I have had problems with Rabbi Glick, stemming from my days as student. This has never been true, and is still not today. Out of all the senior officials at Yeshivah, Rabbi Glick was one of the very few whom I'd respected. I'm not quite sure why, but that is the case.

As per Tzedek's by-now regular process, I offered the complainant the full suite of options available to him—from connecting him to therapy, to going to the police, to sharing his story in some way. As he had already been seeing a therapist for a number of years, at that point he was interested in making a formal police statement. So, at his request, I accompanied him to the police station as part of my responsibilities with Tzedek. I'd let the police decide. After the complaint was lodged and he had been interviewed in private (I was outside the entire time), I asked one of the police detectives who had interviewed him for their view of the allegations. The officer, who told me they had been in the force for many years, said the complainant came across as a credible witness with credible allegations.

The role of helping people take their allegations forward is a vexed one, with an underlying dilemma I have always struggled with. On the one hand, when alleged victims come forward, they are concerned that no one believes them, so I have to give them full support, which includes believing them. On the other hand, I always proceed on the assumption that the alleged perpetrator is innocent until proven guilty. So when I discuss a case with or about a complainant, I refer to them as an alleged victim (or a complainant), and not as a victim, which at times upsets them. In some cases, they feel I don't believe them. I point out that if I accept the word 'victim', it implies I believe the perpetrator is guilty before it has been proven in a court of law. It also makes me vulnerable to claims of defamation.

After careful consideration, and taking soundings from some in my network, as per his request, I also connected the complainant to a journalist at the *Herald Sun*, which published a story on 9 December 2013, saying that Rabbi Glick had been stood down while police investigated the allegations against him. The publication of this story naturally caused an outrage within the community and brought me into the firing line as the person who had facilitated the police investigation, as though I was behind the allegedly concocted story.

The publication of Rabbi Glick's name also raised important ethical questions about 'naming and shaming'. Some of my critics compared this public shaming with the actions of self-appointed community advocacy groups such as the US-based Chabad Jewish Community Watch (JCW), which publishes the names of alleged abusers on their Wall of Shame. However, in my view, there is a huge difference between being named by the media and being named by a community group. The media industry is regulated—media organisations are accountable to industry watchdogs, which can fine or otherwise sanction them—and journalists undergo years of studies and training. So there are in-built protections of editorial integrity. There is no such warrant for naming and shaming by externally unaccountable community organisations. Once someone is named, it effectively becomes a stain for life.

This is not a criticism of JCW—rather, I prefer a different approach. I support JCW's important work and understand their rationale; the fact is, there are many alleged paedophiles roaming our streets who are free simply because of the inability of their victims to bring them to account for a range of reasons (such as legal technicalities, and their desire to protect themselves and their families). So, in order to warn the community, as well as the alleged paedophiles themselves, they post their details online. No doubt this is an effective tool in terms of raising parental awareness and acting as a deterrent. However, despite its potential benefits, I still oppose it. I'd rather focus on education and legislative changes (such as extending the statute of limitations).

Ultimately, knowing the name and location of some paedophiles is not the most effective tool in prevention—education is. The fact is, we have no idea of the identity of most paedophiles; it could be a family member, a teacher, a neighbour, or anyone else. Most will never be caught. So educating children, parents, teachers, and anyone else who interacts with children should be the top priority. In my opinion, no alleged paedophile should be named—not even by the media—until or unless they are convicted of such an offence.

Notwithstanding these dilemmas, the point was that here was a complainant taking allegations to both the police and the media. Just like anyone else, it was his right to do so. And as a victim advocate, I was right to assist and support him. Just as it would be the police's decision whether or not to charge him, it was the media's decision to name him. It's important to remember that Rabbi Glick was neither the first nor the last alleged abuser to be named during a police investigation. The UK's former prime minister and former military chief have both been named. Other more low-profile people, in Australia and elsewhere, have also been named. It happens often. So why should Rabbi Glick be afforded any special treatment? Especially as he was the principal during the period of so much of the institutional abuse and cover-ups, there is no doubt that he should bear some responsibility for it. Of course, his role at Yeshivah doesn't necessarily mean he sexually abused anyone, nor that he should be treated badly. But my point is, as the subject of a complaint, he was treated precisely like any other citizen. And that was appropriate. The police investigation was completed at the end of February 2014 without charges being pursued.

However, while the matter was still under police

investigation, someone posted on the Tzedek website that Rabbi Glick had admitted his guilt. Within a few hours, someone else then posted that he did not admit his guilt. As anyone following my approach on social media would know, my general inclination is to leave posts up, in the interests of free speech and debate. So I left them up for a period of time. The first post was false, and therefore defamatory. In hindsight, I should have deleted it immediately. But it was such a false and ludicrous statement that most if not all would have known it was nonsense. Nevertheless, I should have deleted it immediately. I accept that.

Soon after the Rabbi Glick saga, several of Tzedek's board members resigned. Although the timing appeared made it seem that their resignations were linked to the Glick affair, the reality is that all but one had absolutely nothing to do with it. As it happened, Tzedek had an annual general meeting scheduled for that time anyway. Joel Goldman was the only new member to join the board at the AGM. He joined because he believed in Tzedek and wanted to help out. After having been on the board for around two weeks, he asked to step down, but to continue in his role as treasurer. He wanted to focus on working as a volunteer with Tzedek, without the constraints of governance and political pressures. He would effectively continue doing what he signed up to do—deal with Tzedek's finances. And that's precisely what happened. The others resigned either due to a lack of time or because the board decided at the AGM that it did not want to be constituted with formal interstate representatives. The New South Wales representative was returning to Victoria, and the Queensland representative continued to be Tzedek's informal representative there. But, as expected, this didn't stop the lies and disinformation about what had happened and why.

So it was pure coincidence that the day after these resignations were announced, Rabbi Glick sued me for defamation. On 19 December, the *Herald Sun* reported it as follows:

> The claim alleges Mr Waks posted false imputations and selective material for the purpose of sensationalising his campaign against child sexual abuse at the expense of Rabbi Glick. 'The defendant invited comment to be published on the website and Facebook pages, which led to a torrent of abuse and defamatory statements,' the statement of claim said. It is alleged Mr Waks failed to properly screen, block publication of or remove defamatory comments left by visitors to his site. 'As a result of the publication of each of the online articles and postings ... the plaintiff has been severely injured in his reputation as a practising Rabbi, educator in the State of Victoria and as a responsible member of the community,' the statement of claim alleges.

On advice from my lawyers, and after subsequent negotiations, the matter was settled out of court. As part of the terms of settlement, I issued a public apology to Rabbi Glick on 4 April 2014:

> During December 2013, I posted certain statements on Tzedek's website and on my personal Facebook page and permitted a third party to post a statement on Tzedek's website, which referred to allegations made against Rabbi Abraham Glick.
>
> In particular, I posted certain statements that suggested to some that Rabbi Glick was guilty and permitted a third party to post a statement stating that Rabbi Glick

had admitted to the allegations made. I accept that those statements about Rabbi Glick were false and inaccurate, and accept and believe that Rabbi Glick was at all times completely innocent of the allegations made. I unreservedly apologise to Rabbi Glick and his family and retract those statements.

I had embarked on a steep learning curve about the harsh truths of defamation actions. Once the matter gets into the hands of lawyers who represent insurance companies, as Tzedek's position was at the time, I learned that if you sue, or are being sued, you need a lot of money behind you. It helps if you belong to an institution with deep pockets. Basically, someone with limited resources doesn't stand a chance—at either suing or being sued. And it's important to note that even if you win a case, you may not be awarded costs. I learned this the hard way from both ends.

My apology unleashed a torrent of criticism, from the individual and leadership level, and demonstrated how eager and primed certain segments of the community were to pounce on my every slip-up, to poke holes in my actions and motivations.

Higher up the Yeshivah tree, that same day as my apology was published, the Rabbinical Council of Victoria, headed by Rabbi Meir Shlomo Kluwgant, issued a media release condemning me over the pain and humiliation that the allegations had caused Glick and his family, and calling on Tzedek to consider my position.

Here we had the most senior Orthodox rabbinic body in Victoria, led by Rabbi Meir Shlomo Kluwgant—one of two of Rabbi Glick's nephews on that board—involving itself in a personal and private dispute between two community members. Never before in the history of the RCV had they done this. Never before had they called on anyone to resign for anything. Yet here they were calling for my head.

Even one of my former classmates, who has attacked me publicly and relentlessly, and has been unforgiving due to my involvement with the Rabbi Glick matter, has been happy to forgive Yeshivah for supporting the continued employment of Cyprys, the secret shipping of Kramer to Israel, and much much more, including Rabbi Glick's own culpability as Yeshivah principal. These double standards are something I've become accustomed to from many members and leaders of the Chabad and Yeshivah community.

If I had my time again, I would have handled the Rabbi Glick matter a little differently. The fact that the complainant's claim was dismissed and that no one else was drawn out of the woodwork does not change the merits of my decision. I felt comfortable, based on the information the complainant presented, about accompanying him to the police. However, I would have deleted the singular defamatory website comment straightaway, and I would have been even more careful with my and others' comments on Facebook about it.

Second, I would have delayed putting the complainant in touch with the media until the police had made public the fact that they were interviewing or charging Rabbi Glick. Or at least I would have advised the complainant to wait, accepting that ultimately the decision would have been his to make. This would have made clear that it was the police who had put his name into the public domain—although I suspect I would have been blamed, no matter what.

The complainant was naturally very disappointed that the case did not proceed. But, from my perspective, this matter has now been closed. I've reconciled with Rabbi Glick to the extent possible, even dining with him in his home and sharing a stage with him. While we both seem to have moved on from that episode, a desperate few are still holding on to it, and utilise it at every opportunity to promote their agendas.

After the first year, it became clear that the board of Tzedek was no longer as comfortable with advocacy as it was with education and support. While there was no formal indication of this from my fellow board members, I felt increasingly that I was operating in a vacuum — a feeling that was compounded by the Rabbi Glick affair. In the aftermath of my apology, I had offered my immediate resignation to the Tzedek board, but it had been dismissed out of hand. However, my email contact with Josh thereafter started to run cold — for months, Josh and I barely had any contact. Out of the blue, I received the following email from Josh, in August 2014:

> Board members would like to use our meeting tomorrow to discuss serious concerns that they have regarding Tzedek and your work with it. Given the importance of this, the meeting tomorrow will deal only with that issue. You are invited to bring a support person with you if you wish.

At the meeting, the board, now consisting of four members, basically told me that they felt I was no longer the right person to lead Tzedek. There had been nothing to suggest this was the case before the meeting, nor were they really able to elaborate.

As it happened, I had already informed a number of friends that I was planning to leave Tzedek. My plan had been to do so immediately after the anticipated royal commission public hearing into Yeshivah; but, after that board meeting, I preferred to put the organisation above me and to leave. I was confident of my position, but felt it was not worth remaining. By the end of the month I had tendered my resignation—again—and this time it was accepted. The board acknowledged my contribution in a media release, invited me to join its board of advisers, and announced it would hold a public event of thanks later in the year, which I declined. I finished up in November.

I was very disappointed by how it ended. My departure could have been handled with a quiet conversation, and I would have said I wanted to leave, and leave the country, as we had anyway intended. Instead, I was made a public scapegoat, effectively thrown out of the organisation I had established and led. By every account, I was successful with my work in Tzedek. Of course, this didn't mean I hadn't made mistakes along the way. But Tzedek, and my role in it, was something I was and still am very proud of.

In preparation for this book, my co-author contacted Josh for clarification, in order to try to explain the board's decision. This is how he responded: 'The Board lost confidence in Manny. We reached the conclusion that he was not equipped with the skills to be a CEO of a not for profit organisation. Rather, his skills lay in being an activist.' Bornstein then outlined a series of my failings, none of which had ever been formally raised with me.

Yet this still did not explain what had prompted the board's change of heart after rejecting my offer to resign only a few months before. Pressed for more details, Bornstein said:

[The Board] resolved that a carefully worded statement [about Rabbi Glick] be published in the *Jewish News* and directed Manny to take all steps to place it. The statement expressed regret over the incident and affirmed the Board's view that the rule of law must be respected including the presumption of innocence and the right to a fair trial. Manny did not follow the Board's direction and the statement wasn't published. My guess is that he didn't agree with the statement or felt that it unfairly criticised him. His failure to follow the Board's direction over such a serious matter formed part of the process and deliberations that led to us asking for him to step down.

This claim is false. Perhaps Josh hadn't realised that I had kept my emails from the Tzedek account. Or perhaps he didn't have the time to check our email exchanges. I have a detailed email chain confirming that I did exactly as the board had directed me to do in this regard.

Josh's explanation serves only to highlight the gulf of silence that grew between me and the board, and does no credit to any of the members who ousted me. I didn't receive adequate feedback on my performance, something that should be fundamental in such circumstances.

Notwithstanding Josh's apparent views, I (and many others) feel that I succeeded as both a CEO and as an activist. In my opinion and experience, these are not mutually exclusive. As CEO, I raised the funds necessary for us to undertake our work, I kept to budget, I led and managed a team of staff and volunteers, prepared regular reports, and undertook other tasks that were within my job description. As an activist, I achieved all the goals we set out to achieve. So clearly there were other, unrelated issues driving Josh's (and possibly the board's) apparent desire for change. To me the reasons are clear, and in some ways even understandable.

The confrontations at every level were common—the board wanted a calmer environment. They were never going to get that with me there until I had achieved my goals. Other factors may have been the continuing added tension between my broader family involvement and the fact that the board wanted to focus on a less confrontational approach—on education rather than public advocacy, the latter being the main raison d'etre of the organisation.

After several months serving on the Tzedek board of advisers, I tendered my resignation. I did so for several reasons. After several months observing what they were doing, they no longer had my full support. I could no longer associate myself with them. Another reason I stepped down was because I was in the process of establishing a new organisation to address the issue of child sexual abuse in the global Jewish community. I didn't want there to be a real or perceived conflict of interest.

In hindsight, could I have done anything differently? I honestly don't know.

Would it have been better to keep my advocacy a one-man show, to create Tzedek as an informal outfit, and not to register it as an organisation? Should I have just brought in a few people to help, but kept it informal? Perhaps, but then we wouldn't have received any government funding. Or I could have recruited a different type of board, one with more corporate-governance experience. Yet I am not sure if that would have made it more successful. If I had invited people who had board experience, and with that, conflicts of interest, I might not have been able to achieve what I did.

It's true that I would have antagonised people less by not comparing the intensity of the ECAJ's advocacy with its low public profile on child sexual abuse. People would say to me: *Why did you have to bring Israel into all of this?* But

I don't really regret it. I needed to get people to take this subject seriously. Although the board seemed to think I was too confrontational, too much of an activist, in the end I was fully vindicated. If I had gone softer, there would not have been sufficient impetus to establish the reforms that followed. I can live with myself for having taken a strong line, because I know that it was for the right reasons and that it achieved the desired results.

Chief among these was my work involving the royal commission. When it was announced in January 2013, I declared it my stated mission to ensure that the Yeshivah Centre would be the subject of a public hearing. This took a great deal of work, including sustained lobbying. I had to ensure that victims from this institution went to private sessions to share their stories, provide the commission with huge amounts of material, and then explain the nuances of the process to the Jewish community. I also had to assemble a pro-bono legal team to advise and assist with written and oral submissions. So the fact that there was indeed a public hearing gave me immense satisfaction. It was my greatest achievement, and it was a game-changer. Without that public hearing, I'm confident that we wouldn't be where we are today.

Under my leadership, Tzedek also facilitated a world-first broad public acknowledgement and unequivocal apology to victims/survivors of child sexual abuse by a senior rabbi leading a major Orthodox institution. Rabbi Moshe Gutnick (from the Organisation of Rabbis of Australasia), with whom I'd been working, issued a powerful public apology on the eve of Yom Kippur on 11 September 2013.

Tzedek also led two successful international campaigns, which had to do with two prominent US-based rabbis. The first of these involved Rabbi Manis Friedman, a Chabad emissary from New York who compared child sex abuse to diarrhoea. In another recording, Friedman told a girl from a Russian family: 'What! You think you were the only one molested? You think your mother and grandmother back in Russia made it through their teenage years without being molested?'

After Tzedek instigated actions against Friedman in the Jewish court (Beth Din) in Sydney and Crown Heights in Brooklyn, New York, Friedman backed down and issued an apology over his comments. I spoke to him on the phone, and he seemed to grasp the offensiveness and damage caused by his remarks. Although it was an important victory for Tzedek, and for victims, it underlined the level of ignorance and insensitivity we were up against.

Later that year, in August, another American rabbi, Kenneth Brander, dean of Yeshivah University's Centre for the Jewish Future and the vice-president for university and community life, was invited to Melbourne to speak on 'Ethics in Philanthropy: Should synagogues and Jewish institutions accept tainted funds?' The invitation was issued under the auspices of the Council of Orthodox Synagogues of Victoria (COSV). After checking into Rabbi Brander's background, Tzedek discovered that his university, Yeshivah University, had not properly addressed its own child sexual-abuse scandal. More directly, Rabbi Brander, who led the Boca Raton Synogogue in Florida from 1990–2005 and was its influential Rabbi Emeritus, was accused of hushing up serious sexual-abuse allegations against a congregant, Richard Andron. The same man, Andron, was also named in a class-action lawsuit against Yeshivah University.

When we aired these facts, the president of COSV, Romy Leibler, lashed out and accused Tzedek of shoddy research, in an attack that simply did not stand up to scrutiny. The information is on the public record. Although my statement regarding Rabbi Brander had been strong, perhaps strident, the hypocrisy of his statement is perhaps more troubling. This was the same organisation whose own standard of background research allowed it to appoint Cyprys as a board member of the COSV over several years, going back to 2006. Tzedek's campaign did not manage to stop Rabbi Brander from coming to Melbourne to speak to rabbis and other community figures.

There was, in the end, a silver lining to the pain of my unexpected departure. The fact that I was no longer working for an advocacy group made it easier to differentiate between Tzedek, the organisation I established, and Manny, the victim and public advocate. The extra time I now had helped me with the preparation of my submission to the royal commission and my continuing work with them to ensure we were fully prepared for the public hearing. At the same time, Elise and I had also been discussing the possibility of leaving Australia after the hearing. The relentless public scrutiny and intimidation had taken a heavy toll, and we had concerns for both the present and future remaining in Australia. As previously noted, we were planning to leave after the royal commission public hearing. Leaving Tzedek prematurely simply hastened our departure by a few months. But as I noted at the commission hearing, 'If it was up to my wife, we would have left a long time ago.'

In the meantime, I had the satisfaction of receiving an apology from Rebbetzin Feldman. On 7 October, after a petition against Yeshivah prompted further correspondence between us, which I made public, she issued the following statement:

> In my robust and emotional email I employed offensive language which I remorsefully regret and unreservedly apologize for. I also want to apologize for any perceived trivialization of the impact of child abuse on victims. Molestation is a devastating crime, violating the intimacy and innocence of the pure and defenceless [sic]. The victim is left feeling that there is something wrong with the world in which he or she lives. Perpetrators of molestation should be reported to the police and prosecuted appropriately. Any person, organization or entity that stands by silently is abetting in the crime and must do everything in its power to ensure that children are safe at all times.'

The good rebbetzin couldn't get herself to apologise directly to me—she did so in the public domain, and of course I saw it. Two days before issuing the apology, she drew support from another prominent Chabad figure, Mrs Shyrla Werdiger, a doctor and wife of Shlomo Werdiger, a long-standing member of the Yeshivah Centre's committee of management:

> I don't defend the Grand Most High Pooh-bah Rebbetzin [Feldman] in any way but I do believe that this was a private email to Lord High Executioner Waks, which he chose to publicise. They are all damaged, deranged and generally vindictive and destructive individuals who all bring a *chilul hashem* [desecration of God's name] to the name of Judaism in general, Orthodox Judaism in particular. I could go on but I won't. And yes, poor timing perhaps. But so what.

Clearly, hostilities had not ended.

I spent the last few months of the year working on my submission to the royal commission. Sadly, after my departure, Tzedek almost ground to a complete halt. This, despite the three-month-long handover when I had fully cooperated with the board to achieve a smooth transition. Tzedek contributed very little, if anything, to the royal commission, and effectively abandoned its advocacy activities. As a part of its mission, Tzedek should have put pressure on Yeshivah, and advocated for victims. Instead, this role again fell on me—Manny Waks the individual, the primary reason for which I had established Tzedek in the first place. I should add that at least they sent a representative on most days during the public hearing. This was one better than every other Jewish community organisation, who didn't even bother attending.

Tzedek also showed a serious lapse in judgement when it invited an American Orthodox clinical psychologist, Dr Norman Goldwasser, who practised therapies aimed at 'curing' homosexuality, to be the keynote speaker at its education forum in September 2015. As the *Sydney Morning Herald* reported on 14 August, 'several survivors of child sexual abuse in the Jewish community had condemned Dr Goldwasser's involvement and several Tzedek board members threatened to resign if he attended the event'. Well before this became a public issue, when Tzedek approached me about it, I advised them not to invite Goldwasser. After a public outcry from abuse victims and the LGBTI community, Tzedek cancelled the invitation. The mistake was corrected, but the question mark over its judgement remained.

The bottom line about advocacy in this fraught area seems to be that if an organisation is not led and run by past victims, it will not have the fire in its belly to sustain its mission for justice, accountability, and change. The enduring victims' advocates groups—those with recognised voices in the debate—have been founded by victims and/or run by them. Non-victims, despite their best intentions, will not put themselves in the same vulnerable position, because they do not feel the same depth of transgression, the visceral memory of violation that can never be erased.

It's probably fair to say that non-victims bring a more moderate perspective to the task. They argue, with some justification, that victims are too emotional, and that outsiders bring professional detachment and a voice of reasoned judgment. Of course, we also try to be reasonable, but we know it's not enough. After all, this is about justice for the victim and preventing the same crimes from being perpetrated on others. Sometimes you have to go too far to make your point, whether it looks reasonable to the broader community or not. Without that sense of zealotry, it's too easy to run in second gear. In the specific case of Tzedek, the result is that, after all the sound and fury, the organisation has become largely ineffectual. And ultimately, the community—more specifically, our children—are the biggest losers.

Chapter Seventeen

One step forward, two steps back

The royal commission gave me heart—and something more. The public hearings, admissions, and apologies that extended over two weeks delivered a feeling of genuine progress being made. Thanks to the wonderful work of lawyers assisting the commission, such as Maria Gerace, my own legal team, and the lawyers for the other victims/survivors, the commission ventilated previously hidden ideas and values, and exposed them to the disinfectant of sunlight in the public domain, there for all to see and hear—if they chose to.

In particular, the resignations of Rabbis Glick and Kluwgant were landmark moments. They demonstrated that leaders can be held accountable for their actions, and that public advocacy and community scrutiny cannot be ignored forever. These revelations, and others, at the end of two weeks of hearings, gave me reason to hope, if not yet believe, that the institutions themselves might be pushed into new modes of thinking.

First the leaders, now the boards. With new protocols come new value systems, and a mindset which recognises that the duty of care and trust lies above reputation. According to the old saying, change the behaviour and the thinking will follow. Was I being too naïve? My father certainly thought so. The first fallout between us from the commission was a series of arguments over the prospects for reform and change.

'I don't believe anything will change,' he asserted.

'Give it a chance,' I said. 'I am more optimistic.'

I didn't have to wait long for positive signs. In June, the entire committee of management of the Yeshivah Centre was dissolved. All nine members eventually stepped down. A new organisation, Parents & Friends of Yeshivah Melbourne, was set up after the royal commission public hearing. As an 'inside' group, they added to the pressure. But I did find it ironic that they focussed on accountability, transparency, and the issue of conflict of interest—when three out of their team of five were closely related.

In a statement to stakeholders, Yeshivah announced that an interim board would be appointed under the guidance of 'governance experts', and a new constitution drawn up by December. 'All agree that we must implement the changes with vigour and immediacy to enable our schools and community to continue to thrive,' it read. In addition, the board of trustees, which oversees the committee of management, also announced that it would disband and be replaced by a new governance body before the next AGM in December. However, instead of there being a smooth transition, this descended into a complex dispute involving Chabad Melbourne and New York, and various groups of concerned Chabad members, which I deal with in more detail below.

With hindsight, over a year since the commission's hearings, I see that I was overly optimistic. I didn't think everything would change, but I had hoped for more signs of sustainable progress than have occurred. Indeed, while we have seen significant progress, there have been more indications and examples of regression than progression. So, to some extent, my father was right.

Six months after the royal commission hearing, Rabbi Zvi Telsner announced he was stepping down as head rabbi of Melbourne's Yeshivah Centre. He was one of the biggest names to fall following the royal commission, and it was long overdue.

Rabbi Telsner's seniority put him right up there with Rabbis Glick and Kluwgant. More significantly, I, my family, many within the community, and even the royal commission share the view that he had led the charge against me and our family, especially with the sermons he delivered in synagogue that could only be seen as warnings to the congregation in response to my decision to speak out. Through his position of authority, he was directly responsible for what happened under his watch. Rabbi Telsner went on to bring the entire Chabad community—indeed, the broader Jewish community—into disrepute when he compared paedophilia with homosexuality at the royal commission, and said that both could be 'cured', among several other unfortunate comments he made and the arrogance he displayed.

Although his resignation was inevitable, I did not expect him to do so so swiftly. Certainly, it was the right thing for him to do. I and the other victims I know all feel the same way. Moreover, Yeshivah would not have been able to move forward until he was dealt with. At the time, I was working with the Yeshivah interim committee of management, and I made it clear that I expected the committee to take action about Telsner. I was told they would not be able to do anything because they were an interim committee, and that a formal decision would be the responsibility of the permanent committee, when and if it was constituted. So Telsner's timing caught me off-guard. Yeshivah said the decision was entirely his, and that no one had leant on him.

The Chabad rabbinic panel, which had been recently formed, said it would review the process around his resignation. When they did so, they formed the view that he hadn't been pushed. This new panel was an interesting innovation. In its initial structure, with one member from overseas and the rest local, it was designed as a mechanism to provide more accountability and transparency, by reviewing the inner workings of an independent committee. I understand the idea: the Chabad ethos is being maintained. However, the make-up of the panel leaves me uncomfortable. There are two names in the group that make my antennae twitch. Although I haven't heard anything specifically negative from them about me, I have heard indirectly that they have spoken about me in derogatory ways. There are many people, post-royal commission, who owe me an apology, and I think these two are among them.

Within a week of Rabbi Telsner's resignation, a petition of support started circulating:

Show of Solidarity with Rabbi Telsner

We the undersigned express our dissatisfaction with the events surrounding the stepping down of Rabbi Telsner. Such a matter has a far reaching community impact and requires careful thought and understanding of the feelings of the Yeshivah Centre constituents.

We stand behind Rabbi Telsner in solidarity of both

him as an individual as well as the position of Rabbi as a representative of the wider community. The Koach HaTorah and Halachic principles must be upheld despite there being impediments and hardships.

We further insist that the Yeshivah Centre—true to its title of being 'Under the auspices of the Lubavitcher Rebbe'—follow the directives, principles and spirit of the Rebbe's explicit and inferred opinions in its running and operation. This point is not negotiable.

Ari Schachter

Reuven Centner

I understand that even though people don't like seeing leaders they respect being forced to resign, what this petition effectively said was: *Telsner is a great guy, a great leader, and he has been treated unfairly. We want him to stay on as our leader.* The signatories were saying, explicitly, that despite what we had all seen, despite the fact that he had brought the entire community into disrepute, *Let's ignore it.*

Here, in a nutshell, was the culture laid bare. When Telsner resigned, did anyone from the Chabad community speak out publicly to say he'd made a good decision, and that it was a good outcome? Instead, a week later, this petition appeared, with hundreds of signatories, basically asking for his reinstatement. It begged a question, a really important question: *Why has there never been such a vigorous show of support for victims?* Or what about a petition encouraging victims to come forward to the police? I have not seen anything like that. It's only when the perpetrator of attacks against victims is in trouble that community bestirs itself.

Less obvious than petitions are acts of passive endorsement within the community. For instance, Solomon's Kosher

Butchers in Melbourne still employs Rabbi Kluwgant as its shochet (the person approved to conduct the ritual slaughter of animals according to Jewish dietary laws), and employs Rabbi Telsner as the rabbi to certify that these meats are indeed kosher. What does this say about the broader concept of *kashrut*, of Jewish religious dietary laws? To me, it's completely devalued.

This residual sympathy, reverence, and implicit denial was demonstrated yet again in April 2016, when Rabbi Chaim Zvi Groner was due to make a speech on Shabbat HaGadol, but withdrew the day before, for reasons not made public. Who gave the speech instead? Rabbi Telsner, no longer holding any official leadership status within the congregation. There were no questions asked, no eyebrows raised, no public complaints made.

Another reminder of how hard it is to change a Jewish institutional culture came shortly after the royal commission hearings, when I went to New York and, among other things, met the Chabad leadership in Crown Heights. I met with Chabad's director of operations, Rabbi Mendy Sharfstein, who was welcoming and knowledgeable. I presented two proposals to him.

First, I suggested that that education about child sexual abuse should be provided to every Chabad House around the world, of which there are thousands. I told him that, with respect, most of the current Chabad emissaries and leaders did not have a clue about how to deal with this issue. A lot of them were young, newly married, and uneducated in secular subjects, with almost no sexual education, and had never dealt with this issue. They had probably never discussed sex (except in a brief lesson prior to marriage); they may not have even uttered the word 'sex'. In many cases, they would be victims or perpetrators of abuse themselves. I suggested a campaign to roll out such a program, and even offered myself as a consultant to help address the issue, or to help them find an appropriate person to do so.

Second, I suggested that Chabad headquarters in Crown Heights should employ, or retain someone, in their headquarters to oversee this policy to ensure it was being taken seriously and implemented professionally. This would also allow them to have a go-to person for questions, problems, and advice. In particular, this would provide an avenue for complainants when the statute of limitations (or other reasons) have prevented would otherwise prevent holding perpetrators to account. Instead of resorting to a Wall of Shame, the Chabad leadership could address each case brought to its attention appropriately, and would potentially rule out the need for such a controversial and questionable practice.

I spoke to a person designated as their public-liaison spokesman, and the interview was filmed as part of a second documentary being made about me. Chabad was very receptive to my proposals, describing them as 'great ideas'. I sent them a follow-up email a few months later, to enquire if there were any developments regarding my proposals. I wanted to know what I should say if the media or the public asked any questions about their role and policies after the documentary had been broadcast. I received no response. I followed up a month later. Still no response. Like Yeshivah before them, they chose to ignore me.

To me, the media spokesman seemed to have good instincts, but I feel as though he is under instructions not to speak. The modus operandi is clear. On camera: keen. Off camera: no action. It doesn't mean they're not serious about this issue, but the complexities of pleasing their stakeholders effectively trump the instinct to help and to do the right thing. I suspect there is also a large dollop of institutional arrogance at work. The leadership would be thinking: *Who is this guy who thinks he can come in and tell us what to do?* In this sense, Chabad is acting just like the Catholic Church—a few moments of truth, among the lies, inaccuracies, and chronic amnesia at the royal commission, followed by no real appetite for reform at the grass-roots level. Big religious institutions are very resistant to change. To take another example, Jews like to say that the Muslim community says one thing to the public in English and another to their community in Arabic. In practice, we do the same, with the Orthodox community.

Perhaps I should not have been surprised, given the response that Chabad gave to my brother Yanki when he was considering giving testimony in a sexual-abuse case against David Kramer over charges he was facing in Missouri. Yanki, who had been living in New York for over a decade, sought advice from Chabad headquarters in Crown Heights, and asked a prominent rabbi if he should give evidence. The reply was damning: 'He's already suffered enough [Kramer was in prison at the time]. Leave him.'

This astonishing response encapsulates the resistance of the New York Chabad community to change, and its unwillingness to acknowledge the sexual-abuse problem. And in case anyone thinks this is just paranoia from the Waks family, they should read the insights of a recent former Brooklyn district attorney, Charles Hynes, who spent years trying to prosecute members of the Jewish clergy for abuse. Hynes believes the intimidation of victims is worse than that exercised by the Mafia:

Many victims are fearful that factions within these

communities will ostracize, will terrorize, will do things that are just not acceptable; things that I just think are shameless. I compare it to the Mafia, but at least in Mafia cases we can offer victims witness protection. That does not work in these insular communities, where it is more difficult to leave behind friends and family and go into hiding.

–*New York Daily News*, 20 January 2013

Technically, there is a possibility the royal commission will deliver findings that have legal force—not just adverse findings, but ones that lead to individuals being referred to the police for investigation, with a view to laying charges. For example, it's now indisputable that Yeshivah was informed about Kramer's offences, yet they nevertheless materially helped him get out of Australia. This action effectively aided and abetted someone who was alleged to have committed a crime to escape justice. So one of the Yeshivah leaders from the time may be charged with a crime. If a precedent for this is needed, we need look no further than at the Catholic Archbishop of Adelaide, Philip Wilson, who was charged in March 2015 with concealing the crime of sexual abuse by a paedophile priest who worked with Archbishop Wilson in the Newcastle region of New South Wales in the 1970s. As this book went to press, there was no verdict in that case.

There may be others, too, in the same boat. According to submissions made by counsel assisting the royal commission, Rabbi Glick knew about Cyprys in the early 1990s. The fact that he allowed Cyprys to continue working for Yeshivah, putting at risk the welfare of hundreds of children, cannot be ignored. In terms of achieving justice and sending a strong message, this needs to be taken very seriously.

All of this activity in Melbourne has, however, deflected

the spotlight from Yeshivah Sydney, which has largely escaped post-royal commission scrutiny. While Rabbi Yossi Feldman has rightly been subjected to criticism and ridicule, the commission's hearings have not provoked a series of resignations in Sydney, nor prompted the sort of public soul-searching evident in Melbourne.

Having chronicled this series of stories that has made me feel so pessimistic, it is only fair to highlight an incident which shows that, sometimes, the message has got through to the leaders of Chabad, and that they do understand how to respond. This story directly involved my family—specifically, my parents—in September 2015, on the eve of the Jewish New Year.

At that time, I became aware that a convicted paedophile, Moshe Keller, was staying at my parents' home. Keller had been convicted in New York in relation to one child, and there were additional allegations by several other complainants, over which no criminal action could be taken against him, due to New York's statute of limitations. After years of trying unsuccessfully to sell their house, my parents finally managed to do so—coincidentally, to the daughter of Keller and her large family, who had relocated to Melbourne and had a different last name. My parents have said that at the time of sale they didn't make the link (and, in my opinion, nor should there have been a link to be made—a child should not be held accountable for the sins of a parent). The contract had already been finalised, and the settlement was due in December. As the family needed a place to stay for a few months, my parents generously offered them to move into the house that week free of charge. (Apparently, over Rosh

Hashanah, only Moshe Keller and his wife stayed over, as they'd come to Australia to spend the High Holydays with their daughter and her family.)

I notified the Yeshivah interim committee of management that Keller was at my parents' home so that they could deal with the situation immediately after the New Year (when certain restrictions, such as not using the phone, are lifted). I was delighted to learn that they were already aware of it. Apparently, they'd been informed of this just before the start of the New Year, and had already taken appropriate action.

Almost simultaneously, my parents notified Keller's daughter that Keller could no longer remain there. Both he and his wife left the property that night. Subsequently, my parents again offered the family their free hospitality—this time, on the condition that Keller wasn't present. Keller left Australia two days later, on 19 September.

I wrote at the time, and restate here: 'I view this [response by Yeshivah] as a positive development. It's great to see that the Yeshivah Centre seems to have appropriate policies and procedures in place, and the ability/willingness to address this issue.'

For the record, I am not against convicted paedophiles being allowed back to live in the community. They are humans. But we need proper protocols in place to safeguard children before they are allowed to do so. Just as I am against ex-communicating victims, I also do not believe in casting out perpetrators. If they have been brought to account, they are entitled to try to resume their lives. Moreover, we should resist any calls to vigilantism or extreme punishment. I make this argument not just on moral (human-rights) grounds, but also on personal grounds. Many victims have been abused by people they loved, and they may retain conflicted feelings, of love and loathing, towards their abusers if they are relatives.

Nevertheless, their neighbours and the broader community are entitled to know about the potential risk of someone living amongst them. So I do support the idea of a public registry of convicted child-sex abusers. If I was a neighbour, I would want to have that information so I could take extra precautions. Yet you need public access to the information to be able to act on it. While the US has made this information broadly available to the public, and Britain has as well, to a lesser extent, in Australia, Israel, and many other places, it is only available to the police. This needs to be addressed, and I fully support those calling for such a change in Australia, led by my friend and colleague Derryn Hinch.

Chapter Eighteen

Rabbi behaving badly

The allegations against Rabbi Glick set off a chain of events involving Rabbi Meir Kluwgant, which has not yet been put on the public record. Despite what we now know about Rabbi Kluwgant, thanks to the royal commission, the following story demonstrates the gulf between his public and private behaviour.

Just prior to the matter being resolved with Rabbi Glick, a member of the Glick family posted on Facebook a note that basically said *No one messes with the Glick family*. This was significant because it referred to the power of the extended family within the community. In short, if you take on the Glick family, you take on the whole Chabad movement. Given that his family includes Rabbi Meir Kluwgant (nephew), Rabbi Sholom Mendel Kluwgant (father of Rabbi Meir Kluwgant, and a leading fundraiser at Yeshivah), Rabbi Yaakov Glasman (nephew, and a senior official within the Rabbinate), Nechama Bendet (sister, Yeshivah Centre general manager), and David Werdiger (senior Yeshivah figure, brother of a long-serving member of the Yeshivah committee of management, and cousin of my first abuser), the family has a huge presence within the ultra-Orthodox community.

As noted, Rabbi Kluwgant, the president of the Rabbinical Council of Victoria, called on Tzedek to sack me from my role at the organisation I had founded. He had made his views about me clear a few weeks earlier, on 21 March 2014, in his column in the *Australian Jewish News*, headlined 'An abuse of abuse'. It included the following paragraphs:

> Sadly, the very cause that the vigilantes purport to be championing is actually being undermined in the process, resulting in victims themselves being hurt too.
>
> Innocent people are being targeted, our community is being tarnished, and the course of justice is being interfered with by individuals who use the press as their tool to exact punishment and retribution on a community and one individual whom they feel have let them down.

Exactly one week later, a former Yeshivah Centre teacher and Chabad youth leader, Aron 'Ezzy' Kestecher, apparently committed suicide in his Melbourne apartment. Police confirmed that Kestecher, 28, was facing multiple allegations of child sexual abuse against minors, and had been due to face court in June. In 2012, four charges of indecent acts by Kestecher against minors were withdrawn, but legal proceedings recommenced in 2013 after new alleged victims came forward. A few days after Kestecher's suicide, Rabbi Kluwgant launched another veiled attack against me, as the *Australian Jewish News* reported on 3 April:

Rabbi Kluwgant described Kestecher as 'a very special young man who in his youth spent many a Shabbos meal at my home with friends and family'.

'He was a kind person with very special attributes, but he was also deeply troubled.'

Angry posters took to Facebook claiming Kestecher was subjected to trial by media and driven to suicide because of a presumption of guilt.

Rabbi Kluwgant inferred that the Jewish community had played a part in Kestecher's demise. 'Melbourne Jewish community ... (all of us) need to take a good long hard look at ourselves and see what we can do to ensure that this kind of tragedy never ever happens again.'

Phillip Weinberg, who has been a friend and supporter of mine for several years, wanted to help soothe the tension between the RCV and me. Phillip was a member of the Blake Street congregation in South Caulfield, and approached his rabbi, Ian Goodhardt, also a member of the RCV, to speak to Rabbi Kluwgant on his behalf. He wanted to know why the hopelessly conflicted RCV had involved itself in a matter between Rabbi Glick and me, given neither of us had anything to do with the RCV. He also asked whether the RCV would consider calling on anyone at Yeshivah to resign, or whether their call for accountability only applied with respect to me and my role at Tzedek. To his credit, Rabbi Goodhardt was sympathetic. But Kluwgant sent back a blunt response that the RCV stood by its statement. He was not interested in talking.

Later that year, and only a few months before the royal commission hearing, Phillip met with Rabbis Goodhardt, Kennard, and Genende, and pleaded with them to support victims and to call on those involved in covering up abuse and bullying victims to resign from their positions at Yeshivah. He asked them how they could preach to their communities that as Jews we had a responsibility to speak up against injustice while, at the same time, they remained silent in the face of the greatest injustice our community had ever seen, happening right under the noses. The consensus from the rabbis was that they should not get involved—that it was a Chabad issue and not a Jewish-community issue. However, they did agree to ask the RCV president, Rabbi Mordechai Gutnick, to call on Rabbi Glick to resign. The *Australian Jewish News* got wind of this, and reported it. The following week, Rabbi Gutnick denied everything, and the paper had no choice but to print a retraction and an apology.

One week into the royal commission hearing, Rabbi Kennard eventually came out publicly and called for Rabbi Glick to resign. Kennard also revealed that he had resigned from the executive of the RCV in October 2013, because the RCV hadn't called the leaders of Yeshivah to account when Cyprys was convicted. He said that at the time he didn't comment because it served no purpose, 'but that is no longer the case'. Again, it was great that he took the action, but he undermined his own authority by not making it public, thus preventing his resignation from having any impact on others. Had he made it public at the time, I have no doubt that the attacks against my family and me would have subsided. At the very least, it would have provided credence to my public criticisms of the RCV.

In February 2015, Rabbi Kluwgant was called by the royal commission to give evidence at the hearing into allegations of sexual abuse at the Yeshivah. On the last day of the hearing, on Friday 13 February, under intense pressure, Kluwgant reluctantly admitted to the commission that he had sent a text message to the *Australian Jewish News*'s editor three days earlier, describing my father, Zephaniah Waks, in the following words: 'Zephaniah ... is a lunatic on the fringe. Guilty of neglect of his own children. Where was he when all this was happening?'

In the wake of this testimony, Kluwgant resigned as president of the ORA and also resigned as an executive member of the RCV. He was also forced to step down from a number of other senior leadership positions—with Jewish Care (Victoria), as Victoria Police Chaplain, and as Ambassador for White Ribbon, a secular charity that campaigns to stop violence against women. An e-mail from the chair of White Ribbon confirmed their action:

> White Ribbon Ambassadors have a range of responsibilities ... including not acting in a way that might bring the reputation of White Ribbon into disrepute and/or is contrary to the key messaging of the campaign. In this instance, Rabbi Kluwgant accepted that his actions, as a White Ribbon Ambassador, had breached that requirement and that he was to be removed as an Ambassador.

To make a break with the past, Australian rabbis decided to dissolve the ORA and replace it with the New Organisation of Rabbis of Australasia (NORA), headed by interim president Rabbi Selwyn Franklin. (Ironically, the acronym NORA means 'terrible' in Hebrew.)

Following Kluwgant's admission, Rabbi Goodhardt decided to resign from the RCV. A year earlier, and within hours of calling for my sacking from Tzedek over allegations about Rabbi Glick, Kluwgant had sent a sensational email to

Rabbi Goodhardt and others, falsely and maliciously alleging that a member of Phillip Weinberg's family had engaged in an act of criminal behaviour and that, therefore, the rabbis should ignore his concerns. If this accusation had become public, it would have had the potential to not only humiliate but cause profound emotional suffering to the entire family. After hearing Kluwgant's appalling evidence to the royal commission, on the heels of his description of my father as a 'lunatic', Rabbi Goodhardt decided that Kluwgant's email regarding Weinberg demanded a response.

The email was another turning point, and not just for Rabbi Goodhardt. Up to this point, in the public eye, Rabbi Kluwgant's only error had been to use an inappropriately harsh phrase to describe someone—'just' a member of the Waks family whom many were publicly describing as crazy anyway. To those in the Yeshivah and Chabad community, it was a one-off, a moment of intemperance in a heated environment where many people were using strong language. Many in the community were prepared to forgive him for this single error of judgement.

But to Rabbi Goodhardt, the email about Weinberg's family demonstrated a pattern of intimidating behaviour, and tainted Kluwgant's whole character. He passed on the email to Phillip. That same week, Phillip received a phone call from Kluwgant's cousin, Rabbi Yaakov Glasman, a past president of the RCV, saying that Kluwgant wanted to have a chat with him. Phillip expected that he wanted to patch things up in relation to the 'lunatic' text sent to the *Australian Jewish News* about my father, and move on.

He replied that he would be happy to come over for a chat. Kluwgant did not know that Phillip had seen the email he had written and distributed about his family member, nor that he had printed out a copy of it to take to his meeting with Kluwgant.

When Phillip went over to see him, the rabbi took him by surprise.

Kluwgant: 'I have heard that you have some issues with me. I want you to know that I have never done anything at all to give you or your family any reason to be upset with me.'

Phillip: 'Think very carefully about that statement.'

Kluwgant: 'I swear to you …'

Phillip took the email out of his pocket and handed it to Kluwgant. The email had clearly been sent by Kluwgant from his Jewish Care email account, where he had been employed at the time.

Kluwgant was stunned. 'How did you get this?' he said. 'It was supposed to be confidential.' His reaction was not to deny he had written it, or to show contrition at having written it. He was first and foremost shocked that it had gone beyond a tight inner circle of recipients.

Phillip told him he was a liar, and said he felt like he had just watched Kluwgant giving evidence at the royal commission again. Kluwgant started crying, and begged for forgiveness.

'I panicked,' he said. 'I wanted this whole thing to go away. And I made it up. I made up the allegation. I have not slept in a week. Can't we just tear this up and pretend it never happened? My son is getting married soon. I'm about to become a grandfather. I've lost everything. I can't even pay my mortgage now.'

Phillip was resolute. He told him: 'I have as much sympathy for you as you've had to victims of child sexual abuse who, as opposed to you, have had their lives ruined through no fault of their own. You need to be held accountable for what you have done.'

He left Kluwgant in an agitated state, and waited to see how it would unfold. Within the next few days, the rabbi emailed him: 'Whatever can I do to make this right, I will do.'

Phillip was still reeling from the sheer immorality of Kluwgant's behaviour, and did not hold back: 'Send a written apology to the *Australian Jewish News* admitting what you've done.' He knew this was probably asking for too much. If Kluwgant admitted this in public, his humiliation would be irreversible. So Phillip was not surprised when he did not receive a reply. Indeed, he received no further contact from the rabbi. Kluwgant was in effect daring Phillip to take legal action against him, and, two months later, that is what he did. Phillip sent him a Concerns Notice, and pursued him for defamation. Their lawyers discussed the matter and it was, predictably, settled before going to court. But not without a fight from Kluwgant. Apparently, Kluwgant only agreed to settle after being told by the *Australian Jewish News* that they were about to run a story on the matter if he didn't fess up. As part of the settlement, Kluwgant wrote an apology to Phillip, admitting that he had made up the story and apologising to Weinberg and his family, the people hurt by his allegations. I saw the apology before it was signed, and thus before the terms of confidentiality came into effect.

Kluwgant was also forced to send the apology to the others to whom he had sent the email. Phillip did not seek any financial compensation or damages, and the settlement did not involve any financial payment.

In June 2015, NORA was replaced by a new body, the Rabbinic Council of Australia and New Zealand. Apparently, with significant chutzpah and still in a state of denial, Kluwgant nominated himself to be a leader of the RCANZ, but his fellow rabbis did not vote for him. Humiliated by what was a clear signal of disaffection and loss of confidence, he decided to leave the organisation. He then apparently resigned his membership of the RCV.

Within six months of resigning in disgrace, Rabbi Kluwgant was teaching religious studies at Beth Rivkah Ladies College, which is operated by the Yeshivah Centre.

This was an astounding decision by the college, and one that highlighted the gap between words and actions. And how did the news break? Someone notified me that Kluwgant was teaching there. I told the interim committee: 'This is wrong. It's an endorsement of him, after everything he has said and done.'

The decision was apparently a surprise to them, too.

Committee member: 'We were told he was doing some voluntary teaching last term, but it was a one-off.'

My contact then tells me: 'No, he's still teaching.'

I ask the committee member about this, who responds: 'Yes, my info was wrong. It is ongoing. Why don't you talk to (principal) Rabbi Smukler directly?'

I did. We had a long conversation. Now, Rabbi Smukler is a lovely guy. He and his wife took me out for a very pleasant dinner. He was reaching out to victims. He wanted to listen to my reasons why Kluwgant shouldn't be teaching at the school, and then promised to get back to me in a couple of days. I didn't hear anything. A few weeks later, the media reported the story (without my involvement), and the shit hit the fan. Apparently, Rabbi Smukler has since accepted that it was a bad decision to take Kluwgant on in that capacity. I was disappointed that the good rabbi never contacted me about it afterwards.

Collectively, these events contain several significant objective truths: this was not, and is not, a grievance by the

Waks family. The central issue is Kluwgant's character and pattern of behaviour towards victims and anyone who has wanted to help them. Finally, it sends a clear message about the nature of the culture I have been desperately trying to change. After everything that has been said and done, no matter what you do, there will always be a job for you at Yeshivah.

Chapter Nineteen

Unfinished business

One of the characteristics of the Australian Jewish community is the very high proportion of Holocaust survivors and their families it contains. This has shaped the community's psychological identity in several important ways. These include a highly developed sensibility to anti-Semitism, and a staunch, uniform support of Israel through thick and through thin. Wherever the attack or threat comes from, Australian Jewish community groups are quick and loud in their public responses. Conversely, this trait is also expressed through the restraint that these same bodies exercise in being reluctant to publicly criticise each other, whatever the issue, to avoid giving any comfort or encouragement to those who might try to capitalise on Jewish misbehaviour or transgression. In short, *Keep it within the family so we don't give our enemies any fuel with which to attack us.*

As I noted earlier, the failure to demonstrate a serious, credible response to the culture of child sexual abuse and cover-ups has by no means been limited to the ultra-Orthodox community. If some people regard me as a zealot in my advocacy, that perception has been shaped by the inability and unwillingness of many Jewish leaders to grasp the seriousness and depth of the problem. Or, if they have grasped it, they have failed to demonstrate their understanding by sending a critical message to the broader public.

In this context, two groups have stood out through their words and actions—the Executive Council of Australian Jewry (the peak national body for the Jewish community), and the Jewish Taskforce Against Family Violence, a Melbourne-based group, which was set up initially to address domestic violence in the Jewish community, and later expanded its activities to include the issue of child sexual abuse. Since my revelations in 2011, the ECAJ has failed to address the issue with the same prominence and vigour with which it has tackled other important subjects to do with external threats. It is clear that many children have been sexually abused within the Australian Jewish community—dozens in one institution alone.

Over the past five years, a striking pattern of defensive or limited public statements, interviews, and related responses has unfolded from the ECAJ, a pattern that supports my misgivings about its behaviour. For example, on 14 November 2012, ECAJ president Danny Lamm went on ABC radio 3LO, in response to an article published in the *Herald Sun* that reported allegations of cover-ups of abuse by senior rabbis in Melbourne's Orthodox community.

Here is the transcript of the interview with Rafael Epstein:

Epstein: Danny, thanks for joining us.

Lamm: Good afternoon. We were shocked to hear of the allegations [about sexual abuse within the Jewish community], and subsequently there were charges laid, and matters are going through the court of sexual abuse. It's abhorrent. And it's one that the Executive Council of Australian Jewry, the Jewish Community Council of Victoria, the Organisation of Rabbis of Australia, Rabbinical Council of Australia … all issued a joint statement last year when this came out in 2011 in July, saying that all alleged victims should come forward and provide the police with any relevant information they may have.

We are happy to do anything we can to assist the police with their inquiries, and anyone who has been found to have betrayed the trust of children under their supervision must be held to account to the full extent of the law.

Epstein: I suspect that all institutions have some similar characteristics. You'd have to acknowledge that there is bound to be some cases of Jewish institutions, be they big or small, trying to cover up stories of abuse. Do you think that's likely to be uncovered?

Lamm: In the first instance, we know some of these abuses took place. We now believe they were covered up. These institutions to which these matters were reported have now clearly indicated they are not continuing in that way. They are ready, and have co-operated with investigations, even going back 20 years, to try and ensure this never happens again. There will be no Jewish organisations who will be involved in any cover-up whatsoever.

Epstein: I just want to have a little listen to Shannon Deery. He's a journalist at the *Herald Sun*. He wrote a story in this morning's *Herald Sun* alleging that one of the senior rabbis in Melbourne's ultra-Orthodox community was trying to cover things up. He also says he has been contacted by people today with accusations of a cover-up.

Deery: I have received lots of calls and emails from people within the Jewish community who are not shocked by this story. They say they have been privy to very similar conversations with leaders within Melbourne's Jewish community, who have said: the last thing we should be doing is co-operating with police.

Epstein: Danny Lamm, I spoke to you earlier this afternoon. You were not happy with Shannon Deery's comments. He says he's been contacted by people who are essentially alleging a cover-up. What do you make of that?

Lamm: I refute those comments. He referred to Jewish leaders. There are no Jewish leaders who are representative of the community who are suggesting for a moment a cover-up. Simply not the case.

Epstein: It's dangerous for you to refute that, though, isn't it? You can't take responsibility for all Jewish groups.

Lamm: ECAJ is the umbrella for all Jewish organisations. We have been in contact with Jewish organisations, and we have not encountered one single situation where one current leader is wishing to perpetrate a cover-up.

Epstein: But if you haven't done your own investigation, how can you be so confident?

Lamm: All I can do is refer to the comments that are made to me. I have spoken personally to the leadership of the community that was involved in that serious problem in the past, and they have accepted full responsibility to ensure it never happens again. And that they will co-operate in every single way with any investigation.

And I was just in contact with the executive director [of the Yeshivah Centre] in the last three minutes to ensure ... and they are very keen that this thing will never ever happen again. And those people who were responsible will be met with the full letter of the law.

Epstein: I just wonder why you're so confident in the fact that you've just had conversations with various leaders in the community. Don't you think you're going out on a limb to say there's just no Jewish leader of note trying to cover things up? I mean, the Jewish community is not very big, but it's big enough for it to be difficult for you to be able to plumb all of its depths.

Lamm: Rafael, let's assume that I am wrong. The reported response from all genuine leadership is that this will not be allowed to continue. I don't believe that any of the allegations are recent. But be that as it may, people have been hurt, and hurt badly, and we don't want to see that happening ever again.

We support and welcome the [Victorian Parliamentary] inquiry, and we don't believe that there is any section of society that can say they are clean of this problem. It's a pervasive problem in Australian society. I am president of the Australian body, but from the perspective of the Victorian body from which these allegations arose, this community does not want to tolerate it in any way at all.

Epstein: OK, Danny. Thanks for joining us this afternoon. I appreciate you taking the time.

Lamm: Thank you.

This interview signalled just how out of touch, if not in a state of denial, the ECAJ was. The next day, on 15 November, I wrote the following comment on *Facebook*:

This is the most offensive and despicable interview I have heard on this scandal. Danny is essentially questioning the integrity of the *Herald Sun* journalist (who wrote yesterday's explosive article), Victoria Police (who have made it clear, including in court, that Yeshivah was not fully co-operating), as well as the victims and their families (who have reported ongoing harassment and intimidation by some within the Yeshivah leadership).

Danny is simply accepting Yeshivah's current position, despite overwhelming evidence to the contrary. It makes me wonder how the ECAJ would have reacted at the time the abuse in question was happening—based on their current position, it would probably have taken Yeshivah at their word that no abuse was taking place.

I should add that Danny's acceptance of Yeshivah's position is all the more confusing given that a senior official within the ECAJ had informed me directly and unambiguously that Yeshivah is completely unwilling to engage with any of the peak bodies. So even if Yeshivah changed its attitude towards the peak bodies, the fact that the ECAJ now takes them at their word is perplexing.

It is also interesting to note that the ECAJ belatedly issued a media statement welcoming the Prime Minister's announcement of a Royal Commission. While I welcome this development, it was a shame that it happened (two) days after the announcement and only after I highlighted publicly this lack of interest by the ECAJ and the other peak bodies.

It is also worth noting the major inaccuracy in their brief statement; '[a]llegations of sexual abuse concerning a small section of the Jewish community in Melbourne surfaced in July 2011' is patently false. They have obviously forgotten about the Malka Leifer affair, the former ultra-Orthodox Adass Principal who is alleged to have sexually abused many children under her care and then fled (with assistance?) to Israel. This transpired in 2008. I'm sure her victims, their families and many within our community remember this scandal all too well. Apparently not the ECAJ.

It is difficult for me to rationalise the ECAJ's current position, only to say that perhaps this is part of a second generation Holocaust survivor mentality, where some within the community fear retribution in response to scandals afflicting our community.

While I acknowledge and respect Danny and the ECAJ in terms of their contribution to the Jewish community, on this issue they have gotten it wrong, very wrong. Their position is simply untenable. The ECAJ should clarify its position and/or apologise to those they have offended.

The ECAJ should be standing behind victims, their families and the community—not behind the very institutions that facilitated and covered up the ongoing sexual abuse of dozens of innocent children.

From the time I went public with my allegations, the ECAJ's public response has involved seven media releases, from September 2011 until June 2016. During the same period, the ECAJ issued many more releases on issues related to Israel. I know I upset many people, especially from the pro-Israel communities, by making comparisons between Israel and child sexual abuse. I have been accused by a handful of people of confusing the two issues and their respective gravity. The sensitivity to Israel within our community here means I have put people offside simply by invoking the comparison. But I needed to do something to get attention: child sexual abuse affects the entire community—children, parents, teachers, friends, everyone—and the ECAJ has not dealt with it in the way it should.

Also, the Israel issue is one premised on perceived threats, ones that the Israeli leadership says it can handle. By contrast, if we accept the statistics that around one in five children are sexually abused before they turn 18, which is the figure provided by various organisations in countries such as Australia, Israel, and the US, the sexual abuse of children is rampant (of course, not just within the Jewish community). So it's not only a threat; it's something that happens daily. Kids are being sexually abused, in institutions and in homes. And we are now aware of the destruction this brings with it—to the victims and to those around them, including, often, to the perpetrator's family Why hasn't this been addressed as a major issue, and not just with a handful of broad statements?

I had previously ventilated the problem with a submission to the Victorian Parliamentary Inquiry into the Handling of Child Abuse by Religious and Other Organisations established in April 2012. Submissions were called for on 18 June, and the closing date was 21 September. I gave evidence at a hearing on 10 December. The ECAJ then felt the need to submit a formal response to the inquiry in response to my submission.

ECAJ Submission to Victoria Government re Child Abuse
17 December 2012

The reason for this submission is to respond to certain statements about the ECAJ, which were part of a more general statement made to the Inquiry by Manny Waks on 10 December 2012.

Mr Waks' allegations both of child sex abuse and the covering up by various institutions of that conduct must of course be treated seriously, and we would repeat our numerous public statements urging those making the allegations to provide full particulars to the police and other authorities and to render them every assistance in their investigations and in any resulting prosecutions ... Those victims who have come forward, including Mr Waks, are therefore to be commended for their courage, and for raising public awareness of the issue and encouraging other victims to come forward.

Because of the obstacles—institutional and otherwise—which victims face in making complaints, instances of abuse may not be reported for many years, if ever. It is therefore fair to infer that the incidence of child sex abuse in religious or non-government organizations across Australia is almost certainly far greater than the number of reported cases would suggest.

Nevertheless, caution needs to be exercised in drawing generalized conclusions about entire communities from allegations that concern specific individuals and specific organisations, and especially from those allegations that are yet to be proven, or even investigated.

In his statement to the Inquiry, Mr Waks has described allegations of abuse that he says have been communicated to him by others, and he has characterised the alleged abuse as occurring in 'the Yeshiva community', 'the ultra-Orthodox community', 'the Melbourne Jewish community', and 'the Sydney and Perth Jewish communities'.

These communities vary greatly from one another in numbers, cultural ethos and diversity, and it is a serious misrepresentation to suggest that the Jewish community is a unitary organisation, let alone a hierarchy.

Between the interview by Lamm and the hurried submission to the Victorian inquiry a month later — which was effectively an attempt by the ECAJ to attack my submission, undermine my credibility, and downplay the issue — the ECAJ did not demonstrate an appropriate grasp of the depth and complexity of the problem within the Jewish community. Lamm was the most senior leader from outside the ultra-Orthodox community to make a statement on the subject. Taking Yeshivah responses at face value, and criticising me for doing the opposite, reflected poorly on his leadership of the peak national body.

Lamm's response went to the heart of the difficulties I faced in trying to get leaders, and the community, to take the problem seriously. However, I should note that he was in good company. With just one exception, no federal or state Jewish politician — and there are several, including in the Yeshivah electorate — took a public stand on the scandal. All of these public figures have been very vocal on Israel, anti-Semitism, and the usual subjects relating to the Jewish community. But when it comes to problems in their own backyard, the only Jewish politician to speak publicly and courageously on the issue has been Victorian ALP Legislative Council MP Philip Dalidakis. And he didn't mince his words.

On several occasions, once the full extent of the problem had become clearer, I reached out to Lamm to ask him to retract his comments and apologise for them. I didn't even receive the courtesy of a response. In November 2013, Robert Goot replaced Danny Lamm as president of the ECAJ, for what was his second stint in the role. I approached him about putting a line in the sand and adopting a new spirit of acknowledgement about the example that needed to be set. I did not even receive a response from Goot or from the ECAJ. So it was clear to me who was their target. They just could not see beyond what I was saying and doing. Astonishingly, the ECAJ did not even send a representative to attend the royal commission hearings.

A couple of months later, I sent another message to Goot. He replied, disputing much of what I wrote, and requesting more evidence. I sent this to him almost immediately. As I didn't hear back from him, I sent him a reminder, which he promised to deal with that week. I didn't hear back from him. Weeks later, he sent me another note, promising to deal with it. He never did.

Large community groups don't want to be told what to do by individuals. They can't see beyond the messenger to what is in the public interest. The irony is that I have gone to great lengths to work behind the scenes to effect change, so that these groups won't have to get egg on their faces. Their reluctance to engage in the first place forced me to do what I did not want to do: make the allegations of abuse public.

In my eyes, the ECAJ's credibility has been shot. It couldn't acknowledge its mistakes and relative lack of prioritisation of this life-and-death issue. It did everything it could to try to discredit me and others who were highlighting the problem. We practically begged them to intervene, and they seem to have deliberately refused to do so. I still don't think they realise the profound impact of their actions and inactions on many. They may never know, nor care. But at least they're apparently protecting us from external threats, which have thus far, thankfully, been very limited.

The Jewish Taskforce Against Family Violence is a victim-support organisation, but does not have an advocacy function. It describes itself as 'an organization comprised of [sic] professional women including psychologists, social workers, barristers, solicitors, doctors and teachers. We work closely with Jewish Care (peak community welfare organization), mainstream service providers as well as the Police and the Rabbinate to actively promote awareness through community education at the primary and secondary prevention levels.'

For several months after the royal commission, the task-force website provided a list of names of rabbis who community members seeking rabbinic counselling could contact. The list included Rabbis Telsner and Kluwgant, and stated that they were among rabbis who had completed their training in how to respond appropriately to allegations of abuse. At some point, Rabbi Telsner's name mysteriously disappeared from the list and, eventually, after a complaint about Rabbi Kluwgant, the names of all the rabbis were removed. I was later told that, years earlier, victims had complained to the taskforce about interactions they had had with Rabbi Telsner, and these complaints had apparently been passed on to the taskforce leadership, who apparently had failed to take any material action in response.

A former senior official of the taskforce was aware of at least some of the allegations at Yeshivah, but seemingly did not try to address these allegations, and this same person was reluctant to come forward to the police with information it had in relation to serious allegations of sexual abuse. This same official did not seek to follow up and/or to offer support, advice, or assistance to a victim who had disclosed serious sexual abuse to them.

In November 2014, I wrote a post about this official, Sheiny New, on my Facebook page, as a result of which she indicated that she intended to sue me for defamation. I wrote that she had done 'nothing' regarding this issue. I also noted that her father-in-law was a member of Yeshivah's board of trustees, and referred to her personal association with Yeshivah. I meant she *effectively* did nothing. I should have said 'practically nothing'—even more so in the context of a senior official within an organisation that purports to support victims of child sexual abuse. I also could have said that 'I believed' that she had practically ignored the past abuses at Yeshivah because of her and her family's close connection to Yeshivah. Often this is what defamation is about—playing with words. Add the words 'in my opinion' or 'seemingly', and it makes it difficult to sue (unless, of course, you write something clearly false or malicious). I can categorically state here that, to the best of my knowledge, Sheiny New and the taskforce did not take any substantial action about these allegations involving Yeshivah. Sure, they were providing training in this area to Yeshivah and the Orthodox Rabbinate, but I'm referring to the past—the past that so many others tried to ignore and minimise in some way. And besides, we can now see how effective their training was. Many of those involved in their sessions—not least Rabbis Kluwgant and Telsner—were subsequently forced to apologise and/or resign because of their behaviour.

I mentioned that official's name in my submission to the Victorian parliamentary inquiry:

> The Jewish community in Melbourne is small and tight knit. Hence, the issues surrounding sexual abuse within the Yeshivah Centre reach into the broader community and its ability to combat child sexual abuse. For example: Ms Sheini [*sic*] New, the spokesperson for the Jewish Taskforce against Family Violence, an organisation established to combat family violence and child sexual abuse within the Jewish Community, is married to a member of the Committee. This Taskforce has been silent in relation to the allegations of sexual abuse at the Yeshivah Centre.

Although this paragraph and my Facebook post caused her great offence, Sheiny subsequently did approach Victoria Police about her knowledge of allegations relating to the Yeshivah; but, as confirmed to me by Victoria Police, this was done only *after* I had named her in our submission to the Victorian inquiry. To me, this outcome reinforces the importance of my decision to go public with my allegations. I had first attempted to raise these matters behind closed doors, and had sent Sheiny several emails asking her respectfully to address these issues. Her initial reply was off-topic, and then there was silence. So it was only after *The Age* reported my allegations that the wheels of justice—slowly, very slowly—started to turn.

I issued the following public apology to her:

I wish to apologise to Mrs Sheiny New for the hurt and upset that I caused her by posting a comment on my Facebook page on November 26, 2014 that have [*sic*] false and untrue imputations.

In that comment I questioned whether Mrs New had done anything regarding my disclosure to her of my sexual abuse at Yeshivah Centre because of family connections within the Yeshivah Centre.

I accept that Mrs New contacted the police regarding my disclosure to her of my sexual abuse at Yeshivah centre.

The apology was followed by a clarification, an edited version of which follows:

Along with my above apology to Mrs Sheiny New, a former representative of the Jewish Taskforce Against Family Violence, I would like to make the following known:

In 2001 I attended the home of Mrs New for a Sabbath lunch where I was seated opposite Velvel (Zev) Serebryanski who had repeatedly sexually abused me as a child. Later that afternoon I disclosed my abuse to Mr and Mrs New. I did so because Mrs New was a friend and a representative of the Jewish Taskforce who I believed would support me.

I regret that subsequent to that disclosure, Mrs New never contacted me to offer support, advice, or assistance.

In February 2012, many months after I had made my abuse public, I emailed Mrs New to express my disappointment that she had failed to contact me to offer support. I also expressed my disappointment at the failure of the Taskforce to speak out against the mishandling of abuse at Yeshivah. I asked Mrs New for her support and that of the Taskforce for myself and the many other victims.

I was disappointed to receive a response highlighting the Taskforce's work in ensuring child sexual abuse did not happen again, instead of the support for which I had asked.

Would there have been any arrests, convictions, apologies, and resignations? Would there be new policies on addressing and dealing with child sexual abuse if I had not pursued my approach? Perhaps there would have been some positive developments—but no doubt not as many, and certainly not as promptly as it has unfolded.

Sheiny New's husband, Chaim, was a prominent and long-serving member of Yeshivah's committee of management. In June 2015, Chaim New made a submission to the royal commission, four months after it had finished hearings, claiming that he had offered to arrange a meeting between me and the Yeshivah committee of management in 2012, but that this hadn't proceeded because I had demanded a financial payment as a pre-condition for attending the meeting. This was an outrageous claim—an outright lie—to make at any time, let alone four months after the hearings had concluded. Chaim had had ample time and opportunity to make a submission during the time allocated for the Yeshivah hearings.

In fact, I was the one who had requested that meeting, and I had specifically emphasised that there would be no pre-conditions on my part and that we didn't need to discuss compensation or the like. I proposed that it would just be a confidential meeting to discuss some of the issues. Chaim New responded that he would be willing to try, but that he felt this offer would be rejected. I never heard back from him.

In September 2015, Chaim New, having just resigned from the committee and acting as an individual, instructed a lawyer to apply for his submission to be accepted by the royal commission. New's lawyer told the commission that his client hadn't been able to make this submission during the hearings because of a conflict of interest between his personal interaction with me and his role as a member of the committee.

His application was rejected.

Yet, far from apologising or trying to reconcile with me, Chaim New reiterated these allegations to me, privately, later last year—even after they had been rejected by the royal commission. I will leave readers to form their own conclusions.

My dispute with Chaim was all the more difficult because, despite our 14 years' age difference, we had been close friends for many years before I went public in 2011. Sadly, Chaim died from a heart attack in January 2016, aged just 53. As a younger man, in the early 1990s, I spent many a day hanging out with him, talking about music, drinking, and life's ups and downs. We both loved the song *What's Up*, by the group 4 Non Blondes, and every time I hear it now, I tear up—he wasn't a massive fan of contemporary rock music, but he was a fan of this song. Chaim had an infectious smile, and he could fill the room with his laugh. Once, when a mutual acquaintance—another senior Yeshivah official—was suffering from an illness, and his medications weren't helping, Chaim asked me to procure for him a few joints to help ease his friend's distress. I was happy to help him. His attacks against me, which were sustained over a period of many years, were harder to address than those from others, precisely because we shared these fond memories. Everyone knows you can't just flick the switch from public to private when you go home at night. Chaim New is an enduring reminder of this dilemma. I'm saddened that we never got to reconcile before his death.

Another individual within the Jewish community whose behaviour deserves mention is David Werdiger, a prominent member of the Chabad community. Werdiger's grandparents were among the founders of Chabad in Melbourne; his brother Shlomo was a long-standing member of the (former) Yeshivah Centre committee of management—and the last one to finally resign (and president of the United Israel Appeal Victoria); he is related to Rabbi Abraham Glick; and he is a cousin of my first abuser, Velvel (Zev) Serebryanski.

Werdiger's website lists a variety of his non-profit roles, inside and outside the Jewish community. He is broadly seen as a moderate voice within the Melbourne ultra-Orthodox community—an educated, modern person whose interests and roles extend well beyond the confines of the tightly knit Chabad family. However, in relation to my advocacy over the past few years, Werdiger has been less moderate than his public persona reflects. In 2012, he sent me the following private messages:

19 February
Zev [Velvel Serebryanki], on the other hand, will now be branded a paedophile for life when more likely he's just harmless and messed up [as opposed to David Cyprys].

31 May
[You are] vindictive [because] [y]ou consider yourself a victim of Yeshivah as much as a victim of Cyprys. [And you

are] inflicting additional damage on people or organisations with links to the perpetrators.

In the days after the suicide of former Yeshivah Centre teacher and Chabad youth leader Aron 'Ezzy' Kestecher in March 2014, Werdiger posted the following tribute on Facebook, which seemed like a thinly veiled attack on me:

> Those who helped publicise said alleged sins, who facilitated or conducted trial by media, who acted in a heavy-handed way without thinking about the many possible consequences (or who ignored the obvious consequences following their actions) need to consider to what extent their 'actions' contributed to this terrible outcome.

Despite the fact that I have been vindicated by events since these comments, Werdiger has not even had the decency to apologise for his comments. I have since called on him to resign from all his leadership positions. In my view, he is simply not fit to lead, especially as he's unwilling to be accountable for such conduct.

At least on the subject of attitudes to child sexual abuse within the Jewish community, David Werdiger's behaviour towards me and others has been of a very different character from what he says and does in public. In my view, given my experience, he's a wolf in sheep's clothing. Readers might not be surprised to hear that, for having merely dared to state my opinion that he was not fit to hold a leadership position within the community, I received a letter from his lawyers, stating that my claim was nonsensical (and that they had advised him not to resign from anything), and that all future correspondence should be directed to them. To me, this was an attempt to intimidate me, as lawyers were involved. I wrote back to them, making my case, and, not surprisingly, never heard back.

While I have been critical of many groups and individuals, I do not mean to tar all Jewish community groups with the same brush. For example, the Jewish Community Council of Victoria has stood out in my eyes through the way it has recognised and adapted to the sexual-abuse crisis. Initially, I criticised this group, but they have made the biggest change of all the Jewish community groups, including the setting-up of the now-disbanded Child Protection Reference Group in June 2013, chaired by Andrew Blode, a former chair of the Australian Council for Children and Youth Organisations (safeguarding children from abuse in organisational settings) and a former director of the Australian Childhood Foundation, and Jewish Care—and a man I greatly respect. For the leadership provided by the JCCV, the executive director of the council, David Marlow, deserves some of the credit. This does not mean that there have not been hiccups along the way; but if you want to look at an organisation that has taken feedback and criticism on board, and instead of going on the offensive, has gotten on with the job, the JCCV is a great example.

On the subject of community groups, I would also like to address the role and behaviour of the *Australian Jewish News*. Like many newspapers, the *AJN* has an inherent conflict of interest. It reports the news about what occurs in the local community, but is also beholden to that community and its leaders for its existence. If it alienates readers, many of them conservative, there is a risk that they will stop buying it, and that advertisers will stop putting ads in the paper. So it walks a line between reporting hard news that will ruffle feathers, and self-censorship. It runs columns by rabbis, giving them free rein to say what they want by virtue of their stature, and then on other pages runs news stories that are critical of them and other community leaders.

Given this framework, you never know just how independent the news coverage will be. It was this potential conflict that contributed to my decision not to break my story in the *AJN* in the first place (nor to give them any real scoops), a decision that I believe has been vindicated. However, in general, the paper took a strong stance in its coverage of child sexual abuse. In particular, I commend it for the edition with the front-page headline 'Enough is enough', and for its subsequent editorial that said 'the rabbinate is rotten to the core'. They proved to be fully vindicated.

Given its conflict of interest, the paper has often found itself caught in the middle of complex issues, and has not always covered itself with glory in the way it has resolved them. The first example that comes to mind is the Kluwgant text message that led to the rabbi's resignation. That message was sent by Kluwgant to the paper's editor, Zeddy Lawrence. A journalist at the paper, Adam Kamien, passed it on to me, and I forwarded it to my lawyer, who in turn put it to Kluwgant in the hearing.

Within a few days, Kamien had left the paper. It is unclear whether he resigned or was shown the door—it depends who you speak to. It's my understanding that Zeddy told everyone on the editorial floor about the text, and there was no edict not to share the content outside. In newspapers, once hot information is shared, it usually finds its way outside the building very quickly—and by divulging such a sensitive piece of information so openly, it may have been perceived as a hint for it to be passed on, especially in the midst of the public hearing. On this occasion, Kamien paid a heavy price. In my view, it was an unfair punishment.

I was later told that the tipping point was that the editor's name was mentioned as the recipient, and he then feared that people would not confide sensitive information to him in the future because they could not have confidence he would keep the source a secret. Yet the fact that Kluwgant felt so comfortable writing what he did to Lawrence speaks volumes about the conflicted nature of the editor's role, and that of the paper's.

I stood up for Adam Kamien publicly, and when asked by other media outlets for a comment, told them it was unacceptable that he had left. The *AJN* contacted me, as its publisher, Robert (Bob) Magid, apparently wanted to speak to me about this. The paper wasn't pleased with my public support for Kamien, which was widely covered in the mainstream media. I didn't want to provide Bob with my private phone number in France, and offered to call him back, but I never heard back from the AJN about it.

For several months afterwards, it seemed to me and many others that the paper was effectively boycotting me. The paper did not use a single quote from me whenever a story about abuse came up, which was contrary to what they had always done. They deny it was a boycott; regardless, we clearly have a difference of opinion about this, and I can only repeat my appreciation to Adam for sharing the material with me. Had he not done so, Kluwgant would still have been considered a moderate, if not a hero, to many. And it was also disappointing to read the *AJN*'s view of Kluwgant—that he had apparently become a scapegoat and had paid a much heavier price than the others involved. True, he did pay a significant price. But he also was Australia's most senior rabbi involved in the continuing intimidation of several victims and their families, while simultaneously successfully portraying himself as a moderate and sympathetic voice. And it's not as if Glick or Telsner didn't suffer any consequences—both were forced to resign.

Another sector of the community whose behaviour demands scrutiny are Jewish philanthropists. A number of prominent foundations have continued to support the Yeshivah Centre, seemingly in a 'business as usual' manner, over the past few years of turmoil. I regard this as a slap in the face for the victims, and a denial of the public cloud hanging over the centre. I have been informed that some did in fact either cease or reduce their donations. This should have been made public—no doubt, it would have added to the increasing and sustained pressure on Yeshivah. And imagine if all non-Yeshivah or Chabad philanthropists ceased to fund them until they did the right thing. It would have sent a powerful signal to Yeshivah management that their support depended on certain standards of ethical behaviour, and would have exerted pressure on them to take responsibility sooner.

Instead, many gave Yeshivah a free pass. It was reported that one prominent Jewish community leader donated $100,000 to Yeshivah, even in the midst of its latest governance dispute at the beginning of 2016. It's his money, of course, and he's obviously free to do what he wants with it. But I know that such continued endorsement is deeply hurtful to victims, and is counter-productive in terms of the major reforms we are demanding. In my view, it would have been much more appropriate to give that money—and donations like it—to organisations involved in cleaning up Yeshivah's mess, and in holding them to account.

Chapter Twenty

Confronting the abusers

A few months after the royal commission hearing, I travelled to the US to meet with other advocates, lawyers, and community leaders to address the issue of child sexual abuse within the the Jewish community more broadly. During the commission's public hearing, the producers of *Code of Silence* approached me to make a sequel to their documentary (which became *Breaking the Silence*), with a more international focus. They would be filming the public hearing, as well as some of my meetings and discussions, and they also put a provocative idea to me. Would I be prepared to try and confront my first abuser, Velvel Serebryanski, on camera as part of a sequel to the first documentary?

This was a difficult question. I had also, independently, thought about trying to meet him—but in private. On camera, I knew I might come across as some sort of vigilante, a guy who takes the law into my own hands, who oversteps the mark in the name of revenge or grandstanding. What was I actually trying to achieve? After wrestling with the morality of the proposition, I was reassured by a number of principles and truths. Velvel had been monitoring events in Australia, and was unlikely to return off his own bat because he would face certain arrest—as has been confirmed by the police. So although it was unlikely that confronting him would deliver any measure of justice, I felt sure that I wouldn't be responsible for spooking him into staying away from home—he already had enough reasons not to return to Australia.

In addition, I'd been given what I regarded as reliable information that, allegedly, I was not his only victim. There were two others, but they would not come forward to the police. One was also a victim of Cyprys; he had already gone through one court case, and did not think he could face such an ordeal again, at least not at this stage. However, their existence meant I wasn't alone. If there were two others now known of, how many more were unknown? The idea that this man was living freely and safely in his neighbourhood, free to reoffend, provided a powerful moral argument for trying to do what I could to remedy this situation. I had been told that he would regularly go into a Chabad house, reading the Torah, interacting with children. Yet who knew about his background in New York? I had never seen his name mentioned on the Jewish Community Watch website, or on their Wall of Shame. He had only ever been named once in a US publication, *The Jewish Daily Forward*, and that was soon after I disclosed my abuse publicly. (Subsequently, on 12 June 2016, his name was mentioned in a mainstream US publication, the New York *Daily News*, in a piece reporting on my campaign.)

Velvel lived in a typical Brooklyn brownstone apartment block, the sort you see in American movies. As it turned out, the attempt to confront him failed to flush him out in person.

As soon as he realised I was outside his door, he bolted to the back of the apartment. I caught a slight glimpse of him. I also saw his tallit and tefillin—his prayer shawl and phylacteries—lying on the table. The hypocrisy again struck me. I decided to leave a note, asking him to get in touch with me while I was in New York. Of course, I never heard from him. After it became clear we weren't going to meet, I thought that if I could also talk to his neighbours and alert them to his background, I might be doing them a service. When I did so, I felt fully vindicated. The neighbours told me that their young kids felt as if he was staring at them all the time, making them feel very uncomfortable; as soon as he turned up at the apartment block, they would just run off. Their parents were grateful for the information I gave them. *Now we know to keep our kids away from him.*

Despite their positive reaction, I felt very uncomfortable about the whole scene, about knocking on the door and calling out through his window, with the cameras trained on me, and bystanders wondering what the hell was going on. It also brought back traumatic memories. Although people often see me as forthright and blunt, the truth is that this sort of situation was out of character for me. I don't think I have ever confronted anyone in that way. My discomfort was not due to the scene being 'staged', but rather over the act of going to confront a child molester who didn't want to see me. I certainly wasn't hoping for, nor felt, any 'closure' out of it. In hindsight, I don't regret my actions. I had taken action to protect those children. It was an appropriate thing to do.

From New York, I flew to Los Angeles for other appointments, which also prompted the producers to ask if I would meet with Daniel 'Gug' Hayman, who had been convicted of abuse in Australia and now lived in Los Angeles with his second wife. The director, Danny Ben-Moshe, spoke to Hayman for hours on the phone to persuade him to be interviewed. Once Hayman agreed, this was an easier challenge for me to digest. I remembered Gug from my very young days in Sydney. Everyone in the Chabad community knew him. Gug and I became close friends in the early 1990s when I studied at the Yeshiva Gedola in Sydney. Owing to my erratic past, I was given a long leash there; the rabbis allowed me to go out, and also to watch television. Where did I go to watch TV? Around the corner, at Gug's house. I would go to his house often for meals, and have fond memories of spending time there with him and his first wife. Gug was always funny and happy, a positive guy. I had a lot of fun around him. He made my life easier at a time when I was struggling.

Hayman never tried anything on me during the time I was in Sydney. My motivation for seeing him was an educational one—what I could learn as a victim advocate, and what the community could learn from this interaction. I also wanted to demonstrate that there are circumstances in which we can move forward to some degree. I certainly wasn't trying to speak to him on behalf of other victims, or to minimise the gravity of what he had done and the damage he had caused. We all knew there were more cases than the one for which he was convicted—something that Hayman had admitted to me. Hayman was given a suspended sentence for his abuse of the victim known as AVB. The judge explained that the leniency was due to Hayman's naïvety and sheltered religious upbringing, which had distorted his judgement about what was appropriate and inappropriate behaviour.

I met Hayman and shook his hand. We walked over to a café, and spoke for around an hour. His wife joined us midway. I didn't mince my words: 'If you were my neighbour, I would be warning my kids about you … in a careful, sensitive manner. The reality is you are going to be labelled a paedophile for life.' We spoke about the abuse, and about its impact. I also readily admitted that I was the one who had tipped off the police about him. He said he understood my reasons for doing so.

AVB was very upset that I met with Hayman. On *Breaking The Silence*, he said: 'I think Manny crossed a line. It really, really upset mc. Because Manny wasn't a victim of Hayman. They're not Manny's crimes to forgive.'

My reply to AVB at the time was: 'I'm certainly not holding him up in lights. I'm simply engaging with him. More importantly, this has nothing to do with forgiveness. As you rightly pointed out, it's not my place to forgive anyone for crimes they committed against others.' But I added: 'I think perpetrators have a right to make amends in our community. They should be afforded that opportunity.' This is something I fully stand by—but clearly there will always need to be safeguards in place to minimise the chances of recidivism.

Although I can understand why AVB was upset that I met Gug, I must stress it was never about forgiveness. I had also learned, in the lead-up to the meeting, of the piece of news that he would reveal on the documentary: 'Gug' Hayman had been sexually abused as a child. 'This led to some wrongful actions, which I am certainly not proud of. Had I understood the ramifications of my actions, I would certainly not have done what I did. I hope and pray, that just like God forgives someone who truly repents and changes his ways, so too the victims can forgive and move on with their lives,' he said on *Breaking The Silence*. As AVB then responded: 'It might be difficult for people to comprehend, but I think Hayman was more honest than almost all the rabbis at the royal commission.'

The fact is that Hayman had been caught, exposed in court, and punished. He had been brought to account for at least some of his crimes. I also saw the impact his behaviour had on his family and on his kids. Beyond that, there is virtually no independent research into the Jewish community relating to the issue of child sexual abuse, and here I had a chance to speak with a perpetrator in a civilised, neutral environment. I felt that this interaction would be useful for the community as an educational tool.

The revelation that Gug had been abused as a child meant that all three of the men convicted of child sexual abuse within both Yeshivah centres (Cyprys, Kramer, and Hayman) had themselves been abused as children. While it's premature to judge whether this is statistically significant or just coincidental—you would need to know what proportion of abusers were *not* abused as children—it demonstrates just how much damage abuse can wreak. The impact is viral. If abuse is left unreported and unaddressed, first, the abuser is free to keep offending and ruining many other people's lives. Second, the victims are robbed of the care and support they need to help them get on with their lives. And, third, victims are also at risk of becoming abusers themselves, thus ruining the lives of another generation of young people.

I must admit this kernel of doubt is something that has haunted me personally—especially due to the misperception that most victims become offenders. There is limited research in this area, but it's believed that around 30 per cent of perpetrators have themselves been sexually abused as children. Occasionally, I wonder whether people think this about me. Do they secretly believe I will also become, like Cyprys, Kramer, and Hayman, a victim who might turn out to be an abuser? The idea of being sexually attracted to children disgusts me beyond words. Yet victimhood sows this doubt in the minds of others. It is a sickening legacy, and one that many victims must live with, whether they are aware of it or not.

The abuse of Hayman and Cyprys, both raised in Australia, also points to a pattern of unreported abuse within the Jewish community a generation before mine. In the case of Cyprys, who was brought up in Melbourne, there is a compelling argument that the late Rabbi Yitzchok Dovid Groner, the spiritual leader of the Yeshivah community at the time, presided over a culture of denial and cover-up by rabbis and other leaders that predated my experiences by many, many years. This, in turn, raises the possibility that their failure to act on Cyprys's abusive behaviour was in part driven by guilt, or fear, over their inaction in respect of the people who abused him as a child. In a society as closed as Chabad, it's a vicious cycle that could continue for generations unless someone blows the whistle.

Chapter Twenty-One

Family fallout

One act of child sexual abuse has many victims — the person who was abused, their parents and siblings, their own children and partner, the perpetrator's family, possibly an institution where the abuse took place. The list goes on and on. In the media's obsession with justice and accountability, the range of victims is too often overlooked, yet it is a reality that I am reminded of daily. The fallout from my experiences has radiated throughout every facet of my life, and inflicted a particularly heavy toll on my family — my relations with my parents and siblings, and their relations between themselves.

My father has been one of my greatest supporters, both in private and in public. Anyone who has seen the two documentaries, or read the articles chronicling my campaign for justice, will know how resolutely he has stood in my corner over the past five years. My mother, too, has been supportive, although she has by nature preferred to stand back — and at times wavered — while my father railed against Chabad and the Yeshivah community leadership over their failure to take

action and their persecution of my family. The portrait that
has emerged through the media is that my father and I are of
one mind, one view, in lockstep. Yet this is far from the case.
We have clashed, and continue to clash, on many issues. My
life over the past five years has been dominated by my desire
to bring the Yeshivah leadership, as well as other institutions,
to account, and to instigate reform at Yeshivah and elsewhere
to ensure justice for victims and better protection for children
in the future. My father's life has essentially been focussed
on highlighting the hypocrisies of Yeshivah and Chabad, to
expose the failings and self-deceit of its leaders.

His motivation is easy to understand; he and my mother
have lost most of what was dear to them. He sees Chabad
as a cult, and indeed my own experience and research has
found a strong overlap between the conditions that Chabad
enforces and that cult movements typically create: absolute
authoritarianism without meaningful accountability; the
centrality of a single figure (in Chabad's case, the Rebbe);
no tolerance for questions or critical inquiry; no meaningful
financial disclosures; an unreasonable fear about the outside
world, such as of impending catastrophe, evil conspiracies,
and persecutions; and the disallowance of any legitimate
reasons for leaving, so that former followers are always
wrong or even evil if they do so (see Families Against Cult
Teachings.org).

My campaign has been about creating something new,
better. His has been relentlessly negative. He admits that. My
behaviour has involved trying to build bridges, engaging with
the community leadership while at times, even often, also
criticising them for their ostrich-like mentality. He has found
fault with me for sometimes being too soft. He wants nothing
to do with Chabad any more. He believes, as do many others,

that it has been corrupted from its original ideals, and he does not have a good word for the movement.

In 2014, my parents moved to Israel, primarily at my mother's instigation, to get away from the spiritual and physical isolation imposed on them. These days, he has trimmed his beard and walks around the house wearing shorts in summer—both outward signs of just how far he has moved from the values he once held dear. Although he attends synagogue regularly, he does not belong to a community, as he used to in Melbourne. He still works a little as a computer consultant, but has a lot of time on his hands. He is even getting flak from his mother-in-law over his lack of religiosity. Chabad took his whole life away from him. He is seething with anger, but he doesn't know what to do with it, except vent in words, on Facebook (at least until my mother banned him) to anyone who will listen. He no longer classifies himself as Chabad, or even ultra-Orthodox. By contrast, my mother has remained within the 'fold'—a proud and loyal Chabadnik. Perhaps their early background has played a part; she was Chabad from birth.

But that is not the main reason for our differences. The key to our tension has been the way he has behaved as a parent. He is an intense, extremely intelligent person, but a highly controlling father who has found it difficult—even now, although to a lesser degree—not to meddle or intervene. In some ways, I understand this: as a parent of 17 children, you'd have to be on top of everyone and everything, literally all the time. In a group, his natural tendency is to take over, to niggle and push.

This became evident at the royal commission. I organised a lawyer to help prepare him for his appearance, and when we came to have roundtable discussions, he took over, consistent with his domineering nature. Then, during the hearings, he would text our legal counsel incessantly—occasionally, several times a minute—with a running, angry commentary on his frustration with the rabbis' responses. To the public, he seems impassioned and colourful. To me, his son, at times, he is maddening, and I often find his behaviour counterproductive.

It's been like that in my family from the beginning. The Waks family was a laboratory of human stress long before anyone was sexually abused. My parents, and my father in particular, raised their children with a strict routine, fierce discipline, and a regime of physical punishment for transgressions by the boys against our religious values.

The beltings were common and, as the eldest boy, I led the way. If I got into trouble, my father would give me a fierce look and growl: *Go upstairs and wait for me*. I knew what was coming. My dad kept the belt on the kitchen shelf, so often when we were playing up in the house, he would just have to point to it, and say 'Be careful', and he knew that we understood. So we would try to toe the line. When I did cross the line, he would send me up to my room, where I would wait, scared. Quite a few times he would come upstairs, and my mother would follow and just sit there—and watch, seemingly trying to put on a brave face. He would give me five or ten hard lashes with the belt on my bare bottom; the number would depend on the gravity of the 'crime'. This was around the time I was being sexually abused, though they were not to know that. One of my younger brothers once refused to go to prayer on a Sunday morning, according to a story recounted to me by a family member. This brother was 12 or 13, and wanted to stay in bed, as you do at that age. My father belted him and locked him in his room for two hours. His screams could be heard throughout the house.

In their defence, my parents would argue that, with so many children, discipline had to be this direct. My mother was also occasionally physical, pinching or slapping us to bring us into line. They would say examples needed to be set and that there simply was not the time to talk things through at length, as smaller families do; that there was no time or space to devote to our individual emotional wellbeing. To be blunt, I believe that, with 17 children—or, for that matter, any more than around a handful—you cannot be a good parent. You just don't have the time or energy to do it properly, irrespective of who you are.

As a result, we missed out on much of the love and care that comes from getting individual attention. Indeed, the need I have to speak my mind publicly as an adult may not only be due to the enforced decades of silence of the abuse, but also to the feeling that I did not have my own voice while growing up; I felt more like a number than an individual child. The rights of the individual are not genuinely valued in ultra-Orthodox Judaism, and remain a distant second to the reputation and health of the community. Which is why, in many ways, I don't really blame my parents. They were living and acting within a framework that encourages and values this approach and lifestyle. It was about having as many kids as you possibly could—and, of course, in this case, it's worth recalling the Rebbe's specific blessing to my parents. And it's about doing everything you can to mould your children into followers of the ultra-Orthodox branch that you, as parents, follow—because, apparently, it's the Truth.

By contrast, over the past generation, western secular society has begun to recognise the rights of the child and to enshrine them in law through legislation, the creation of human-rights commissioners whose role is to promote the interests of the child, and so on. Although ultra-Orthodox Jewish values have evolved in this sense, progress has been much slower than in broader society. While it is the subject of robust public debate in secular society, there has been little acknowledgement within the ultra-Orthodox world that the rights of the child are something even worth being discussed. There, it's still very much about the community, and their interests, rather than about the rights of the child. *What rights?*, they'd ask. They'd see it essentially as their right as parents to mould their children into what they believe is in their best interests, which is ultimately the interest of the community. In Chabad's case, this is all about doing whatever they can to bring forth the Moshiach (the Messiah). And how will this happen? Through them studying more Torah, and doing more *Mitzvot* (religious commandments). Everything in life is geared to these goals.

So although I have rich memories of feeling joy and happiness during religious and family celebrations, we led a tough, regimented existence day in, day out. My father is an all-or-nothing type of personality, and was charismatic but unrelenting in his past devotion to the Chabad lifestyle. My mother is more flexible, softer — only slightly — but a brilliant organiser, having raised and fed so many children and run a successful wig business. She and my father have always been warm and welcoming. Yet all families have their dirty laundry, and our family has several baskets full. We are, after all, around five times larger than the average family. And our strong personalities compound some of the problems.

To his credit, my father acknowledged the excesses and mistakes of his parenting in a public statement in March 2015. Here is an edited version of it:

There is no doubt that I regret some of my past parenting techniques. To provide some context, I became a parent in Israel during the 1970s, and raised eight of my children in one of the most ultra-Orthodox cities there, B'nei Brak. A common form of discipline at the time was the use of corporal punishment, both in the home and within the school environment. Of course this was not unique to Israel or the ultra-Orthodox community. Indeed, it was common in Australian homes and schools. I suspect, however, that the approach to discipline within the ultra-Orthodox community was even more rigid. This no doubt informed my future parenting skills and habits, even much later when I relocated with my family to Australia. In hindsight, I certainly regret this.

Moreover, I fully understand that having a large number of children carries with it a great responsibility: to care for the well-being of each child in every possible way. On reflection, I fully acknowledge, however, that this is an almost impossible task with 17 children … In hindsight, with so many children, it is difficult for me to see how any parent can possibly provide completely for the unique needs of each and every child, and I obviously did not.

I would like to make it clear that I have apologised to all my children individually in the past for my above-mentioned errors. I have sought to make amends. Of course, I acknowledge that it is each individual child's prerogative to choose whether or not to accept my apology.

It is important to emphasise, however, that to try to conflate the parenting issue and that of the issue of child sexual abuse that was perpetrated against three of my children under the auspices of the Yeshivah Centre is more than inappropriate. Clearly, it has nothing to do with the sexual abuse, cover-ups, and ongoing intimidation by the Yeshivah Centre. It should be clear that anyone attempting to conflate these two separate issues is promoting a personal agenda.

I again reiterate my acknowledgment of past mistakes, and accept that in some cases nothing I say or do will compensate for the hurt I have caused to some of my children. I take full responsibility for my actions, and extend my sincere apology to each and every one of them.

In addition to the problems I have experienced, some of my brothers have variously grappled over the years with drug addiction, alcoholism, and gambling habits. Some have been thrown out of home as teenagers for rebellion against Chabad values; others are dealing with broken marriages and divorces; and most have renounced the ultra-Orthodox lifestyle. This is not as surprising as it may sound, given that there were 11 boys, and also in view of the general trend among young ultra-Orthodox members to question their faith as they mature. Moreover, as the eldest boy, I was a role model for some, which may have encouraged and/or empowered them to follow in my footsteps—as one sibling directly told me. According to a recent figure published in Israel, the number of people leaving 'the path' is one in ten. A growing number of international groups offer guidance and a voice to people who have made this decision, which is often called *Off the Derech* (the Hebrew word for 'path').

My father accepts that there have been casualties of our upbringing. He once described this to me as the result of the law of averages. If you have three kids in a family, one of them is going to have problems—that's just the way of human nature and families. Is he right? Well, it's not that easy to reduce human character to numbers. Whether it's through genes or upbringing, many of my siblings have strong, unique personalities.

My father reminded me how one of them at one point started to associate with criminal gangs, hardened criminals, and decided he needed to impress some of them to gain their confidence. He thought about how he could achieve that, and worked out that if he went and hit a police officer in the face, in front of the gang leaders, the police would not kill or hurt him, and in fact he would gain credibility in the eyes of the guys he wanted to impress. So that is what he did. My father says he attacked a cop and got bashed by the police afterwards—but he became a person of substance.

Several of my brothers have gone to live in the United States. One of them became, for a time, a successful real-estate developer in New York after having arrived there, around twenty years ago, as an illegal resident with one dollar in his pocket. Eighteen months later, he had made a million dollars. Since then, however, he has had many problems to deal with.

Although I won't go through them all, I mention these two brothers to highlight the unpredictable life choices that have emerged from our tightly knit religious home. Yet while the boys have been all over the shop, the six daughters have led more stable, secure lives. Was that due to my mother's greater influence over their upbringing, or because my father did not get as involved with them as he did with his sons? Whatever the reason, my sisters have not been as directly affected as the brothers.

One result is that all six have remained religious—only one ventured out of the fold for a period of time. Perhaps because my father was much softer with the girls, they did not have as much reason to rebel by dumping their religion.

And their school, Beth Rivkah College, did not have the sexual-abuse problems that the boys' school endured. They were more comfortable, so did not have the same reason to look elsewhere in life for meaning and happiness. In turn, they all finished high school, and all but one went on to university—one is a dentist, while others studied commerce, media, science, and nursing. Our family has been quite modern in that sense, although the corollary is that boys were expected to go to Yeshivah (religious seminary). I think it's fair to say that the girls grew up in a more normal family environment than the boys did, although they were certainly affected by larger family dynamics. Some of the brothers have been able to lead stable lives, but others have not.

Gender difference is one way of understanding our upbringing. Another is age. With 17 children spread over 21 years, there is a full generation between the oldest and youngest. While I am on good terms with most of my younger siblings, the age gap meant I didn't have the time or opportunity to stand in their shoes and to get their perspective on our family dynamics—nor to interact with them as 'real' siblings. I was already out of the house in dormitories from the age of 15, and I was permanently out of the house when I relocated to Israel at the age of 18.

While I have been out of touch with many of them as the years have gone by, opportunities always pop up for us to reconnect—whether we're in the same city, or there is a specific reason to get together. I've also had to come to terms with the fact that I may never have anything to do with some of them. Time heals, and anything can happen, but if the schism that exists between some of us is maintained I'm sure it's something we can live with. I feel that I can. We can all pick and choose who we want to be close to. Living in Israel,

I now have the chance to renew relationships with some that I was more distant from in the past. That also means becoming re-acquainted with their own families. I have about 40 nieces and nephews dispersed around the world, but can't recognise most of their faces. This was made clear to me on a recent trip back to Melbourne, when a nephew I knew fairly well—at least, I thought I did—came up to me all excited to see me. While he looked familiar, I didn't recognise him at all (notwithstanding the fact that he's not a Melbourne boy and that I hadn't seen him during the growth-spurt years).

I now understand how different it is to have been born at the other end of the production line. In contrast to the intensity of my upbringing, many of the younger children felt neglected by our father. Unbeknownst to me, for example, he kicked one of my younger brothers out of the house as a 15-year-old—I would have thought he'd have learned from past experiences that this approach doesn't work. My parents kicked me out briefly, as well as a couple of the others, at that age. As one of my siblings put it to me, at least the tough discipline he imposed on us showed that he cared. For the younger ones, it felt like he didn't care anymore. By contrast, my mother remained relatively hands-on and engaged with all the children. It seems that these younger siblings are now reflecting on the quality of the parenting they received.

In some ways, I don't blame my parents (in particular, my father) for their more recent disengagement. They probably want to focus more on themselves than their children and grandchildren. After all, they've been dealing with many children for most of their adult lives. The trouble is, irrespective of the number of children one has, it's one's responsibility as parents to love and nurture them.

Interestingly, I was struck by a different dynamic whenever

I visited my parents' house for Shabbat as a grown-up. There were only six or eight children there, and the house was calm. No one was fighting or screaming. My mother had become more assertive, and my father more restrained, almost subdued. I would occasionally feel jealous of this peaceful atmosphere, giving the impression of something close to a normal family. It also stung me when I saw that the younger ones were getting pocket money and presents. I remember getting pocket money only a handful of times—and that was for a specific reason, such as taking a friend to buy a pastry or for summer camp. My parents seemed to have relaxed in many senses. But, as I can now see, looks can be deceiving, as this is not necessarily how all my younger siblings feel.

The anatomy of my family's faultlines is important, because it is the template that has shaped their responses to my experiences, both as a victim and an advocate. It is fair to say there has been a backlash among some of my siblings against me and my father. Although the dynamics are complicated and multi-stranded, the common denominator is my alignment with my father. I have fallen out with several of my siblings and their spouses through my campaigning. Some of the religious ones believe I have blackened the Chabad reputation more than I needed to. Some have felt that my campaign was about bringing down Yeshivah or Chabad—a common (but deliberate, I believe) misperception among many within Chabad and Yeshivah, at least prior to the royal commission public hearing. When I disagreed with these siblings, and explained why I needed to ruffle feathers, we often fell out. Some preferred to stay on the sidelines and not get involved. This was a cowardly approach, in my opinion, but at the same time one that I sympathise with (although I have different expectations of different siblings, based on a number of factors, but predominantly on their ages). As a result, I am no longer in communication with some siblings. But, as I have said, I still have around a dozen to choose from.

However, the broader view—call it discomfort—among my siblings springs from the popular perception that my father and I are a united team. Until recently, many of them did not realise that tensions even existed between us. Their discomfort can be explained as follows.

My father is popularly seen as something of a saint for his support of my work. The media pieces and television documentaries have spread this message, and also focussed entirely on his relationship with me, giving the impression that the experiences of his other children are not really important. While that is the nature of documentary—to simplify stories by applying a narrow lens to the protagonists—it has had the effect of heightening our relationship above all others. Many, if not most, of my siblings are uncomfortable with my father's crusade against Chabad. After all, he spent most of his life immersing them in its ways, rituals, and values. He made it central to everything about their lives, and now he has walked away from all of it. Some of them feel a little betrayed by his response, despite how clearly justified his grievances are. That is a parent's burden. You set the example, and it becomes the touchstone for all your children's lives.

Yet this, too, is not the main reason for their anger. The kernel of the problem is this. Some of my siblings believe that the physical punishment handed down by my father amounted to its own form of abuse. In my opinion, this is an extreme and jaundiced view of a complex issue. Based on my personal experience—as the eldest boy, who probably copped the most beltings—it is inaccurate and wrong. But it cannot simply be dismissed out of hand, because of the ramifications it has had for all of us. First, let me say that I do not see my parents' punishment of their sons as abusive. It was sometimes harsh—very harsh—but it was not abusive. I see it as misguided discipline, a horrible form of discipline, but discipline nevertheless. The fact that my mother was often in the room when I was getting belted reinforces my view that this was a consensual, calculated form of discipline.

Their ideas of parenting must also be seen in context. They drew on the experiences of the community around them. They became parents in B'nei B'rak, where modern models of parenting skills were hard to find. It was a closed society, where you did what your parents did, or asked your friends what they did—as, so often, community members, even in Melbourne, approached my parents for parenting advice. That's where and how they learned to become parents. I can see, from first-hand experience, that this was the way ultra-Orthodox schools and parents disciplined their kids. It doesn't justify it, of course, but it does contextualise it.

Of course, there has been a revolution in social attitudes towards parenting and discipline over the past 25 years. Likewise regarding child sexual abuse. But the latter has always been a crime, and one that should be reported to the police, and yet it took a long time for our understanding to progress. Similarly, the goalposts on parenting have shifted: physical punishment is now outlawed at schools and frowned upon within the home, although it is still widely practised in very moderate form. Yet this upheaval in western society does not necessarily infiltrate closed religious communities, who do their best to resist any change, especially liberal reforms from the decadent world that threatens the stability of their controlled world. For evidence of this, you need look no further than the taboo on TV and movies, and even secular books, during my childhood. And the sad fact is that many children within the ultra-Orthodox community still experience corporal punishment—both at school and in the home.

The view that my father, who supported me so publicly in my campaign against child sexual abuse, was a physical abuser has driven deep divisions within my family. My father is painfully aware of the schisms. Several children no longer speak to him, and he does not wish nor expect to speak to some of them ever again—unless there's a radical change in their approach. While most of my siblings have chosen to keep their views about this subject private, or at least within the family, one of my brothers—the one who once punched a police officer in the face—has been conspicuously public about it. This involved a Facebook campaign against my father, which was expanded to attacks on me, on the grounds that I was ignoring the child abuser in our own family. Such were the depths of the enmity felt by a son and brother.

The rest of my siblings have been more or less able to get on with their lives. Online communication has been both a blessing and burden for a family like ours. With my family now spread all over the world—in Australia, Israel, and the United States—it is hard for us to ever get together in the way we used to. The last such occasion was the wedding of one of my sisters, shortly before I went public, when 14 of the 17 children gathered together. It was a joyous, happy time, and especially because we could feel the size and strength of the Waks family in one place again.   ·

Yet thinking abut it now reminds me just how much we have endured as a family. The schism between my father and brother has become a running sore that won't go away. When I stand back for a minute to reflect on it, its true impact is revealed. Child sexual abuse has torn my family apart. Whatever anyone thinks or says about my father and his behaviour, it should never be conflated with the undeniable facts that at least three Waks boys were sexually abused at Yeshivah, that Yeshivah attempted to cover up these horrific crimes, that we faced continuing and significant intimidation and re-victimisation for speaking out, and that, in stark contrast to his community, my father stood up for me, and on the right side of history. My parents and siblings, their spouses and their children—every one of us is a victim.

Chapter Twenty-Two

The lightest I've felt in years

Although I have been criticised for a range of shortcomings, perhaps the most common has been that I went to the media, instead of community leaders, with my allegations. I keep hearing from people, in Australia and overseas, that I should have tried to work within the ultra-Orthodox community and not expose their dirty washing in public. Every time they say this, I have given them the same two-pronged response. First, I did initially go to the community, and the Yeshivah leadership did nothing. In fact, they actively attempted to cover it up (not just my abuse, but the abuse of others by more than one perpetrator—at the very least, by both Cyprys and Kramer—and I'm aware of several other allegations as well). Second, look at the progress and reform that has occurred, albeit slowly and with pain felt on all sides, by my allegations having been placed in the public domain.

However, my advocacy has been conducted on many fronts, and the media is just one of them. Over the past five years I have also worked with the Jewish community leadership in Australia and internationally, and in particular the interim committee of management at the Yeshivah Centre, created to replace the old board that was dissolved in the wake of the royal commission. Despite my estrangement from the Chabad community, and the ostracism of me and my family, I have long understood that any genuine progress must be desired from within, not just imposed from outside. In the wake of the bloodletting at the royal commission, the interim board, their appointed bodies, and other relevant stakeholders have sought my input and advice on various matters relating to this issue. I have been happy to help out, volunteering countless hours with no remuneration, even as I have lived overseas since early 2015—ironically, in exile because of them. More than that, this working relationship has given me a sense of acknowledgement and hope that people—especially Yeshivah people—really do care about doing the right thing and moving forward.

Early in 2015, prompted by the royal commission public hearing, we began preliminary discussions about the possibility of the centre holding a public forum for the Yeshivah community, at which I and others would speak. It was envisaged as a way for Yeshivah to acknowledge its faults with regard to the child sexual-abuse scandal, provide a forum for open and frank discussion, and, hopefully, create a momentum for reforms that need to be put in place. As part of this process, I first raised this broadly with Rabbi Moshe Kahn, a senior Yeshivah and rabbinic official, when he contacted me during the royal commission. After I approached Rabbi Glick subsequent to his post-royal commission resignation from all leadership positions at Yeshivah—something I had committed publicly to doing—I then met and spoke with him and his wife at their home. Rabbi Glick and I had a private, candid, and comfortable exchange, a meeting attended by genuine goodwill. He conveyed what felt like his sincere and profound apology, which I accepted, and I reciprocated over how some had seemed to interpret my involvement in the sexual-abuse allegations against him. During that meeting, he asked whether I'd be willing to speak at a Shabbat event at Yeshivah that he'd be willing to try to facilitate. I responded affirmatively and with great enthusiasm.

As negotiations towards the Yeshivah landmark event gathered pace, and flyers were sent out, I started to be on the receiving end of inquiries, raised eyebrows, and murmurs about 'selling out'. I felt it necessary to explain why I had decided to participate in this event:

Some people have asked me why I have agreed to participate at an event hosted by Melbourne's Yeshivah Centre, including alongside former Yeshivah College Principal Rabbi Glick. I still have major issues with the way Rabbi Glick has conducted himself in recent years. I am profoundly troubled by his evidence at the Royal Commission in relation to a victim known as AVR. But to his credit, Rabbi Glick did apologise to me in our private meeting and I accepted his apology. And so I view this event as an opportunity for Rabbi Glick to publicly accept responsibility and apologise for his role in the events which led to the Royal Commission. And if Rabbi Glick can do that, and we can show that our rift has started to be healed, then perhaps there is hope that a divided and traumatised community can start to get back on track.
[Edited blogpost on my website, 20 November 2015]

A date was finally set down for early December. In tandem

with this community forum, the Yeshivah Centre was also formulating its own victim-redress scheme, drawing on guidelines set up by the royal commission and also those used by Jewish Care. Although the Yeshivah Centre had informed me of the Redress Scheme details in advance of its launch, I had no input into the framing or determination of the scheme. So it was with a mixture of optimism and trepidation that I flew back to Melbourne in early December from our new home in Israel, where I had moved my family a few months earlier, to attend the launch of the victim-redress scheme on 7 December, and the community event, two days later, on 9 December.

The redress launch at the Beth Rivkah Ladies College had been publicised within the Yeshivah community and the media. Yeshivah had apparently asked all the departmental heads of all its schools and other entities to attend the media conference to announce the scheme, and several major media outlets indeed attended. The launch was a formal event, which I saw as a great opportunity for me to prepare for the community event; I was much more nervous about the latter, because it would be far less structured and open to more hostile elements in the crowd.

Nevertheless, as that Monday morning unfolded, my stomach began to tighten. I could not face food. It would be the first time I had returned to the college since my 2011 public disclosure of sexual abuse. I was in the middle of a radio interview with the ABC when Craig Goldberg, a member of the interim board and someone I came to regard as a friend, came to pick me up from my friend Tony Fink's house. As I walked out, my mobile phone at my ear, I checked my pocket to ensure I had put my kippahh in there. We arrived at the college, and my nerves went up a notch. The room was full, with around 50 people present, and the air of friendliness was accompanied by an underlying tension. This was no less than I had expected. We were greeted by a warm welcome from the Yeshivah teachers and staff from Jewish Care, some of whom shook my hand before the launch began. As I scanned the room, I saw Rabbi Chaim Zvi Groner, son of the late Big Chief, who had officiated at my marriage. Four of the eight members of the Yeshivah interim board of management were also there (of the remainder, two were interstate, and two were unavailable).

I also noticed two prominent figures who seemed like they did not want to be there. One was Shmuel Gurevitch (known affectionately as Mr G), the former Beth Rivkah principal, a member of the board of trustees, and a son of one of the Yeshivah founders; the other was Rabbi Sholom Mendel Kluwgant, the father of Rabbi Meir Kluwgant, and a leading fundraiser at Yeshivah. Rabbi Telsner was not there, having stood down a few months earlier, and Rabbi Glick was also absent, as he no longer held any formal leadership position at the Yeshivah Centre.

The first speaker was Yechiel Belfer, the centre's official spokesman, who, in an excellent opening speech, made clear the responsibility that the Yeshivah accepted. He was followed by Michael Debinski, the president of Jewish Care Victoria, and John Leatherland, a former executive with the Victorian Department of Human Services—both Mike and John had been tasked with administering the Redress Scheme as independent administrators and assessors. I was particularly pleased with their appointments, as I had full confidence in them. I had worked with them previously when I was leading Tzedek and they were administering the Jewish Care Redress Scheme. They were the perfect candidates.

The redress scheme covers anybody who was a victim of sexual abuse at the centre's schools or through its activities, and who was under 18 when the abuse occurred. It includes ex gratia payments for three categories of abuse (ranging from significant to extremely severe), therapy, and the opportunity to receive a personal apology.

As I waited to speak, butterflies filled my stomach. By now I was an experienced speaker, but this would be different—very different. How would people react? Here is the edited text of my remarks:

> From the very beginning of this journey, I said that one of my aims was to return to the Yeshivah Centre—to be welcomed back.
>
> Today's announcement of the Redress Scheme is a watershed moment for our community. It sends out a clear message. That the Yeshivah Centre is finally taking this issue seriously and is trying to right past wrongs.
>
> I warmly welcome Yeshivah's Redress Scheme, which I know has been considered very carefully to take into account many important and complex issues. It demonstrates a great deal of sensitivity and compassion towards victims of the Yeshivah Centre. It prioritises the needs and rights of victims. Things that have been completely lacking in the past.
>
> I'm particularly pleased that Mike and John have been tasked with this challenging work. They have my full confidence. On a personal level, my presence at this event, and the event later this week, supports what I've been saying all along. Despite the campaign of demonisation that has been waged against me—that I'm being vindictive towards Yeshivah and that my motivation is to bring down this institution—in fact, the complete opposite is true; I

want the Yeshivah Centre to thrive. I want it to undertake the critical work that it does, such as providing a Jewish education to so many, assisting the less fortunate, and much more.

And I want it to be a safe place for children. It is clear that it can only thrive on the condition that there's transparency and accountability for the past, and into the future, and that steps are put in place to ensure the safety and well-being of our children.

In conclusion, I want to express my gratitude to the interim leadership here. I've had the opportunity to work closely with some of them and they have my full support and praise. It would not have been easy to step up during such a dark time—but they did, and hopefully they and the Yeshivah community will start to reap their rewards. I'm confident that the Yeshivah Centre has turned a corner and brighter days are ahead.

I did not specifically comment on the terms of the redress scheme outlined above. The key thing about the scheme is that it is not a compensation scheme, but effectively a mechanism to acknowledge sexual-abuse victims of the Yeshivah Centre, and to grade the character and extent of their abuse. As such, the scheme does not prevent an individual from taking civil action against the Yeshivah Centre.

While in general, I still believe the scheme is well thought out and comprehensive, there are two worrying aspects of its structure and governance that I noted at the time. The first was that, at the time of the announcement, Leah Balter, who was not only a member of the Yeshivah board, but its chair, was also on the board of Jewish Care Victoria, which was intimately involved with the Yeshivah redress scheme.

Although Leah was technically on leave from Jewish Care at the time (despite her name being on their website), it invited the perception of a possible conflict of interest, no matter how slight that might have been, especially when so many of Yeshivah's problems seemed to have occurred due in great part to the conflicts of interest and lack of transparency and accountability there. I understand this may have been a plain oversight, but the Yeshivah board, while they considered the issue, did not move to address it after being alerted to it.

The second aspect was that although Mike Debinski is a figure of substantial and appropriate experience, nevertheless he is Jewish, working within a small, tight-knit community. I initially believed he was a perfect candidate, as I've written above, but I came to the view that it would have been preferable for the person who oversees the scheme to be from outside the Jewish community—to counter any perception of potential conflict of interest that might flow from being part of the community. This is in line with my public view, and that of the royal commission, that such schemes should be as independent as possible. I want to emphasise that I am not implying that either of these figures has demonstrated, or might be vulnerable, to showing bias in any of their decisions. My argument here is about the perception of independence.

A general sense of relief and celebration swept the room when the media conference ended, and I felt vindicated, empowered, as people came up and shook my hand. The media stepped up to shoot some footage, take photos, and grab a few quotes from me and others. SBS also wanted some footage of me walking into the Yeshivah Centre, and, after getting approval from the school principal, Rabbi Smukler, the camera crew got a lot more than they expected. Before I knew it, we were standing in front of the mikvah where Cyprys had molested me all those years ago. This was a challenging moment, one I had not considered having to confront at that point. It seemed much smaller now than I remembered it, seen through the eyes of a child. Yet I could not help but reconstruct in my head the scene from my abuse as we walked around the building—the feeling of blacking out, and saying 'I have to go.' Did I actually murmur those words, or was it just in my mind? I am not really sure any more.

When that was over, I went back to Tony Fink's house, and then on to other friends for lunch. These friends had guests with them from overseas, and after we chatted about the redress-scheme launch, one of them came over and confided in me regarding two additional victims of child sexual abuse. They were neither Jewish nor Australian. (It is not uncommon for events like the launch to spark disclosures, and it has occurred many times to me in the past. For example, at Tony's house, a husband and wife once both independently confided to me that they had been sexually abused as children—something that neither had previously disclosed to anyone, including each other.) The guest at the lunch asked for assistance, so I made some connections. Like it or not, I have become a go-to person for anything to do with sexual-abuse disclosure, networking, or assistance. I don't particularly enjoy the role—responding adequately depends on being able to deal with a range of circumstances, yet I cannot ignore who I am, the expertise I have gained, and the responsibility that comes with it.

The next day, I met with the Rabbinical Council of Victoria—a meeting that came at my initiative, not theirs, which was a source of disappointment to me. The RCV had not yet offered me a formal apology, and I had emailed them ahead of my visit, asking for a chance to speak candidly with the rabbinic leadership. We had a history of tension stretching back several years, and although the RCV was not ready to offer an apology at that meeting, I came away confident that one would come, in writing. I also encouraged them to reach out to anyone who had been mistreated by them, or as a result of their inactions—such as, for example, the man known as AVB at the royal commission. I'm pleased to report that, several months later, I did receive a written apology from them. Like so many of the other apologies, it is meaningful—and it's also vindicating and empowering. Unfortunately, at the time of writing they have still refused to apologise to others.

Two days later came the main event, the community forum in the evening, which was open to anyone. This was the occasion I was really nervous about, the one with the potential for things to go wrong or turn nasty. So I was edgy from the moment I woke up. I couldn't face breakfast, and went off to run around Caulfield Park three times to shake out the cobwebs. The run cleared my head. By the time I went to some friends for dinner before the forum, I was feeling a lot calmer. Another speaker and friend, Dr Cathy Kezelman, president of Adults Surviving Child Abuse, who had flown in from Sydney especially for the event, was also at the dinner, and she gave me some advice about how to help the person who had approached me two days earlier about an abuse experience. During those last few hours before we left, every manner of potential problem flashed through my mind: awkward questions, accusations, tears, and finger-pointing from people in the room; tears from me; people walking out; or my troublesome brother turning up to hijack the evening.

Cathy and I arrived together, and the first people I saw were two close supporters and friends, Phillip Weinberg and David Benau. My mood lifted. Upstairs there were so many familiar faces, among them my friend and colleague Andrew Blode, as well as members of Yeshivah and Tzedek, with whom I was less comfortable. But as more friends and supporters turned up, especially Yeshivah guests, I felt more at ease. There was a great buzz in the air, I felt a genuine sense of excitement, and, within a few minutes, I was comfortable and looking forward to speaking. As I took my place on stage with Cathy, I scanned the room to see which prominent members of the Yeshivah community had decided to turn up and acknowledge what had been organised in their name.

In the room of about 300 people, I noted Rabbis Groner, Telsner, and Glick (the latter was also presenting), and also the media personality John Safran, who had been a student there and whom I remembered well. I didn't see or identify any members of the Kluwgant family; Chaim or Sheiny New; David, Shlomo, or Shyrla Werdiger; or Don Wolf. Neither could I see Rabbi Mordechai Gutnick, president of the Rabbinical Council of Victoria. These people may have been there, but I didn't see them. In addition, it appeared that many Yeshivah staff, including senior staff, were absent. This was disappointing, although it must be said that the event fell in the middle of the Jewish festival of Chanukah, which may have created clashes with religious and family commitments. But, as someone said, there are thousands in the Yeshivah community, and more of them should have attended. Nevertheless, as I've repeatedly stated, this was significant progress—my mere presence at the Yeshivah Centre.

The evening was moderated by Yudi New (a Yeshivah member, lawyer, and former classmate and friend), and was addressed by Rabbi Glick (who had told me privately, prior to the event, that he was disappointed not to have been invited by Yeshivah to the previous Redress Scheme event there, which I appreciated); Cathy Kezelman, who provided an overview of the impact of sexual abuse on victims; and, in a pre-recorded interview, an American called Rabbi Yossi Jacobson, from Brooklyn, who has spoken publicly about child sexual abuse in the past. Rabbi Jacobson (the younger brother of Rabbi Simon Jacobson, who also speaks on this subject) gave a very powerful interview on video, although to me it was a little too animated, lengthy, and evangelical.

Yeshivah also arranged for three other students who were sexual-abuse victims to speak briefly at the forum. One was AVB, and only two of the three others turned up and spoke; the third one still felt intimidated, and asked a friend to convey his feelings on his behalf. Interestingly, all three had spoken 10 days earlier at a synagogue on the grounds of the Yeshivah Centre, in an event with the former premier of Victoria, Ted Baillieu. So although their identities were somewhat known within the Yeshivah community—especially that of AVB and another from within a prominent Yeshivah family—the possibility that they might be revealed within the broader public spotlight still inhibited them.

I spoke after Cathy, and before the other Yeshivah victims said a few words. I was given up to 20 minutes to speak, but only spoke for a few. I said they'd heard enough from me—usually through the media—so now it was their turn to speak to me, and I'd respond. I did refer to the scale of the abuse, saying there were dozens of victims, a point I was concerned may not have been fully appreciated by the community, since I had been the only person in Australia to publicly name myself as a victim. I emphasised the Jewish concept of 'lashon hara', which means 'the evil tongue', deliberately making the point in their language, Hebrew, and using a concept they specifically understood. This refers not only to saying something horrible about a person, but also about hearing, or overhearing, such remarks. 'Reflect, for a moment, if you ever spoke badly, not just about me or my family, but about other victims. Reflect, if you ever listened and did nothing about that, and just consider that for a moment,' I told the room.

Some people later admitted to me (in person and on social media) that they were indeed guilty of the evil tongue—at least one even apologised publicly during the event's Q&A. That was very important to me. People would feed on the rumour mill, without ever meeting or engaging with me; make judgements based on hearsay; and, before you knew it, the story would become one big mess. After raising this fairly confronting subject, I gave my time over to the floor, and my fears soon dissipated. The tone and subject of comments and questions was respectful and positive.

During a break in the Q&A, I was invited to light the Chanukah candles. This was a powerful moment: by inviting me to participate in a religious ritual, the Yeshivah Centre was symbolically welcoming me back into the community tent from which I had been cast out. Further, this was to light the Chanukah candles; to bring light to the community, both physically and metaphorically. It was powerful and symbolic. I was very moved, and also a little nervous, because I could not remember all the blessings and in which order to recite them. I had recited them occasionally with my own family, but could no longer reel them off by heart. (To some extent, I get a sense of satisfaction when this happens, as this was one of my ambitions when I left my family, at the age of 16, back in 1994.) One of the blessings is only meant to be recited on the first night, when the first Chanukah candle for the year is lit, so it's only said once. As this was my first candle lighting for the year—on the fifth night of Chanukah—I remembered to say that blessing as well. I almost made a smart-arsed comment: *Is there a blessing for the first time in five years?* My hesitation over the blessings was a poignant reminder to the group that the former yeshivah boy had moved far away from his earlier life.

When the Q&A started, a few people, especially the rabbis, left to attend their own Chanukah and keep other commitments. Nevertheless, the atmosphere in the room was excited, and questions kept coming at a rapid pace. The event went way over time. At the conclusion, a steady stream of people lined up to speak to me (and others contacted me later), many of them apologised, and I was left with a very warm feeling at the end of the night. I didn't leave till 10.15. The adrenalin was pumping, and it would have been nice to have an after party, but I settled for a few drinks with Tony at his place. Despite one or two caustic messages the next morning (for example, a Yeshivah member bizarrely felt that I should've also taken the opportunity to apologise to the community for what I had done), the general response to the forum was overwhelmingly positive. As I wrote on my Facebook page: *It's the lightest I've felt in years. Literally. And it has nothing to do with my weight as I'm probably the heaviest I've ever been!*

The only shadow over this experience was cast by my father, who still remains unreconciled with Yeshivah. First, he applied to be considered as a secondary victim under their redress scheme, arguing that the ostracism he and my mother had endured, and the disruption to our family, had contributed to his heart attack (which was corroborated by his doctors) and their decision to leave Australia. He was advised that he did not meet the criteria for eligibility. On a personal level, Rabbi Glick has not yet apologised to him, and he says he will not take him seriously until that happens. After I reconciled with Rabbi Glick, I was pleased to be able to play a constructive role by connecting the two of them in their attempt to reconcile — they used to be fairly close friends over many years. This process continues.

For the record, I believe my father deserves an unequivocal apology from the Yeshivah Centre and that he should be made an ex gratia payment under the redress scheme — although this would mean altering the scheme's terms of reference. He can't make a claim because he is not a direct victim, but I believe his experience should be somehow acknowledged and addressed. In my view, he should also be entitled to take civil action against Yeshivah. Due to all of the above, and despite his years of support for my campaign, my father took no interest in, nor showed any support, for my involvement in the forum. While he does not hold it against me for participating, it is fair to say that there are significant differences, and often tensions, between us in our approach and attitudes to the Yeshivah and Chabad communities. But I do understand his perspective, and do empathise with him. And, to be fair, he too has been vindicated.

Fundamentally, I have been agitating for justice for victims and accountability for perpetrators, and for reform of the Jewish institutions whose leaders and governance were found to be so lacking. My father's agenda over the past few years has been driven more by profound disillusion with the way of life that he lived and breathed so dearly. In short, he believes Chabad is a dangerous cult, like other religious cults, that has corrupted the very ideals and values on which the Lubavitch movement was built.

These two events with Yeshivah represented a personal watershed moment. I now feel that I have done everything I can to achieve justice for past crimes, and to prevent them in the future. It feels as though I have come full circle. *I am handing over the mantle to you, Yeshivah and your community.* Ironically, if Yeshivah had engaged with me and not shirked their responsibility in the first place, I would have been denied the opportunity to experience this journey over the past five years. It has been hard yet rewarding, but this work—relating specifically to Yeshivah—has occupied my life for too long.

I have told the leaders that it is now up to them to address sexual-abuse matters in their own community and backyard. I don't feel it's my responsibility any more to advocate for them. Indeed, they have stepped up to the plate, at least to some degree. They have shown that they acknowledge and are prepared to take responsibility for the past and the future. And now that they are in the middle of doing so, I realise that I have significantly reduced the enmity I felt towards Yeshivah. Sure, there are still some outstanding issues to resolve, but they're generally more at a higher level, or over specific issues that generally I can try to disconnect myself from—although at times they're frustrating to observe, and at other times have a more profound impact on me. It seems that, to some extent, I still care about the community. But now that I've been vindicated and more (by being invited back, for example), I feel I can let go more than previously. As upset as some of them apparently are with me, their anger is not really a concern to me.

Besides, there is only so much I can do personally, and I don't have the physical or emotional energy to keep doing this on my own as a private individual any more. My relentless focus on the issue has probably stopped people from ever considering how I and my family actually live. I have not had a permanent job, or a reliable income, since I left Tzedek. My time, energy, and resources have been focussed on this issue more broadly, doing what I can to fill the vacuum that still exists, by establishing a new initiative—among other things—to address this issue within the global Jewish community. The redress scheme is helpful as a temporary measure in this transitional period, but more will be needed.

Over the years, my critics and supporters have come and gone: they weigh in to the debate, some stay, and most depart. But this has been my life, day in, day out. And it's time to move on.

Chapter Twenty-Three

Living with myself

Over the past five years, I've focussed a huge amount of energy and resources on the words and deeds of others — leaders, politicians, teachers, abusers, police, and victims. This is partly because of the responsibility I feel, but also because I derive immense satisfaction from addressing this issue and helping other people in this area. More than that, currently it feels like the only thing I'm capable of doing. It's basically my calling. That's not necessarily because I chose it — rather, it feels like it's been imposed on me. However, this commitment has left me little time to focus on myself. My advocacy has tended to push under the carpet the trauma and emotional stress I continue to experience as a result of being abused, as well as the vicarious trauma of hearing about the abuse of countless others, and the harassment from some segments of our community, especially the ultra-Orthodox community.

Despite how I might feel on any given day, child sexual abuse is a 24/7 experience for me. It never goes away. Other people can pick up a newspaper, watch a documentary on

television, or graze the internet. They may be affected by
what I am doing, or by the stories of others. They may talk
to their friends, reflect on how it affects them, and then get
on with their life. My reality is different. When I wake up in
the morning and go to bed, the issue is still there with me.
Sometimes I have nightmares and flashbacks, filled with the
faces of abusers, or police, or rabbis, or victims, or others.
There are just so many people I deal with in a traumatic
context.

Because people feel comfortable sharing their stories with
me, my waking life is filled with the vicarious trauma of
other victims' experiences. I am often inundated with stories.
Sometimes it's once a week; other times, five times a week. A
message comes in, online or on my mobile: *Manny, my father
has abused my daughter. How do we respond? We still want
to have a relationship with him, but how do we protect the
children? What do we say or do when they come to eat at
our table on Shabbat? We don't want to put my dad in jail.
How do we get around all of this?* Then there are people who
want advice about school. *We're not really part of Chabad or
Yeshivah, but we want to send our kids to school there. Is it
safe? What is really happening?*

While it's deeply rewarding to help others navigate the
pitfalls and confusion of their personal problems, I sometimes
make myself too available; I just can't help it. As a result, often
some don't stop to think that I also need personal time or that
I am entitled to a private life. Except for the period when I
worked at Tzedek, I have delivered advocacy and assistance
as a private individual, rarely getting paid for it. I am taken
for granted as a public resource. *Have a query about this
issue? Contact Manny Waks.* Many people have offered to
assist me over the years, but many also have not followed

through. As a result, I no longer have any expectation that someone who offers help will necessarily deliver it. I know that if I don't do something myself, it will probably not get done. Despite the large network of friends and supporters around me, deep down I feel isolated, alone.

Sometimes I am even expected to speak out on other issues, such as domestic violence, or refugee and other human-rights matters, and get criticised for not doing so. If those people only knew how much time the requests for advice on sexual abuse take up. People approach me—via emails, phone calls, or social media—from all over the world. They come mainly from the Jewish community, but also beyond it. I am invited to speak in public frequently, and by the end of each talk, I am just knackered, completely drained from re-living my story, and having to adapt it to the audience for a particular event. Of course, after you speak, people come up and want to share their stories. Once they start talking with me, I am expected to respond in some way. This is not the sort of subject where you can just say, 'Thanks, but I'm really busy. It's probably best to go elsewhere.' I can't just switch to being a paid consultant. It would not solve anything, because I am not driven by money (although it would at least help pay the bills); it's addressing the issue that matters to me. To some extent, I am caught in a bind of my own making. It is a bitter-sweet dilemma. But I much prefer to remain in the position where I can make a much-needed difference. At this stage, the alternative—ceasing my involvement in this work—is not an option.

While I may present as a confident public speaker, and as someone who is comfortable with the media—I certainly have had plenty of practice by now—beneath the big talker lies a man who has struggled for many years with complex post-traumatic stress disorder, depression, anxiety, and other symptoms typical among victims and survivors of child sexual abuse. This has manifested itself in many ways. There have been days when I just lie in bed and stare at the ceiling, paralysed, unable to move—or with no desire to move. Other days, I have headaches for lengthy periods. Concentrating becomes a challenge. I have also swung between an inability to sleep and too much sleep—mostly, too little sleep. The common denominator is instability. I have found it hard, almost impossible, to reach a happy medium, and over the years I have resorted to a range of substances, to help get me through those times when it all seems too hard. Some days, especially over the past couple of years, my darkness goes deeper, and I have found myself thinking about something previously unthinkable.

Clinically, the doctors call it suicide ideation. The whole idea of disclosing this feeling, as well as my other symptoms noted above, reminds me of the anxiety that enveloped me when I prepared to disclose my sexual abuse. Both are so difficult to even admit that it's far easier to keep them to myself, hidden from the gaze and judgement of others. The feeling has been fleeting, but it has been recurrent. Some nights I even find myself writing suicide letters in my head, wanting to put everything in order, in case ... But when these confronting thoughts arrive, I realise I can't do it to my family, especially my children, or because there is still unfinished business. Thankfully, it's not a constant thought. But one of my concerns is that it may easily become this way—what's the transition between ideation and practice? I don't want to think about it. But I do, and discuss it with my therapists.

Although I have often been able to function, despite chronic anxiety and depression, the events of the past couple of years have combined to bring my emotional difficulties to a new point. As I write these words, I am having intensive therapy—four weekly sessions—to get a better handle on my life. Each time I must travel to another city to see a psychologist who specialises in treating child sexual-abuse victims. This has necessitated significant time, energy, and financial commitment—unfortunately, Yeshivah is only paying for six months' worth of therapy. But it's the first time ever that I've had systematic therapy. I've always had therapists along the way, but never like this. It's a major relief, but the challenges are enormous, and some of the therapy sessions are particularly confronting. I often consider quitting therapy. It's painful.

For example, as I lay on the treatment bed one day, mentioning an email I had seen that morning from the Yeshivah Centre regarding their proposed governance restructure, I had a completely unexpected response. My heart started beating uncontrollably, my legs shook, and I was overcome with emotion. All indications had been that the Yeshivah-appointed Governance Review Panel (GRP) were going to recommend the continued involvement of the current trustees in the new governance structure, and I knew when I got this email that my worst fears were being confirmed. My body reacted involuntarily to the realisation that, after everything that had happened over the last few years, and despite the pleas of so many victims, the seven remaining trustees of Yeshivah were still refusing to simply go. Rather, they were proposing to formally embed themselves in the running of the Yeshivah Centre for the next few years, and in the case of Rabbi Chaim Zvi Groner, for life (as per the previous GRP recommendations, which I didn't expect would change).

As the session continued, I found myself needing to get

up, sit on the bed, and then walk around to try to calm down. Despite arriving the most relaxed I'd ever felt at any therapy session, this was the most stressed I had ever become. Eventually, I returned to the sitting position, the way I had when I first started these sessions, and I continued talking. Before long, I said that I needed to face my fears, and I lay down again. My therapist asked why I felt like lying down, and instinctively I said, 'I don't want to let them win. They've caused me enough pain and suffering that I wanted to fight it and do things on my terms.' I stayed lying down for the rest of the session, refusing to be driven into agitated movement by the stress I was feeling. Needless to say, the rest of the day was pretty much a write-off. And the next day I was still struggling with that confronting session.

There is a reason I have gone into considerable detail about my difficult personal circumstances. As with other parts of my life, I think it is important to be open about the full fallout that comes with being abused. This is not just to demonstrate the ups and downs, but also to help other victims—and my fellow victim advocates—by letting them see that they are not alone in their private suffering. It's also to educate the broader community: irrespective of who you are or what you do, the impact of abuse is often profound. My life continues to feel not grounded, and I don't know where things are heading. On a bad day, I think I'm heading for the grave—like everyone else, but a whole lot sooner. On a good day, I think I'm going to achieve incredible reforms, not just in the Jewish world, but beyond—the sky's the limit. Most days lie somewhere in between, so I have to balance my global-initiative plans, the needs of my family (which have too often taken a back seat behind my advocacy), re-acclimatising to Israel, practical matters such as buying the basics in a new country, my personal problems, and a drawn-out lawsuit against Yeshivah.

The past few years have been a rollercoaster ride, wilder than even before. It's been consumed by the stress of preparing for the royal commission, and its aftermath: our desire, or need, to leave Australia; our move to France and the isolation of living in a small village, without knowing for how long or where to next; moving the family again, to Israel; having no steady income while trying to build a global initiative to address this issue; and being constantly exposed to victims and this issue more broadly. All this has pulled me in a thousand different directions all at once, and cut me adrift from any genuine sense of security. Where is home? What is home? What is my future? Our future?

Our stay in France was always intended to be temporary. It provided us with a number of opportunities—not least to live in and experience Europe, in particular the beautiful French countryside. As we all had European citizenship, we had intended to remain in Europe, in a different location. However, as I was continuing to develop my global initiative, it became apparent that Israel would be the most viable option for us. The problem was that, culturally, Israel had never felt like home to me. Worse, I recall the desperation with which I'd left back in 2000. So I'd always said to myself that I would never live there. I have some family there, but, with all due respect to them, that wasn't compelling enough. Nevertheless, it seemed for now that Israel was the best place to base our life.

We are now living in a progressive city, Ramat HaSharon, about 20 minutes' drive north of Tel Aviv. It's a great city, cultured and secular. My family enjoys it here. I enjoy aspects of it—it's a great place to live, probably even my ideal place to live within Israel—but admittedly, I'm still uncomfortable living in this country. I must admit that it has been difficult to resettle twice within a year, finding a home and settling into new routines. I know now that I have to accept the fact that we are going to be living in Israel for some time. That is hard for me to accept because, right now, I just don't feel Israeli, or that this is my home. Although I am comfortable with the concept of dual loyalties (unlike those who argue that once you relocate you can only have one allegiance—suspiciously, this issue seems to arise only in the Israel context), I do desperately miss my close friends and family in Australia. I miss living there. I would probably feel more comfortable living in Europe, or even America, than Israel. I feel closer culturally to those countries than to Israel. It will take time and patience—probably my biggest weakness.

In the interim, I can't avoid the political debates and tension that make life here so interesting. The impasse between the Israeli government and the Palestinians needs to be resolved through a two-state solution. Sadly, we are a long way from that right now, especially given the Palestinian attitude to terrorism and incitement, and the Israeli government's policies in a range of areas, including some of their responses to terrorism—such as increasing the settlements. It is obvious the Palestinians need and are entitled to their own state. We need to focus on Israeli behaviour, not just the Palestinians'. We must always try to act correctly, do the right thing, regardless of what they do.

The immediate practical need I have now is to support my family and put bread on the table. Some may think: *Why doesn't he just go and get a job?* To be honest, I'm incapable of doing this at the moment. I don't feel I can do anything else but focus on the issue of child sexual abuse for now. We sold our property in Melbourne with the intention of purchasing a property here. However, soon after the sale, I received news that one of the two co-buyers had pulled out when they saw that I was the owner. No specific reason was given, but we understood. The party involved comes from Caulfield, deep in Jewish territory. The uncertainty was enormously stressful, and brought back those horrible memories of the years of intimidation and harassment in Melbourne. The problem was eventually resolved, the sale proceeded with only a minor delay, and the funds belatedly came into our account to give us some breathing room with rent and other transitional costs.

It seems I can never really get away from Yeshivah, not even over here in Israel. After the sense of closure I felt after the forum in December 2015, I deliberately tried to stay out of the continuing crossfire and incremental point-scoring over local disputes. Then Chabad headquarters dropped a bombshell and, almost against my will, I was drawn back into the debate by people seeking my advice, media asking me for comments, and participants seeking clarification. As much as I want to stay at arm's length from Yeshivah, I can't. I have a deep emotional connection to the issue.

In February, Chabad headquarters in New York issued an astonishing statement that seemed to veto proposed new governance arrangements by the Yeshivah Centre, effectively saying that it has always been in charge of its branches—any Chabad institution—around the world, and that it bears responsibility for their actions and responses to child sexual abuse within the community. After a massive outcry, Chabad then issued a clarification that suggested they had done a massive backflip. The clarification asserted that, contrary to the initial letter, they did not have any power or authority over the Yeshivah Centre.

Beyond the confusion this caused, it is important to remember that the original reforms proposed by the Yeshivah-appointed GRP had plenty of flaws, and although I originally wished to stay out of that debate, I cannot endorse them, no matter who claims authority. The current trustees must not be involved in the leadership of the centre in any way, shape, or form—not now and not in the future. They have proven, time and again, that they are unfit to be involved and that they must leave, as they claimed they would. Just as important, the detrimental impact on the many Yeshivah victims of the current trustees' continuing involvement should in and of itself be a cause for their immediate collective resignation.

My uncompromising position left me conflicted about Yeshivah's recent accomplishment of being awarded child-safety accreditation. On the one hand, I wanted to congratulate them publicly. On the other hand, it was deeply offensive that the same leaders—those who oversaw the period of sexual abuse, cover-ups, and intimidation—were still there. To many of us, Yeshivah cannot move forward until it holds its entire leadership to account. In fact, neither can we. At the very least, the entire leadership must resign. Anecdotally, it was sad to read the *Australian Jewish News*'s coverage of the accreditation—it read like Yeshivah's media release, with absolutely no reference to its past.

However, a more practical conflict soon overtook the Chabad edict. The potential conflict of interest that I had noted when Yeshivah launched its redress scheme in December was never rectified, and now it became all too real. In February

2016, at least four Yeshivah victims refused to be involved in the scheme in any way, after a private email sent by a board member of Jewish Care Victoria allegedly leaked the identity of one of the victims to Yeshivah. Jewish Care tried to hose down the leak, claiming the email did not contain information about the victim. But that missed the point. The victim issued his own statement, saying he *felt* his identity had been revealed to Yeshivah. The bond of trust had been broken, and, with it, the promise of confidentiality for other victims, some of whom have since told me they are now sceptical, even distrustful of the integrity of the redress scheme. In that same month, Jewish Care and the Yeshivah Centre saw the light, and ceased their redress-scheme arrangement.

All of this had occurred due to a conflict of interest — at the very least a perceived one — that had been known about for several months. I had personally pointed it out to Yeshivah at the time the redress scheme was announced (see chapter 22). Leah Balter, who was chair of the Yeshivah board, and also on the board of Jewish Care Victoria, even offered to resign for the benefit of everyone. For some reason, she didn't. I have a lot of respect for Jewish Care and its principled behaviour over the past few years, in particular as demonstrated by Bill Appleby, its CEO, and Mike Debinski, so raising issues that may in some way portray the organisation in a negative light is not easy for me. Yet I cannot avoid the fact that they made a mistake which needed to be rectified — although, having said that, it wasn't really a Jewish Care mistake, but something they became drawn into.

I republished *The Age* story regarding the Jewish Care matter on my website and Facebook page — without a comment. After Jewish Care publicly responded to *The Age* article, the victim involved in the story asked me to publish his response to it, which I did, again without comment. Yet, despite this, within a couple of days I received a Concerns Notice from Leah Balter's lawyer, threatening legal action unless I removed the links to both items. I never received an email or phone call from Leah Balter or anyone else asking me to delete the links and explaining why. Instead, I received a legal letter on behalf of none other than the chair of the Yeshivah board, one of the new Yeshivah leaders, apparently one of the 'good ones', the more progressive ones, threatening to sue me for having republished a mainstream newspaper article and a response to it from a victim. It was astounding.

To me, this was a clear attempt to intimidate me. I felt the legal communication was a form of bullying—consistent with what I'd experienced from the old Yeshivah leadership, only now the new leadership was involved. More importantly, the fault was hers, not mine. She was the one who had opened herself up to a potential conflict of interest and who had nothing to remedy the situation, yet she claimed I had done the wrong thing simply by posting an article from *The Age* and a victim's statement in response to it.

As a gesture of goodwill, but without conceding any wrongdoing, I took down the posts, and she dropped her claim. I have spent so much time dealing with litigation or threats of it that I managed to resolve the dispute myself. And as my generous and strict go-to defamation lawyer emailed me: 'I like it when you resolve them before I have to deal with them.' I was pleased to learn that as a part of the continuing restructure process at Yeshivah, Balter (and others) had resigned from their positions—although I should note that this was purely procedural, as she'd been part of the interim board, and in fact was meant to resign at the end of 2015. As I write these words, the story is still unfolding, and it's worth noting that Tzedek—which issued a warm, bland statement of support when the redress scheme was announced—has been conspicuously silent since the politics of it have got complicated. But one thing is clear from this incident. The sense of entitlement and inability to admit mistakes that defined Yeshivah's leadership in the past has not yet been eradicated—not by a long shot. Again, perhaps my father's scepticism is more reasonable than I had initially thought.

The incident reminds me of the constant line of criticism that has been made of my advocacy over the past several years, which can be summed up as follows: *I agree with what you're doing. I just don't agree with your methods.* This refrain was put most succinctly by New York Chabad rabbi and counsellor Simon Jacobson in an interview with the BBC in August 2015: 'The bottom line is someone has to yell, and if you don't yell and scream, no one is going to do anything about it. He [Manny] has definitely gotten everyone's attention. So even though I may not agree with all his methods, he's like a burglar alarm. You've got to get the alarm going.'

All along, that has been the theme of the main criticism against me. What do they really mean by 'his methods'? Do they mean I called a spade a spade, or a shovel? Or is it that I called out in the first place? The unspoken message is that no one likes the surface of life to be disturbed by uncomfortable truths, and they cannot reconcile the importance of truth with the pain of seeing their lies and falsehoods challenged and torn apart by facts and evidence.

I am not surprised by their inability to understand this process, but I resent the blaming and vicious name-calling that has been hurled against me, my family, and my supporters.

However, the real issue is this. What else could I have done? I tried doing it by the book.

I went to the police, and they put it in the too-hard basket. I went to community leaders, and the Yeshivah leaders stalled, covered up, lied, and did nothing. I tried to do it quietly, and I got nowhere. I had no alternative but to go the media. In fact, I've repeatedly stated publicly that I invite anyone in the Jewish community who has an alternative approach to the resolving of these matters to come forward. Not a single person has done so—not with anything of substance. Their criticism is negative, and never constructive. When my critics mention that phrase, 'We are uncomfortable about your methods', I say, 'I have been uncomfortable standing in front of journalists outside the court. I have been very uncomfortable sharing my story repeatedly. I have been uncomfortable being hounded. I have been uncomfortable living this difficult life. Very uncomfortable.'

What else could I have done? Ostensibly, I could have chosen the path that the victim known as AVB took, staying within the community, agitating for reform and justice while remaining a member of Chabad. AVB had been abused by both Hayman and Cyprys. His identity is an open secret within the Yeshivah community, but he has chosen to keep it out of the broader public view. AVB chose to fight from within.

In *Breaking The Silence*, AVB spoke for the first time in public, without revealing his identity:

The reason I don't want to be identified is that I don't want to be defined by those events of the past, and I want to be judged for what I accomplish on a conscious basis, for something that I have decided to do. I didn't decide to be a victim of sexual abuse. It was something that was forced upon me.

This is what happened to AVB. He decided to work behind the scenes. In June 2011, he sent an email to victims and members of the Yeshivah community, urging them to go to the police: 'As a community, we must ensure a full and proper investigation is conducted. Ongoing silence is not an option.' AVB's plea led to the first sermon by Rabbi Telsner against those speaking out on the issue of child sexual abuse and making calls to assist the police. As a result, AVB and his family became outcasts. AVB then called members of the board of Chabad to seek their support. They told him they didn't want anything to do with him. Instead, he was subjected to bullying, intimidation, and ostracism.

For example, in March 2016, the lawyer who represented Cyprys early on in his case in 2011, Alex Lewenberg, was found guilty of professional misconduct and subsequently suspended from practising the law for comments he made about AVB at one of the hearings and during a phone call—Lewenberg complained about AVB helping police by invoking the crime of mesirah, of reporting on another Jew to outside authorities.

AVB has been denied employment opportunities, and his family has been shunned in their social relations. His wife said at the royal commission public hearing that 'the night before my daughter's batmitzvah party, my daughter was very distressed and told me that everyone hates us, and that she was nervous that no one would come to her batmitzvah party'.

AVB also told me he had been the victim of fictitious stories alleging, among other things, that he was the product of an affair, which, under Jewish law, would make him a *mamzer* (bastard), causing ramifications for AVB and his children lasting 10 generations, adversely impacting upon whom AVB's children could marry. He has also been forced to take out a number of Personal Safety Intervention Orders and Undertakings against individuals from within the community—including David Werdiger. Yet AVB continues to wage battle on his own terms. He goes to synagogue every day, and they can't stop him. They have to face it. He wants to make life uncomfortable for the Chabad leaders, just as it is for him.

In hindsight, AVB told me that he would not have gone to the police had he known then what he does now. He now believes he was naïve to think that morals would guide the Yeshivah's response, and that they would appreciate him raising the issues in private.

While I deeply respect AVB's courage and persistence, I also believe that, for all the suffering he and his family have endured, his decision to remain a member of Yeshivah has held him back somewhat in his mission to achieve justice for victims, accountability by the leadership, and reforms of governance for children and the Jewish community at large. Nevertheless, we have been complementary to each other's efforts. He is doing the work from the inside, which brings another unique perspective. We regularly communicate, and have what I'd describe as a close working relationship, indeed a friendship. We have known each other since we were children, and have a long mutual history. Our unfortunate experience—fate, if you will—has brought us together for this fight of a lifetime.

I also recognise that, having chosen this path, he can't just get up and leave, and join a new Chabad community. Everyone knows everyone, he would lose his anonymity, and he can't just leave his past behind. There is also the practical issue of uprooting a whole family with deep ties to the community and its institutions. In the end, each victim must choose and forge his or her own path. I am following mine, wherever it leads me, and he is doing the same. I wish him and his family all the very best. They deserve it.

Chapter Twenty-Four

Where to from here?

We all make choices in life. Do we accept the hand we're dealt, replace the cards we don't want or like, or reject the whole lot and strive for something different? Looking back on my life to date, it now seems clear that I am not the type who makes do with a poor hand. I have fought, and will continue to push, for something better. I owe it to myself and to the many people who have suffered like I have. With the benefit of experience, I might be a little more patient from now on. Between my sense of mission and tendency to work at full throttle, I have often moved a little too fast.

With this in mind, I have spent more than a year working to establish a global advocacy organisation for Jewish victims and survivors of child sexual abuse. It has been a massive undertaking, in many ways. First, there was the challenge of me understanding my identity. I am 40 years old. Who am I? Am I Manny Waks, the abuse survivor and advocate who spent five years of his life fighting for justice, but is now ready to become another person, to move on to a new, different path in life? That is an identity I have spent many nights contemplating while I lie awake in bed, trying to make sense of everything. When I think about the family sacrifices and adjustments we have undergone, now in Israel and before in Melbourne, I would love to flick a switch and transport myself into that future for a while to see what it's like.

Yet deep down I know the answer, even though I might regret it. I know I would flick the switch back. I can't just turn off and say the past five years is in the past, done, finished. Life is not like that. I am not like that. There is still so much unfinished business—personally and communally. Moreover, for all the troubles I have experienced, all the arrows that have been aimed at me and all the fires I have started, I cannot avoid the vindication and satisfaction I derive from the life of advocacy. I was an advocate long before I became a voice for victims—whether of child sexual abuse or anti-Semitism. I am suited to it, and some say I was born to it.

I also realise that an opportunity beckons to build on the work I have done—the knowledge, skills, and contacts I have gained—to speak out on behalf of the thousands of Jewish, and other victims, around the world. As I investigated the global body of research available on child sexual abuse within the Jewish community, it became clear that there is so much we don't know, so much that needs to be brought to attention. Learning this, in the aftermath of the royal commission in 2015, has provided me with a renewed sense of purpose—and patience.

On a practical level, there have been countless dead ends and false dawns, as the network of people who have lent me moral support become nervous about committing resources, time, and money to a project that is unique, sensitive, and controversial. Everyone understands local and national advocacy groups. Tzedek started off in that mould, although its trajectory kept pushing into international cases (as in the case of the American rabbis, Manis Friedman and Kenneth Brander). So a global initiative was a natural next step. But when you go global formally, it raises questions that are not easy to answer. What is your key responsibility? Are you trying to take on too much? What can you achieve that smaller, committed, local organisations cannot?

At the start of 2016, I launched Kol v'Oz—Hebrew for 'voice and strength/courage'. As founding CEO, my aim is to give truth to its name—to speak out with courage, and to make it the leading voice on child sexual abuse in the Jewish world. I will not, and must not, duplicate existing services. On the contrary, I want it to become a representative body for the other organisations in this field, working closely with the other existing service providers.

After around a year of hard grind, endless meetings, and correspondence with a range of stakeholders around the world, and the submission of proposals to potential supporters, I am proud to say that, at the time of this book going to press, Kol v'Oz is active and out there, making a difference in major Jewish global centres.

In March, I was invited to speak in the Israeli parliament, the Knesset, with the Knesset's chair of the Committee for the Rights of the Child, Ms Yifat Shasha Biton. I invited colleagues from other organisations in this field to join me. It was a powerful experience, not only meeting the head of the committee, but feeling acknowledged and heard in Israel, another country, my new home—the Jewish homeland—for the work I had been doing. I left the event on a high, my adrenalin pumping. It was hard to relax afterward, but then again, I have to come to accept that I am forever vigilant, always on the alert. Here in Israel, the issue of sex abuse has another, unique dimension, thanks to the Law of Return, which allows Jews from anywhere in the world to migrate here, regardless of their situation or status. During the Knesset meeting, I came out strongly against the unintended consequences this caused. The prominent newspaper *Haaretz* reported my comments:

> 'Sex offenders tend to move from country to country to avoid jail, but what makes Israel unique is the Law of Return, which essentially grants unhindered access to anyone who is Jewish to come here without any real screening,' said Manny Waks, the chief executive officer of (newly formed) Kol v'Oz.

It's an easy get-out-of-jail card. While one obvious beneficiary is Malka Leifer, the loophole is clearly available to anyone. And I shared several recent examples to make the point.

By April, we had appointed a New York-based project manager, and, soon after, made another New York-based appointment. At this stage, all the positions are pro bono. Obviously, this is not sustainable, so I hope that in due course we'll secure the funding required to run this organisation professionally and with adequate funding.

In April, Kol v'Oz also wrote to the UK Independent Inquiry into Child Sexual Abuse, urging the inquiry to investigate sections of the British Jewish community as part of its probe. My letter outlined a range of media reports about sexual abuse within the Jewish community in England over the past few years, arguing that collectively, they merited attention from the inquiry. We received an acknowledgement letter from them, indicating they would be in contact if indeed they pursued the Jewish angle.

In May, we put together a Jewish coalition of over a dozen organisations and over 150 leaders and rabbis from New York and around the world to support a Bill seeking to end the statute of limitations for child sex crimes in the state of New York. Currently, victims of these crimes only have until their 23rd birthday to seek justice. The initial Bill was sponsored by Assemblywoman Markey, and has been stalled in the New York State Legislature for around ten years. The current statute is considered among the four worst in the US—on a par with Alabama, Michigan, and Mississippi. I flew to New York twice to join in the lobbying efforts. I was honoured to speak at two press conferences, one at the New York State Legislature in Albany, and the other after a public march, which attracted hundreds, over the Brooklyn Bridge. Unfortunately, we were unsuccessful in having the Bill passed in that session, and at the time of writing are in the process of doing all we can to ensure that a Bill passes as soon as possible. The coalition did secure a commitment from New York Governor Andrew Cuomo to work closely with us to ensure that this indeed does happen in the next session.

I can see that this is the start of a future involving increased travelling, potentially more clashes with authorities in different countries, and a relentless mandate to speak out. There is so much more work to do, which is why we have an ambitious agenda. Yet I am still unsure whether I will even remain in this field, and if so, for how long. It's taken a massive toll on me. Some days, I feel significantly restricted in what I can do. Paradoxically, although I know that from a health perspective I should move on, this work is often healing. So, at this stage, I simply can't move on.

There have been many wonderful moments, as well as many dark times. My internal turmoil continues, but that is the nature of life. Even when specific problems are resolved, in all probability my demons will continue to hound me. But, ultimately, at this stage I feel in control, and I'm determined to make it all work: for me, for my family, and for my community.

My life has gone down a very different path from the one I was brought up to lead. Yet I would be less than truthful if I did not also admit to harbouring strong feelings for the spirit of Chabad, a connection with rituals and pleasures instilled in my upbringing. I still put my shoes on most days according to Chabad rules. I slip on the right shoe first (according to its teachings, right is the side of strength), then the left shoe, then tie the left shoelace, and then the right shoelace. Often, I find myself singing the nigunim, songs we sang at farbrengens and around the family table more than 20 years ago. They give me pleasure, as a connection, an anchor, to something comfortable in a time of flux. My reverence for the Rebbe also remains intact. Whenever I watch footage of him, I still feel deeply emotionally drawn to the man.

Although it's been over twenty years since I left Chabad and a religious lifestyle, it's been hard to fully let go, at least on an emotional level—and I know I am not the only one with these ambiguous feelings. It's been well documented that many ex-Chabad people feel this way. They post photos of themselves putting tefillin on themselves or on others, reading the Torah or other scriptures, and attending farbrengens—often noting somewhat sarcastically that once a Chabadnik, always a Chabadnik. There's some truth in that.

On a religious level, I remain an agnostic, not an atheist. I want to stay on God's good side, just in case He happens to be there. But in almost all other ways, this is not the path I would have imagined heading along. I accept, and embrace, the fact that this is my life now. As with everything I have ever done, I intend to pursue it wholeheartedly.

Victims all over the world deserve that. So, too, does my family.

Acknowledgements

I would like to thank my dear parents, Zephaniah and Chaya Waks, for their continuing support—and to those siblings who have stood by me, especially my dear brother Shneur. Thank you also to the many relatives who have supported me, especially my uncle Nathan, his life partner, auntie Candice, auntie Sheree, and their children.

I would also like to thank some of my dear friends who have supported me in various ways throughout my life journey: Tony Fink, Jodi Climo Lancelot, John and Bronia Witorz, David Benau, Efrat Condrea, Woolfu (Moshe Wolf), Isaac Maman, Hymie (Chaim/David Rosen), Amnon Trebish, Yudi New, Phillip Weinberg, Menachem Vorchheimer, Nick Scheuer, Munzie (David Munz), Bruce Cooke, Vivien Resofsky, Yossi Goldfarb, Sandy Waislitz, Christine Leick, Raphael Weil, Dov Zwerling, Eli Hacco, Melissa Kahn, Shannon Smith, Heather Lang, Adam Tilove, Daniel Kotzin, Libby Burkeman, Gabi Sulcas Nudelman,

David Jacobson, Brandon Srot, Yuval Agassi, Nadia Levene, Rabbi Jeni Friedman, Samantha Castiel Menda, Catia Valdman, Tali Margolis, and Bruce Gurfein.

My mentors and friends: Geoffrey Winn, Dr John Serry, Kim Williams AM, and Sam Lipski AM.

The documentary filmmakers of my story, my friends: Danny Ben-Moshe (Identity Films), Dan Goldberg and Adam Kay and their team (Mint Pictures), and the Australian Broadcasting Corporation.

My various legal teams: Viv Waller and her team from Waller Legal, Lennon Mazzeo law firm, Maurice Blackburn, George Newhouse, Dan Star, Colin Golvan, Anton Herman, Melissa Marcus, and Duncan Fine.

My therapist Orna Sheratzky.

Former prime minister Julia Gillard and her government for establishing the Royal Commission into Institutional Responses to Child Sexual Abuse, and the royal commission itself, especially The Hon Justice Peter McClellan AM, Justice Jennifer Coate, Maria Gerace (counsel assisting in the public hearing into the Yeshiva(h) Centres), Pia Van de Zandt, Louise Amundsen, Sian Hutchinson, Brydie Cameron, and Aaron Tang.

The media, for playing a critical role in addressing the issue of child sexual abuse, and for providing me with a platform to undertake my work in this area — in particular Jewel Topsfield for breaking my personal story in 2011 with great sensitivity and professionalism.

My co-author, Michael Visontay, and my publisher and editor at Scribe, Henry Rosenbloom, and the Scribe team.

All the volunteers and supporters who have been there along the way, especially those who were there from the very beginning. There are simply too many of you to mention—but a profound thank you to each of you.

All the organisations and individuals—especially victim advocates—who are working to address the issue of child sexual abuse.

Index